DECEPTION

TINA BROOKS MCKINNEY

ISBN: 09821089-1-5
ISBN-13: 978-0-9821089-1-8

DEDICATION

As always, I would like to thank God for giving me this talent and the ability to share with you. To my husband, William McKinney, I don't know where I would be if you weren't in my life. I love you more than the law should allow. My children Shannan and Estrell are the biggest blessings in my life. They have made me so proud. I could not ask for better children. My mother Judy and father Ivor, I love you. Thanks for spending so much time making me the woman I am. A final shout out to my readers who have supported me in this journey. Every time I think about giving up, you are right there pushing me to continue.

ACKNOWLEDGMENTS

To my readers, I know how much you hate for authors to re-release a book without explanation. Some of you have been loyal readers of mine for years and have everything I have written. I really appreciate you for that, but sometimes it is necessary to recreate a project to keep it from dying. This is the case with this title. I am no longer affiliated with Urban Books thus, in order to keep this book alive, I am republishing it. There have been some changes to this book but the basic concept has not changed.

Thanks for your continued support. I will be providing new titles shortly as well as sequels to Fool, Stop Trippin and Snapped 3.

Special thanks to my ride or die supporters: Angie Simpson, Valerie Nixon, Kim Floyd Moss, Patrice Harlson, Muriel Broomsfield-Murray, Joyce Dickerson, Sharon Jordan, Theresa Gonsalves, Maureen, Antionette Gates, Marvin Meadows, Sabrina Meadows, Barbara Morgan, Detris and Candace Hamm, I love you guys to death.

CHAPTER ONE
ARIANA MENDOZA

"Ten more minutes and I'm out of here." I was not in the mood for this crap today. I was still fussing when my younger brother Ramón walked in the room.

"Look who the cat drug in."

"Oh, you've got jokes." I shot him an angry look because I was pissed at the world. Rummaging through boxes in my old room for discarded baby clothes was not on my list of things I wanted to do.

"What are you doing over here?"

"I promised Madre Sita that I would come by today to look through these old clothes to see if I could use them for my baby."

"She don't know your uppity ass ain't gonna allow that?" If he wasn't telling the truth I would have popped him.

"Guess not." I chuckled. There was no way in hell I'm going to put a child of mine through that torture. Been there and done that.

"You're right, but I promised Madre I would look. Where is she?"

"Where else, she's writing at her desk. Do me a favor and take all that crap with you when you leave," Ramón said as he left the room.

"Like hell. The only thing I'm taking home with me is my fat ass. Besides, I thought I'd save them for your children."

"Over my dead body," Ramón yelled back. I suppressed a smile as I listened to him going down the stairs.

"Whew, I needed that," I said aloud as I braced my back to stand up. I had been bending over boxes for the last half hour and my lower back had begun to vibrate. I wobbled to the hallway and grabbed the phone, thankful for the temporary reprieve. Although it had stopped ringing by the time I got to it, I still picked it up and heard a strange voice. For a split second, I heard Madre Sita mutter something but it was so garbled I couldn't understand it.

"Canary, prepare your nest," the voice said with a heavy Spanish accent.

I was about to hang up the phone. I thought they had the wrong number, but the call piqued my curiosity. "Hello?" My voice was met with silence. An eerie feeling came over me. I wasn't sure why. I wanted to hang up but I could not get my fingers to release the phone. I played the waiting game.

Another few seconds passed and the caller repeated the alien words: "Canary prepare your nest." His voice was low and guttural. It sounded like the voice of a man who'd been chain-smoking for years. He struggled with his English. Irritation won over curiosity. I had little patience for people living in the United States who barely managed to speak the language.

"I'm sorry, you must have the wrong number." The voice spoke again as I attempted to return the phone to the cradle.

"Nest or grave? Prepare," he said as if he didn't hear me telling him he had made a mistake.

"Excuse me?" *Did he say grave? What the hell was he talking about?*

A distinctive *thud* followed by the sound of our downstairs phone hitting to the floor startled me. I snatched the phone from my ear, straining to hear what was going on downstairs.

"What the hell?" I muttered aloud for the caller to hear, even though I wasn't speaking to him. That's when his next words stunned me.

"Ariana," he barked my name like a command. "Prepare," he hissed as he elongated the word, using his native Spanish language. His voice, no longer coarse, irritated me with its familiarity. Who was this person? Before I could ask who he was and—more important—what he wanted, I was summoned downstairs.

"Ariana!" My brother's voice jolted me.

"Oh shit! Ariana hurry…it's Mother."

I slammed down the receiver, all thought of the mysterious call dismissed from my mind. I navigated the rickety stairs as quickly as my girth allowed. Fear, the likes of which I'd never known, gripped me. I wrapped my free hand around my stomach as I clutched the handrail to keep my balance. My petite body struggled to handle the heaviness of my unborn child. By the time I had reached the bottom of the stairs, I was winded.

Madre Sita was lying on her back on the kitchen floor. Laying next to her was the cordless phone that she had apparently dropped.

"What happened to her?" I gasped as my mind fought to understand what my eyes were seeing. My feet refused to move.

"I don't know. I was in the living room when I heard a noise. I came in and she was lying on the floor." Tears were streaming down my brother's face. To stunned to cry, I pried my stubborn feet from the floor. I had to do something.

"Madre," I yelled as I attempted to lower myself to the floor. With the exception of a small knot growing on her left temple, she looked to be sleeping. Her face held a terrible grimace as if she were in dire pain even as she slept.

"She must have struck her head against something, look at that knot on her head." I smoothed my hands across her face as I noticed the gray that had streaked through her hair, especially around the temples. Her flesh was chilly and hard. I was attempting to pick her up and position her on the nearby sofa but Ramón stopped me.

"What are you doing?"

"We can't just leave her on the damn floor."

"But…the baby…"

He was right. I wasn't in any condition to lift her up, even though she couldn't have weighed more than ninety-eight pounds soaked and wet. Ramón weighed less than Mother so he couldn't do it either.

I grabbed her shoulders and began to shake her but immediately stopped. If she suffered from internal injuries, I wanted to make sure I didn't complicate the situation.

"Is she breathing?"

I pressed my nose close to her face but couldn't be sure. My heart was beating so loudly I couldn't hear anything else.

"Hell, I don't know." I wasn't sure if the breath I felt was my own or that of my mother. I pounded on her chest, hoping it would help and not hurt. I did not do the breathing 'cause I was unsure of how that worked. I took a CPR class once, but I could not remember a damn thing I was taught.

Tears burned the backs of my eyes as I looked on helplessly. "Dial nine-one-one," I demanded. As the oldest child, I knew I would have to be the strong one in this situation. Grabbing Madre's hand, I started to massage it, hoping she would open her eyes. I willed away the panic that wanted to overtake me.

"Now dammit!" I yelled when I realized Ramón was still fixed in place and had made no effort to pick up the phone, which was still laying on the floor. The harshness of my voice seemed to break his trance as he scrambled to pick up the phone.

"Hello…hello? There's something wrong with the phone," Ramón whined.

The sound grated on my nerves. In his haste to dial, he had forgotten to clear the line. Getting up from the floor, I snatched the phone from his hand and pressed the button to clear the line and made the call myself. Once connected, I gave the emergency operator our address. She advised me that help would be on the way. I handed the phone back to Ramón, then I continued to massage Madre's hand.

"Do you know CPR?"

"No, do you?" Ramón cried.

"They will be here soon," I spoke to Ramón, but I prayed Madre Sita heard me as well. I looked over at Ramón to see if he was going to be all right.

He was seventeen years old but didn't run the streets like most boys his age; instead, he preferred to stay at home playing video games.

"What if she dies?" I slapped Ramón's face before I could stop myself.

"Don't talk like that." Ramón walked over to the couch and sat down. I regretted hitting him but it was done

"What's wrong with her?" Ramón asked. If he was angry with me for hitting him, he didn't allow it to show.

"She'll be fine. She's breathing, so that's a good sign. Call your sister and tell her she is needed at home as soon as possible. Don't tell her what happened, just tell her to get here." I tried to keep my voice confident and calm despite how terrified I was on the inside.

"Can't you call her? She's going to yell at me if I do it."

I didn't have time for this shit. I fought the urge to slap him again, but the look in his eyes tore through my heart. Thankfully I heard the ambulance in the distance and realized it was too late to call my other sibling, Gabriela. "Never mind, they're here now. We'll call her from the hospital." I was in control once again now that help had arrived.

Ramón appeared to have breathed a sigh of relief. He raced to open the door and allowed the paramedics inside our small living room. They questioned me as they tended to our mother.

"Is she allergic to anything?" one of them demanded.

I didn't like the impersonal tone of his voice. I started to let his ass have it, but I held my temper. "I don't know."

"Is she taking any medications?" He was checking her vital signs.

"No, not that I am aware of."

"Does she have a history of fainting spells?"

"Uh…no, I don't think so?" I hadn't realized how little I knew about Madre until I had to answer all those questions.

"What was she doing before she lost consciousness?" he said as they wheeled the stretcher out the door.

"I was upstairs. I assume she was on the phone because it was laying next to her when I came downstairs." I recalled the four words I'd heard—*canary prepare your nest*—before she fell, but they made no sense to me. I wondered whether they held meaning to Madre. I made a mental note to give it more consideration when things got back to normal.

CHAPTER TWO
ARIANA MENDOZA

There wasn't enough room in the ambulance for me and Ramón so I decided to drive my car and follow the ambulance. I was afraid I might lose them because they travelled quickly with their sirens blaring, but I tried to keep them in sight without getting into an accident. I had no idea where they would take her, so it was imperative that I remain behind them if it were at all possible. I prayed the entire time that they would take her to the closest hospital to our home, DeKalb Medical.

We drove through the lunch-hour traffic, in relative silence, each of us lost in our own confusion. Chasing behind an ambulance reminded me of my childhood, and that trip down memory lane depressed and frightened me. My thoughts wandered as I weaved through the traffic. Fortunately, most drivers pulled over to clear a path for the ambulance, which enabled me to fall right behind it. "Had Madre been sick?"

"Not that I know of. She was fine before you got there."

I looked at him to see if there were any accusation in tone, but there wasn't. Ramón wasn't thrilled to be the only child left living at home with Mother, and sometimes he was very vocal about that when we were alone. Tears continued to roll down his tiny cheeks.

"What about medicine? Did she take any that you know of?"

"If she did, I never saw her."

I nodded my head to indicate that I had heard him. If he noticed, he didn't say anything. Since I no longer lived in the house, I assumed Ramón would know something even if I didn't.

"Remind me to ask Gabriela when she gets there."

"Okay."

"Wipe your face. You don't want anybody to see you cry, do you?"

"I don't care," he mumbled but wiped his face with the bottom of his T-shirt just the same.

I had some nerve talking about the way he looked when I knew that I looked a hot mess as well. My makeup had run all down my face and my eyes stung from mascara. Up ahead I noticed the ambulance took a right turn, going away from DeKalb Medical. I turned on my blinker and got into the right lane to make the same turn.

"I guess they are taking her to Emory instead of DeKalb Medical." I could've kept that comment to myself since Ramón knew Atlanta better than I did, but I felt compelled to say something. Once I realized that we were almost there, I felt better.

I turned into the emergency-room parking lot. We managed to get to the ambulance before the paramedics lifted Madre out of it. I looked back at my car, knowing I could not leave it there for long. I decided to come back out and move it once we knew what was going on. We were unable to follow the gurney through the double doors of the emergency-room.

"Are you with the patient who was just transported?" a nurse asked as I struggled to hide my irritation at being stopped.

"Yes, we are," I answered for myself and my brother.

"And are you over the age of eighteen?"

"Of course, I'm twenty-two." I could not understand what that had to do with anything, but I continued to answer her questions.

"What is your relationship to the patient?"

"I'm her daughter and this is her son," I said, pointing to Ramón.

She looked around the room as if she was looking for someone else. I started to get an attitude.

"Follow me." She walked in the opposite direction of the double doors that I so desperately wanted to go through.

I wanted to tell the bitch she was going the wrong way. If I could at least find out if Madre had awakened, I felt I would be more cooperative. Torn, I decided to follow her anyway. "Wait over there," I instructed Ramón and pointed to the crowded waiting room.

He looked as if I had asked him to stand in a puddle of pissy water, but he eventually did as he was told.

"What is the patient's name?" the nurse asked, getting into her seat.

"Alelina Mendoza."

"Uh, can you spell that? No, better yet, write it down for me?"

I was not surprised by her request, so I took the pad she had handed me and wrote down Madre's name in English. She stared at the paper and I waited for her to repeat what I had written. I hoped that she wasn't about to clown Madre's name, because I was sure to go off on her.

"Thanks. And her date of birth?"

"June 2nd."

"Year?" She looked up at me. My attention, however, was being diverted by a new patient that was raising all kinds of hell in the waiting room. A large black man had entered the waiting room and from the looks of it, he had been either shot or stabbed. He talked as if he was more intent on getting back on the street so he could retaliate on his attacker than getting medical treatment.

"Miss, I need the year."

"Huh?" I didn't know what she had asked me.

"The year your mother was born," she calmly said.

"Oh…uh…I'm not sure. I think she's forty-three; she does not talk about the year." Once again I felt like I didn't know enough about Madre Sita.

"I understand. I don't tell my age, either." The nurse attempted to make light of my ignorance.

Feeling like I dodged a bullet, I answered the next few questions about Madre's address, place of birth, height, and weight fine. I started to get nervous, though, when she asked about insurance. If I had thought about insurance before we had gotten there, instead of giving Madre's name, I would have given my own. That way I would have had an insurance card to give her. Tears started up again as I tried to think of something to say that would prevent the nurse from denying Madre medical attention. Madre was self-employed, and, to my knowledge, she had never applied for insurance. Perhaps she was covered under a plan with Padre, but I had no way of knowing about that since he still lived in Columbia. "I left her purse at the house. Can we fill that part out later?"

She gave me a stern look, but I believed she was moved by my tears because she proceeded to ask me the rest of the questions on the forms. I said a silent prayer of thanks.

I knew I wasn't out of the woods yet, but I would cross the insurance bridge when I got to it.

She finished the paperwork and instructed me to sign them. She then asked for my driver's license and told me to wait while she made copies of it. I was glad that I didn't lie about Madre's name, because I would've been busted the second she took a look at the license. She returned my license and instructed me to have a seat in the waiting room. I breathed a sigh of relief as I hurried back to my brother before she changed her mind.

"Do you know if Madre has insurance," I whispered to Ramón.

He shrugged his shoulders. He was trying real hard to be a man and I felt proud of him. I pulled out my cell and called Gabriela, to inform her of what had happened.

I spoke low into the phone, "Gabriela, please don't get alarmed, but Madre passed out. We are at Emory Hospital right now."

Immediately, she started shrieking. I pushed the phone away from my ear. My younger sister was very high strung and easily excited. We were as different as night and day. She was the loud and boisterous one, while I was more quiet and timid—unless you pissed me off; then it was a whole different story.

"What happened?"

"Will you calm down for a second?"

"Where are you?"

"I just told you." I held the phone away from my face to get a breather.

"Well, tell me again!"

"We're at Emory—"

"Why didn't you call me?"

"Wait a minute—I tried to call you but the ambulance got there before I had a"

"You should have called me as soon as you called them!"

"I didn't know where they were taking—shit." She wasn't giving me a chance to finish my sentences. "Gabriela, shut the fuck up for a minute and let me finish telling you." I held the phone away from my ear again. I counted to ten before I put the phone back to my ear. "There was no sense in calling you before I knew where they were taking her."

She continued to rant and rave.

I'd had just about enough of her mouth. "Are you coming or what?" I demanded.

Of course I'm coming…that's my mother."

I wanted to scream at her that she was my mother too, but I held my tongue. "Good. See you when you get here." I closed my phone and shook my head. It was a good thing she didn't have high blood pressure, because she would have stroked out on my ass.

"See, that's why I didn't want to call her." Ramón smiled for the first time. He had a point for real.

Gabriela tended to be over dramatic and always wanted to be in control. I returned his smile and placed my arm around his shoulder. He positioned his head next to mine. We sat this way in silence, each of us lost in thought. For me, the worse part about being at the hospital was the waiting.

I looked around the waiting room and noticed the melting pot of faces, separated by gender and race. Lately, I had been paying more attention to color lines. Black people sat on one side of the room amid the Spanish people, while the few Asian people in the room sat closer to the white people. I had never paid particular attention to the obvious alliances before, but idle time allowed me time to speculate why Latinos seemed to gravitate to blacks and not white people.

"I guess I'm going to have to call Padre."

Ramón jerked away from me as if I had slapped him. "What for?" he hissed as he narrowed his eyes to mere silts. If it were possible for them to change colors, they would have turned red.

"What are you saying? He has a right to know. It's his wife that's back there."

"Like he cares," he muttered loud enough for me to hear.

"Whether you like him or not, he is your father and Madre's husband, so he has a right to know what is going on with her."

"Humph." He folded his arms across his chest, mumbling something under his breath in Spanish.

He moved a few chairs away from me. His apprehension about sitting alone in the crowded waiting room was obviously forgotten.

I felt conflicting emotions about making the call. While I understood Ramón's anger toward Padre, I viewed it as a sign of disrespect the way he acted whenever anyone brought his name up. As children, we were taught to revere our parents, and Ramón's attitude defied those teachings.

Ramón had never formed a close relationship with Padre because Ramón was too young to remember what it was like when we all lived together in Bogota, Columbia. Our parents moved us to the States shortly after he was born. Padre was forced to return to Columbia when his parents refused to relocate. They thought it would be too difficult to learn another language and they wanted to stay at home with the things they were familiar with. By the time Ramón had learned to say his first words, Padre was but a vague memory to him. Each time Padre had visited, he made false promises to Ramón about coming to live with us. Ramón believed those empty promises for many years until he finally stopped caring. Over the years, Padre visited less and less. Now that Ramón was about to turn seventeen, he felt he didn't need a father any longer. At least Gabriela and I had gotten to spend some time as a family unit before tragedy ripped us apart.

CHAPTER THREE
GABRIELA MENDOZA

"Shit!" I said as I put my phone back in my pocket. An unfamiliar feeling of helplessness settled over me as I looked around the room, searching for a pair of jeans to throw over the shorts I'd been wearing while I painted my bedroom.

My things were thrown all about the room and nothing was where it should've been. Ever since I moved into an apartment that I shared with a coworker, I had become a total slob. Not having to worry about my mother fussing at me to clean my room, I allowed stuff to fall wherever it may. This was also the first time in my life that I had a room to myself, and I wasn't used to all the space. As I searched to find my tennis shoes, I realized the error of my ways and vowed to clean my room the moment I got back from the hospital.

I grabbed my hooded sweatshirt off the closet floor to go with my jeans and my backpack that was miraculously hung on the back of my door and ran out the apartment. Halfway to the car, I remembered to go back and lock the door. My roommate wasn't home from work yet, and she would have been pissed to come home and find the door unlocked.

I threw my backpack onto the passenger seat and slid on the baseball cap that I normally kept in the car. From the front, I looked like a small boy because of my flat chest but from behind, I was all ass. Although it was a warm summer afternoon, I could never be too careful with the weather. Georgia was unpredictable in the summer. I never knew when a late summer storm would pop up, not to mention the rash of tornado-like weather we had been having lately.

As I drove, I tried to keep my mind off what was happening at the hospital. To my knowledge, my mother had never been inside a hospital before. She was proud of the fact that all of her children were born at home. She and my sister had gotten into the biggest fight because Ariana planned to have her child in a hospital. My sister said she wanted all the modern conveniences—including all the drugs they were willing to supply.

I chuckled at the memory because my mother liked to have had a fit at the mention of my sister taking drugs. Hell, if she only knew how Gabriela used to get down before she married Mike and got pregnant, she would have really lost it. Mother was old-fashioned and stuck in her ways. She clung to outdated Latino traditions and despised the ever-changing world we were living in.

The drive to the hospital was short. I pulled into the emergency-room lot next to my sister's Honda Accord. As I got out of the car, I looked at my attire and almost turned around and went home. My mother thought only Spanish girls with no class wore jeans and tennis shoes. She wanted me to dress more like the traditional idea of a woman, but I hated that crap. I liked to be comfortable—to me, there was nothing comfortable about a dress. Normally, I would try to find some balance when I planned to visit with her, but today I just didn't have that type of time. I shrugged my shoulders as I briskly walked through the doors with a false sense of bravado.

The hospital was cold. I was glad I had donned a sweatshirt instead of a tee. I spotted my siblings immediately in the waiting room and rushed over to them. I could tell that they had been crying, but I also detected that they had been fighting as well since they were not sitting next to each other. "How is she?" I asked.

Ramón didn't say anything. He was pouting but that didn't faze me.

"We don't know anything yet. They haven't come out to tell us anything since we got here," Gabriela answered.

"Well, what happened?" I hated feeling left out of anything. The fact that I was the last to find out about my mother pissed me off.

"I stopped by the house to get those baby clothes Madre had been bugging me about. I told her that I didn't want them—too many bad memories—but she insisted I take them. I was upstairs and the next thing I knew Ramón was calling me because she had passed out on the floor."

"That's it? She wasn't sick or something?" I said, turning to Ramón, expecting to hear something different from him. I was closer to Ramón than I was with my sister, so I knew he would keep it real with me.

"Nah, she was fine," he said. "She was in the kitchen cleaning up the breakfast dishes the last time I saw her."

"Did you ask the nurse for an update?" I was halfway to the desk by the time Ariana grabbed my hand to stop me.

"Please don't create a scene. I'm sure they will come get us when they have something concrete to tell us."

"Fuck that. You can sit here all night if you want to. I want some answers, and I intend to get them now." I pushed her hand off my arm and brushed past her, stopping short of the reception desk. "Excuse me?"

The lady never raised her eyes from the computer screen. I could tell by the way her eyes jumped back and forth that she wasn't reading a chart. That heifer was playing Candy Crush.

"I said, excuse me."

She tore her eyes away from the computer. "Yes?" Her tone implied that I better take it down a notch if I wanted any assistance from her.

I decided to revise my tactics. It wasn't that I was scared of her or anything like that, I just realized there was a time and place for everything and this was not the place to act an ass. "I'm sorry to bother you…but I was hoping you could tell me something about my mother. She was brought in here over an hour ago, and we haven't heard anything yet."

"What's the patient name?"

"Alelina Mendoza," I reminded myself that I could get more results from sugar than with shit. She punched a few strokes into the computer before she looked back up at me. "They have not updated the computer. The doctor will come see you as soon as he can. I made a note in the computer that the family is waiting."

I knew she was lying immediately because she didn't ask for the spelling of my mother's name. I wanted to snatch her ass over the counter but I attempted to remain calm. "Could you check again? Her name is spelled A-d-e-l-i-n-a—"

"I know how to spell." She looked at the screen once more, but it was evident to me that I had been dismissed.

"What did they say?" Gabriela said when I sat down.

"Nothing. She said the doctors would come to speak to us when they were ready."

"Gabriela, do you ever recall a time when Madre was sick? Do you know anything about her taking any medicine?"

"No, she's as healthy as a horse. Remember how she ragged you about going to the doctor about your baby?"

"Yeah, I'd forgotten about that. We were just trying to think of something that would have caused her to pass out like she did."

I looked around the hospital and realized that Ariana's husband, Mike, was missing. "Hey, where's Mike?"

She moved her hand to her stomach and began to rub it. "Oh God, I completely forgot to call him. He's going to be pissed. I should've been home hours ago. I'll be right back." She grabbed her purse and wobbled out of the waiting room.

I used that time to find out what was eating at my younger brother. Placing my arm around his shoulder, I pulled him closer to me. At first he resisted, but eventually gave in. I was slightly larger than him, and he knew I could whip that ass if I had to.

"So, what's up with you?" I ran my fingers through his hair because I knew he hated when I did it. He had taken to using mousse in his hair to slick it back and it annoyed the hell out of me. A majority of Latino boys were doing the same thing. I wanted Ramón to make his own statement and not follow behind the masses.

"Stop that," he said, batting at my hand, which made his hair even more messed up. He pulled away from me again, but I managed to maintain my hold on him.

"So what's up?" I repeated.

"Gabriela wants to call Padre."

"Oh, and that got you all bent out of shape?"

"Yeah, she acts like calling him is going to solve everything. It ain't like he's gonna come back here, so what's the point of calling him?"

"Ramón, there are a lot of things that you don't understand about Madre and Padre's relationship. Regardless of how you feel about it, you have to respect the fact that they are married." Truth be told, I didn't understand their relationship either, but it wasn't for me to understand.

"I understand a lot. I understand he doesn't love us," he replied. His voice started to rise, attracting attention to us.

"That's not true. He loved us enough to bring us here. That was a big sacrifice on his part."

"So you say."

"There are things you don't remember." Unknowingly, I had pushed a button I should have left alone.

He jumped up and screamed at me: "Like what? If you want me to understand, than why don't you tell me instead of beating around the damn bush."

This was the first time that he'd ever used that tone with me. If we weren't in the middle of a crowded waiting room, I would've knocked his silly ass down. I was only three years older than he was, but I was old enough to take him down if I had to. "Sit your silly ass down and lower your voice before you get us thrown out of here!"

He looked around as if he'd forgotten where we were, and, more important, why we were there. Humbled, he sat down, but not next to me as he was before. He moved over a seat.

I gave him a few seconds to compose himself. I had promised my mother that I would never speak of those days again, but I could see that withholding that information had taken an ugly toll on my brother. Taking a deep breath, I started to speak. "Do you remember Dezi and Fabio?" I hadn't said those names in years. Hearing them again evoked so much pain, I felt as if they had just died all over again.

"No, why should I?"

"They were your older brothers," I said quietly.

A look of confusion crossed his face. He just stared at me but I could feel his pain. I didn't want him to know the agony we had gone through. I always wanted to spare him of that, but if telling him would make things better between him and my father, I was willing to hurt him.

"What are you talking about Gabriela?" Before I could answer him, Ariana came back into the waiting room. Her faced was etched with worry, and I was afraid for her and her baby. I wanted to fix her pain too, but again, I felt helpless.

"Is Mike on the way?" I asked, not wanting to finish my conversation with Ramón in front of Ariana. I gave Ramón a look that told him we would finish our conversation later when we had some privacy.

"I told him not to come unless I called him back," Ariana said. "It makes no sense for him to come over here until we knew something. Besides, I can't deal with him right now."

I raised my eyebrow at the inference of her words. Was there trouble brewing in paradise? Ramón sunk back in his seat with his arms folded across his chest. I could tell that he was still troubled by my words. Before I could address either of my siblings, we noticed a doctor—or at least a man dressed as a doctor—heading our way. My heart clinched in fear. I tried to read his face to see what he was about to say, but his expression was unreadable.

"Good evening. I'm Dr. Haywood. Are you the Mendoza family?"

"Yes," we collectively answered.

I reached for the hands of my brother and sister and held on tightly to each of them.

"Your mother appears to have suffered a stroke."

"Oh my God!" I cried.

"A stroke? Surely there must be a mistake," Ariana argued.

Ramón was silent, his eyes wide with fear. None of us had expected the news to be so grim.

I recovered first. "Is she going to be okay?" I was scared of his answer but we needed to know.

"I think so, but she is not out of the woods yet. Her heart is enlarged and we're not sure why. Does your mother have a history of heart disease?"

Who was this man talking to us? I wanted to see his credentials because he obviously didn't know his ass from a hole in the ground. Ariana yanked my arm before I could fly off the handle.

"No, sir, not to our knowledge," Ariana stated. She was crying again; we all were.

"We have her heavily sedated. She is resting comfortably. We will run some more tests in the morning. Hopefully she will respond to the medication we are giving her."

"Can we see her?" I asked.

"I'm afraid not. She is in ICU so we can monitor her heart. The next forty-eight hours will be crucial for her. We want her to rest tonight. Please go home and get some rest. There is nothing for you to do here. Hopefully you will be able to see your mother in the morning."

"No disrespect, Dr. Haywood, but there is no way that I can go home without seeing her. Please! Won't you just let me look at her? I promise I won't get in the way. I just need to see her face."

He looked as if he was going to refuse me but something in his eyes softened as he nodded his approval. "All right but just you, and only for a few minutes. She needs her rest." He turned to leave.

It didn't occur to me to allow Ariana to go instead of me as I quickly followed him.

"I'll be right back." I said over my shoulder. I hoped they understood my decision to be the one to see our mother.

We took the elevator to the second floor but neither of us spoke. This wasn't the first time I had visited a hospital, but it was the first time that a member of my family was ever admitted to one. When the doors opened, I followed Dr. Haywood down a series of corridors until we reached a glass-enclosed room.

He paused with me outside the door.

"Are you sure you want to do this?"

I thought that was an unusual question for him to ask, but I ignored it. "Of course," I said as I stepped around him and entered the room. I wasn't prepared for what I saw: My mother was laying in the middle of the hospital bed attached to every machine I could possibly have thought of. She had a breathing tube in her mouth, plugs and wires going everywhere, and IV wires in her arms. Even though it had only been a few days since I'd last seen my mother, she appeared to have shrunk. The bed practically swallowed her up. Her skin was no longer vibrant; it was more milky and somewhat faded in color. I searched her face to find the woman I knew and loved, but she wasn't there.

The woman laying in that bed did not resemble my mother at all! I wanted to snatch out the tubes and wires and carry her out of there. At the same time, I didn't want to touch this stranger who lay in front of me. I felt a hand on my shoulder. I turned to see that the doctor had followed me into the room.

"What happened to her? She doesn't even look like the same person." I slumped against the wall to keep from falling.

"As a physician, we sometimes try to shield the family, especially if there are extenuating circumstances such as your sister's advanced pregnancy and your brother's youth. We recognize your rights to know, but sometimes, in cases like this, we withhold information until we have a better idea of what we are dealing with. Since you insisted on seeing her, I had to respect your wishes. Come with me so we can talk." He led me away from the room.

I didn't look back. I couldn't. We went into an empty office not far from the ICU room.

"It is true that your mother suffered a small stroke; however, she also had several heart attacks en route to the hospital."

I gasped, unable to comprehend what he was saying to me.

"We had to sedate her to allow her body to rest, which is why she is on a ventilator."

"But what happened?" I knew I sounded dumb, but this was so unexpected, I just didn't understand. When he had told us forty-eight hours, I assumed he meant that in forty-eight hours our mother would be allowed to walk out the door.

"We don't know. The good news is that she is young and otherwise, appears healthy. She is in good hands here. I promise you that we will do everything we can for her."

"Is she going to die?" Whoa, where did that thought come from? I wanted to snatch that thought back because I didn't want that thought out in the universe, but it was too late to grab it back.

"I honestly don't know," he replied.

That's it? That's all he can tell me? What am I going to tell my family? Oh my God. Suddenly, I was so angry I wanted to hit him. I slid out of my chair and unto my knees on the cold floor and prayed like I'd never prayed before. My tears blinded me as sobs wracked my shoulders.

After a few minutes, Dr. Haywood pulled me from the floor. "You must be strong for your family. We will call you if anything changes."

I was being dismissed, pushed toward an elevator, and left alone with my fears. During the short ride down to the waiting room, I composed myself as best I could. I would follow Ariana home and take Ramón with me. He didn't need to sleep in the house alone, and I couldn't go back to that empty house—at least not tonight. Once I was sure that he was asleep, I would call my father. He would know what to do.

I felt comfort in my resolve until the enormity of our situations slapped me. This realism stopped me in my tracks. If I called my father, there was a good chance he would come to Atlanta. That would mean he would discover that we weren't as obedient as he thought we were and the secrets that we had kept from him for years would be exposed. As much as I hated it, I was not going to be able to make this decision on my own. I would have to discuss this with my sister and perhaps my brother.

CHAPTER FOUR
GABRIELA MENDOZA

As soon as we got to Ariana's house, I understood why she didn't want her husband at the hospital with us. I loved my brother-in-law dearly, but he got on my damn nerves the way he hovered over my sister.

Mike opened the door before she could even turn the key. "Where have you been? I've been worried sick." He took her purse and guided her over to the sofa. He pulled over the footstool, took off her shoes, and propped up her feet. He went in the kitchen and came back with a cup of tea, and this was all before he kissed her and said hello to the rest of us.

She put her feet down. He immediately put them back on the stool, holding her small ankles in place. "The doctor said you should keep your feet elevated when you sit down." He smiled at us and I wanted to puke.

I understood this was their first child and all, but enough was enough. They made a strange couple. He was a tall and lanky white man, standing well over six feet tall with a burley chest and slim waist, and a cute, boyish face—a virtual giant compared to my sister. Every time I envisioned them fucking, I laughed out loud. But I guess they worked it out because now they were having a baby.

My thoughts wandered because I wasn't ready to spoil the evening. Part of me wanted to have Mike leave the room so I could speak to my sister in private, but I needed him there to support her just in case things went to the left.

I took a deep breath and began. "Come here, Ramón. I need you to sit next to me."

He got up from the easy chair he was sitting in and came over and sat next to me on the love seat. Mike sat next to my sister and held her hand.

"I think we are going to have to call Padre."

Ramón tried to pull away from me.

I pulled him back. "Before we do, each of us has to understand why I am saying this and what it will mean."

"Of course you should call your father. That's a no-brainer," Mike said.

If looks could kill he would've died instantly. He didn't have a clue what this revelation meant, and I wasn't going to be the one to explain it to him. I told Ariana over and over again that she should have told Mike about our father but she refused.

"Madre had several heart attacks in route to the hospital." I let the words sink in before I continued. Shocked faces met mine as I looked around the room. "The doctor is not sure what is going on, so they are keeping her sedated. She's on a breathing machine and didn't even know that I was there." I didn't tell them that she looked like a stranger. Hopefully, they would never have to see that for themselves.

Mike pulled Ariana closer to him as she cried. Ramón edged closer to me. His eyes were rimmed with water. Thus far, he had not allowed the tears to fall.

"What are you waiting for? Your father needs to be here. You can't make these kinds of decisions yourself," Mike insisted.

Ariana pushed herself away from her husband and got up from the sofa. She paced as she cried. "My father will never accept this." The anguish she was experiencing was clear to us all.

"He has no choice but to accept it—she's in the hospital."

"No, Mike, he will never accept that I'm married or that I'm pregnant."

"He doesn't know? You told me he knew all about us."

I saw the hurt on Mike's face.

"I couldn't. He wouldn't understand." She came and sat on the love seat next to me.

As much as I wanted to walk away from this entire situation, I knew I had to help my sister out: "My father is from the old school. He believes that Latino people should marry other Latino people. He won't understand my sister marrying outside her race."

Mike was clearly upset by this news. He was raised in a foster family and we had become the only family he had ever knew, that's why Ariana refused to tell him about my father's prejudice.

"You lied to me?"

Ariana did not respond. She hung her head as more tears found their way down her face and dripped on her lap.

I had spoken up because I didn't want the situation to get any worse than it already was. "I don't consider it a lie—" I was about to say more but he interrupted me.

"I wasn't sleeping with you," he spat back at me.

Things were starting to look very badly.

"Mike, you don't understand my father. He didn't want to move his family to America in the first place. He was afraid that we would get corrupted by American ways and values." I couldn't help but notice that Ramón had reddened with anger.

"Then why did he do it?" Mike was sulking like a kid who had gotten his Tootsie Pop taken from him at lunchtime.

"He made the decision after the disappearance of our brothers," Ariana said.

I jumped up shooting Ariana a warning glance.

"Ramón and I are going to go." I gathered my things and looked all around the room, everywhere except at my brother, who stared at me as if we had lost our happy minds. This was not the way to have this conversation with him.

"No, I want to hear this. What are y'all talking about?" Ramón demanded.

I shared a look with my sister, silently asking her what to do.

"Wait, we are losing sight of what we are here to talk about." She turned to Ramón and addressed him. "There is much that you don't know about our family, but now is not the time to discuss it." Her plea was directed to both my brother and her husband. She reached for Mike's hand and he accepted it.

I breathed a sigh of relief. One down, one to go, I thought to myself. "I agree. Right now we have to decide whether to call Father or not." I looked at my watch and it was past midnight.

"It's morning in Columbia," Ariana said. "I think we should call him now. Since I am the one who deceived him, I will deal with him privately. After we make the call, I will explain everything else, okay?"

Without waiting for anyone else to say anything I jumped up and went to get the phone. I didn't envy my sister at this moment. My father was a difficult taskmaster and he was going to be very upset when he learned that she had not only married a white man without his knowledge, but also carried his child.

CHAPTER FIVE
ARIANA MENDOZA

I went upstairs to find my phone book. In the twelve years that we'd been living in the states, I had never once phoned Padre. Because of the time difference and the expense of the call, he would call at an assigned time. All of us were expected to be there just in case he wanted to speak with us. Normally, he didn't, because he believed that children should listen rather than speak. If he was interested in how we were doing in school and what was going on in our lives, we never heard it from him. If Madre needed to speak to him privately, she would leave the room, but most times their conversations were strictly about business.

When we had first arrived, Padre would call once every two months. Over the passing years, those conversations had dwindled down to every six or seven months. This didn't bother me, because I knew that Padre loved us, but I still felt sorry for Madre Sita. She never complained, however—that's just how she was.

It wasn't always like that. I remembered a time when there was plenty of love to go around. Each day we would wait eagerly by the door for Padre to come home from work. He would lift us up and give us a big hug and a kiss on the cheek and pull a small gift from his pocket for each of us, then he would go in the kitchen and lift Madre up too, spin her around and give her a gift too. In those days, she used to laugh, but that was before he lost the sunshine in his life.

I found my phone book and went back to the living room to make the call. Three heads lifted and six sets of eyes followed my steps into the room. The tension was so thick you could feel it as it moved throughout the room. I went back to the sofa and sat next to my husband.

Gabriela handed me the phone. "Don't tell him about your marriage just yet. Let him know about Madre and find out what he wants to do. He may not be able to come, and you'll upset him for nothing."

I nodded my head, but I sought my husband's eyes to make sure he was in agreement with the plan. He nodded his head in stiff agreement but I could tell I had hurt him deeply. I felt such pride for the man I married. Without knowing the full story, he accepted how difficult this was for me.

My fingers shook so badly that I had to get the operator to make the call for me. I kept dialing the wrong number. Lord only knew how much those misdialed calls were going to cost us. Although Mike and I made a decent living, we had to use our money wisely because of the baby. The phone was answered on the third ring. My father spoke in Spanish, which shouldn't have surprised me but it did.

I pressed the speaker button and placed the phone on the coffee table so that everyone could hear the conversation. "Padre, it's Ariana. I am here with Gabriela and Ramón." I felt stupid. I was speaking to my own father and didn't know what to say.

"What has happened? Where is your mother?"

He didn't say *hi, how are you, or what a pleasant surprise* and that hurt me. Ramón got up and left the room. I understood exactly how he felt. I expected some warmth in his voice but it was like we were speaking to a stranger.

"She has taken ill and is in the hospital." My voice was devoid of emotion just like his, but inside I cried. I needed him to tell me that everything was going to be all right and that he would take care of everything. I had never felt so alone in my life.

"I...don't...understand." He switched from Spanish and spoke choppy English. He struggled so badly with the words, he quickly switched back to his native language. He began rattling off questions and I couldn't catch them.

"Padre, I can't understand you. Please slow down." It had been a minute since I had heard so much so fast. My heart began to race. Gabriela slipped over next to me and grabbed my hand.

"Where...is...she?" Padre stumbled over his words.

"She is in the hospital. She just passed out. The doctors said it's her heart." I felt like a damn had burst inside of me and I was little girl all over again. When my father didn't respond, I kept on talking. "The hospital wants insurance; I don't know what to tell them."

"We have money." He huffed as if I had insulted him.

"Padre, you don't understand. Hospitals here cost a lot of money."

"We have money," he said again with attitude.

In Columbia, our town was small. The nearest hospital was over one hundred miles away. Although I was still a child when I had left Columbia, I remembered enough to realize that we didn't have much. How was I going to make him understand that in America I spent more on a single lunch than he'd probably spend in an entire week for a family of four?

"What are we going to do?" I didn't ask if he was coming; it was not my place to question Padre.

"I need to make some calls. I will call tomorrow." He switched back to Spanish and hung up the phone without saying good-bye.

"The son of a bitch didn't even cry," Ramón said in an accusing tone as he walked back into the room.

I wanted to chastise him but I felt the same way. I had expected to feel some relief just from speaking with my father, but I didn't.

"You've got to call him back," Gabriela said.

"Call him back for what?"

"He thinks we still live at home with Madre. Give him your cell number or give him mine. You can tell him that we are staying at the hospital." Gabriela was using her head. Her scenario made sense.

I didn't think about that while I was on the phone, but I was reluctant to phone him again. Sensing my discomfort, Gabriela snatched the phone from me and made the call herself. She wasn't angry with me. She just took control like she always did.

"Padre, it's Gabriela. We didn't give you a number to call us back."

Before Gabriela could hang up, I asked to speak to him. She looked at me strangely and gave me the phone.

"Canary, prepare your nest." Those words had replayed in my mind all day. I didn't think they would mean anything to Padre, but I was willing to try them. Far too many things about the day were not adding up in my mind.

"What did you s—say?" That was the first time I had ever heard Padre stutter.

"Those were the last words Madre heard before she passed out."

"Shit! Why you not say this before?" Choppy English again.

"I didn't know it was important."

He hung up on me. I was stunned, holding the phone away from my ear. If I didn't understand a word he had said before, I understood that one.

"What's the hell does that mean?" Gabriela asked.

"I wish I knew," I replied. Lying back, I lost myself in the comfort of my husband's arms. I was tired and the baby was ready to eat. "Do y'all want something to eat?"

"Nah, I got to get home. Ramón, are you coming with me?" Gabriela stood up and grabbed her purse off of the coffee table.

"No, I think I want to stay here tonight if that's okay." He looked at me.

"Sure it is. Let me get you some blankets." I was a little surprised that Ramón opted to stay with me instead of going with Gabriela, but I tried not to let it show as I started upstairs to get the blankets.

CHAPTER SIX
GABRIELA MENDOZA

Ariana was heavy on my mind as I drove home. Not only was I worried about how her husband would react to her news of keeping their marriage a secret, there was also the added threat that my father would be coming home. There was no way she was going to be able to disguise the fact that she was pregnant. Although he had never hit any of us, we had never given him reason to. He ruled with an iron fist, and we never thought to defy him.

Exhaling, I turned off my car after I parked it in the lot in front of my apartment building. I really should have stayed with Ariana, but I wanted to sleep in my own bed. I said a prayer for my mother before I left my car: "Dear God, I know I don't come to you often…but you know my heart, and I truly love you. I come to you tonight not to pray for me. I wish to pray for my mother, who, as you know, is fighting for her life. She's worked hard, God, making a way for me and my family, and I just wanted to ask you to wrap your arms around her. Thank you."

I wasn't embarrassed to pray—I was embarrassed that I didn't do it more often. It wasn't a conscious decision. I was like a lot of other people who only remembered to pray when things were going bad. I made a mental note to change my bad habits immediately.

The apartment was dark when I opened the door. I didn't really expect my roommate, Tilo, to be up since it was almost three o'clock in the morning, but it would have been nice since I really needed someone to talk to. I tiptoed down the hallway and paused before her door to see if I heard any movement. It was quiet, so I went into my room and softly shut the door behind me.

My clothes hit the floor, one article at a time. I was so exhausted, I decided against taking a shower. My luck, once I got finished, I would be wide awake and unable to go to sleep. I pulled back the covers and crawled into bed but sleep still did not come easy to me. I could not get the image of my mother hooked to all those machines out of my head.

As I tossed and turned, another unpleasant image played out in my mind—the night that had driven us to flee Columbia in the first place. My older brothers were outside doing chores. We had a small garden in front of our house. They were supposed to clear the weeds and water the plants before coming inside for dinner. We always ate promptly at six, which was around the time my father came home from work. One night my father was late so my brothers used the extra time to play and frolic in the setting sun.

They were just supposed to get the weeds, leave the water running, and come back into the house. Children sometimes disappeared in our village. Mostly girls, but we found out the hard way that wasn't always the case. The only reason Padre let them pick the weeds at all was because he got home too late to handle it himself. He thought our brothers would be safe.

The wails of my father scared me when he realized that my brothers were not in the house. He searched the village for hours but we never saw them again. That was the only time that I'd heard him cry and it frightened me. His anguished cries still haunted me.

"Damn, girl, you okay?" Tilo said, shaking me awake.

"Huh?" I wiped the sweat from my forehead. I was bathed in it. I looked down and noticed that I had kicked off my covers, and I quickly gathered them to my chin.

"You screamed. Scared the shit out of me," Tilo said.

"Sorry, I must have had a bad dream."

"You think?" She sat on my bed with a baseball bat clutched in her hand.

Laughing, I said, "What were you going to do with that bat?"

"Beat the hell out of whoever was in here fucking you up." Her face was so solemn I couldn't help but to laugh.

"Shit ain't funny." She tried to sound hard but failed miserably.

"Thanks, Tilo. Sorry about that."

She didn't answer as she closed the door behind her. I didn't want her to leave, but I had too much pride to ask her to stay. In any event, I knew I would not be going back to sleep—of that much I was sure.

I got up to take a shower. It was five-thirty and way too early to be up on a Sunday morning, but I refused to lay back down until I was sure the images that plagued my sleep were gone. I let the water get hot before I stepped into the shower. I was hoping the hot water would clear my head, but it didn't work. I couldn't get rid of the apprehension I felt in my bones. Dissatisfied, I turned off the water and stepped out the shower. I quickly dried myself off and went back to my room to put on a pair of shorts and a t-shirt.

Careful not to awaken Tilo, I tiptoed down the hall to the kitchen to make myself a cup of coffee and some toast. I was surprised to see her already seated at the table with two cups.

"What are you doing up?"

She looked at me as if I had three heads, but didn't respond. I sat down across from her and sipped my coffee. We sat in silence for a few minutes. Apparently, the silence had gotten to her because she broke it.

"So, are you ready to tell me what had you wailing like a banshee?"

"I did not sound like a banshee," I replied, watching her sexy lips.

"Like hell you didn't. You were making enough noise for two or three people. At first I thought it was your television."

"I had a nightmare." I couldn't look at her any longer because she was getting me horny, and I shouldn't be considering my desires at a time like this.

"No shit. Now tell me something I don't know."

"I don't even remember what it was about," I lied.

She gave me a look that said she didn't believe me. Although Tilo was my best friend, I wasn't ready to share that part of my past with her.

"What happened to you last night? I thought we were going to the movies to see *Sex In The City*?"

"Damn, I'm sorry. I completely forgot."

She pushed her chair away from the table and took her empty cup to the sink. "If you didn't want to go, you could have told me so I could have gone with someone else."

"I did want to go. Hell, I'm the one that turned you on to the show. You used to hate it because there weren't any black people on it."

She laughed. "Yeah, you're right. What about today? Do you want to try to catch the matinee?"

"I can't. My mother is in the hospital, so I've got to go back over there this morning."

She came back to the table and sat down. "What's wrong with your mother?"

I didn't want to talk about that either, but I needed to tell someone. "She had a heart attack."

Tilo got up and placed her arm around my shoulders. Unwanted tears welled up in the back of my eyes and threatened to fall.

"Is that where you were last night?" She massaged my shoulders, releasing some tension.

"Yeah. We were there most of the day, and I don't know what today is going to bring."

"Why didn't you call me?" She continued working her fingers on my shoulders.

"Tilo, it was crazy. Ariana and Ramón were there, too, but they wouldn't let them see her. There was no need for you to come down there too and just sit."

"You still could have called me."

I could tell she was hurt. I knew something that would soothe her wounded feelings, but now wasn't the time. "Have you ever felt that if you didn't say something out loud maybe whatever you were dealing with would go away?"

"Yeah, been there and done that."

"That's how I felt. If we didn't talk about it, my mother would come through the door like nothing had happened," I said in a low voice.

"What did the doctor say?"

I didn't answer her right away. I didn't want to admit, even to myself, that she might not leave the hospital. "He said she's young and the next forty-eight hours would tell the story."

"I'm sorry, Gabriela. I want to go back to the hospital with you. Let me go get dressed."

Shit, how am I going to tell her that I don't want her there without hurting her feelings? "Tilo, you really don't have to come. Nine times out of ten, they won't let us see her. I don't even know how long I will be there. I need to get with my sister so we can figure out how we are going to pay for this. To my knowledge, Mother didn't have insurance, so we have got to get with my father to see what to do."

"I still want to be there for you."

"I know you do and I really appreciate that, but let me find out what is going on first. The doctor said they would be running test this morning, so we won't know anything for a while."

"Okay, if you're sure. But if you need me, just hit me up on my cell. Since I'm up, I think I'm going to head over to the gym," Tilo said.

"I'll call you as soon as I know something."

She left the room, and I was happy Tilo let it go so easily. She was sweet as pie most of the time, but when something got under her skin, she was like a dog with a bone trying to get to the meaty center. She was the first friend besides my sister that I have ever had, and I didn't want to lose her friendship. I went back to my room and got dressed. I wanted to head over to the hospital to see if I could speak with the doctor again before he left the hospital.

I was about to leave the house when my cell phone rang. "Hello," I said.

"Ramón and I are on the way to the hospital." It was Ariana.

She must have been reading my mind because I was going to call her from the car. "Good, I'm headed that way too. See you there." I found it strange that Mike wasn't going with them, but I knew Ariana would tell me if she wanted me to know when I saw her. She kept a lot of things to herself. But who was I to judge—we all had our share of secrets. I knew that I had mine, so I could not be mad at her. When I got home tonight, I was going to have a long talk with Tilo. I had some explaining to do, and the sooner I did it, the better I would feel.

CHAPTER SEVEN
ARIANA MENDOZA

I dropped Ramón off at Madre's house before I went to the hospital. He was a complete basket case, and sitting in the hospital all day long wouldn't do anyone any good. Because of his age, the hospital would not let him see Madre Sita anyway.

"I promise to come get you if things change. and, of course, I will call you as soon as we know something." He stood on the sidewalk, looking uncertain. "I still think I should be there," he said, sulking.

I don't know who he thought he was fooling, his heart wasn't in it. "I know, baby, but someone needs to be at home for Madre's customers. They might come by the house to pick up their cleaning, and it wouldn't be good if no one was home." That was a cheap trick and he knew it. We seldom had customers come to the house. He accepted the lie, though.

Madre Sita had been doing laundry in our home for some of the most elite families in Atlanta. It was a business Padre had set up for us, but it hardly paid the bills. Over the years, Madre washed less and less. Oftentimes she sent to the clothes to the dry cleaners, removed their tags, and packaged them as if we had done all the work.

"All right," Ramón said, but make sure you call me if anything changes. I'll get somebody to drop me off if you can't come back to get me."

I had a lot on my mind as I drove to the hospital. I was scared we were going to hear something today that we didn't want to hear. Not to mention, I was still afraid of what Mike would do when he finally met Padre. Although we had been married for over three years, there was never any motivation for me to tell him about our strange family dynamics. After Gabriela had left, Mike hardly said two words to me and did not once attempt to hold me as he normally did during the course of the night. I knew he was hurt, but I could not change that. He misunderstood my reasons for keeping our marriage a secret. He assumed it was because I didn't love him, and I refused to go into it in front of Ramón. Our family kept a lot of secrets, and it appeared as if all of them were trying to rear their ugly heads at the same damn time.

A car pulled out in front of me and I narrowly missed hitting it. The sudden stop forced my belly into the steering wheel, causing a sharp pain in my pelvic area. "Shit," I exclaimed as fresh tears welled in my eyes. I pulled over to the curb to get myself together. The pressure from the last few days was catching up to me, and I felt like I was on the brink of losing it. I waited for my hands to stop shaking before I pulled back into traffic. I was eager to speak with the doctor and, at least, put some of this anxiety behind me.

I saw Gabriela as soon as I walked into the waiting room. She appeared to be arguing with the lady at the reception desk.

"Gabriela, what's going on?" I ignored the lady who looked as if she was about to come over the desk and kill my sister.

"All I asked this bitch to do was call the doctor and she started asking me all these questions about the damn bill. I ain't—"

I spoke in Spanish, "Gabriela, calm down. She is only doing her job." I gave the lady a tight smile while I pulled my sister away.

"Calm down, hell? That heifer doesn't know who she's talking to."

I practically dragged Gabriela out the door because she had called the lady out her name one time too many, and she was about to make an example out of her. "Gabriela, stop it. That woman has every right to ask us about insurance. When I brought Madre in here, I told them I would be back with her insurance information. Yelling at that poor woman ain't gonna change this situation. Now we are going back in there and you are going to apologize."

She just looked at me like I had lost my damn mind, but she finally nodded her head in agreement.

We approached the desk again and this time the lady just rolled her eyes and ignored us. I could tell that Gabriela was about to lose it again so I hit her in her side, warning her not to start anything.

"Miss, I'm so sorry for the misunderstanding. My sister didn't know that I was supposed to be bringing back our mother's information, and she is sorry for calling you names." I looked at Gabriela as we both waited for the apology.

Gabriela chewed it over for a few seconds and spit out a miserable response. "Sorry."

All of our emotions were running on high, but I wanted to wrap my fingers around my sister's neck and choke her.

It was clear to me and the lady that penitence was the last thing Gabriela felt, but the woman acted professionally and let it go.

"The doctor will be down to see you shortly," she said and dismissed us with a wave.

It was my turn to catch an attitude. I was ready to dog walk that bitch around the building but Gabriela dragged me away. "When we leave here, we need to go over to the house to see if we can find out anything that will help us pay this bill. We're also going to have to call Padre back. If he has some money, he's going to have to wire it or they will likely transfer Madre to Grady."

Gabriela said, "As far as I'm concerned, they can transfer her 'cause I don't like this uppity-ass hospital anyway. It's a damn shame they care more about a person's insurance than they do the welfare of the patient. At least at Grady you know you are getting the best health care, regardless of how much money you can afford to pay."

"I don't know if you've been listening to the news or not, but Grady ain't in all that great shape these days. I heard they were even thinking about shutting it down." Before I could go on any further, Dr. Haywood came over to us.

His face was haggard, but his steps were brisk. He looked around the waiting room before he began speaking to us. "Can you both come to my office?"

I wasn't sure why we had to follow him, but I assumed it was because of the scene Gabriela had put on. I figured he wanted us away from the general population just in case we decided to get rowdy again.

He led us to a small office behind the intake desk. It was only big enough for a small, round table and three chairs. He instructed us to have a seat and closed the door behind us. "I don't know an easier way to say this so I'm going to just say it. Your mother passed away this morning. We did everything we could to save her, but the damage to her heart was too extensive. I'm sorry."

"Huh?" I bolted from my chair. Those were not the words I had expected to come from his mouth. My heart sprinted and I felt myself slipping sideways. I tried to sit back down. Unfortunately, the chair had moved and I dropped to the floor. Dr. Haywood knelt down next to me on one side. Gabriela was on the other. I could hear them talking, but I could not understand what they said. The last thing I remembered before I blacked out was asking Gabriela to call Moses.

CHAPTER EIGHT
GABRIELA MENDOZA

"Hey boo, you scared the shit out of me," I said when Ariana opened her eyes and finally focused on me. I had sat by her side for two hours waiting for her to wake up. All kinds of crazy thoughts were running through my head.

First and foremost was why she had asked me to call her boss and not her husband. Dr. Haywood was worried that she'd go into premature labor so he ordered a room for us. I was so afraid that I didn't call anyone. Surely she had to be delusional if the first person she thought of was her boss, Moses Ramsey. Our madre was gone and the first thing out my sister's mouth was to ask me to call her job? What the hell was up with that? I've had dreams about work before but she took it to a whole different level.

"Was I dreaming?" Ariana asked as worry began to etch a pattern on her face.

"No, sweetie, Madre's gone. I saw her and she looked peaceful." The words sounded foreign coming out of my mouth. I was trying to remain calm but I really wanted to scream. I wanted to break down, but someone had to hold it together.

"Oh God, how can this be? How did this happen?"

"I don't know. You've got to think about the baby right now. You fell pretty hard, and we were afraid that you were going to lose the baby."

She started to rub her stomach as the tears fell from her eyes. "I've got to talk to Moses."

"Moses? Why are you so concerned about him? Shouldn't you be trying to call your husband?"

She struggled to sit up in the bed. She had an IV running in her arm and a fetal heart monitor attached to her stomach. "There are a lot of things you don't understand." She gave me a look that told me to leave it alone but I couldn't, this was too important.

"Ariana, what the hell is going on?" I had a bad feeling she was about to say something that would change the way I looked at her.

She didn't answer me right away. She kept looking around the room as if she were contemplating escape. "Did the doctor say how long I would have to stay here?"

"Don't try to evade the question. What the hell is going on?"

She took a deep breath and let it out slowly. "Mike and I had been trying to have a baby for two years; it just wasn't happening. Every time I came on my period, Mike would get so depressed. I just had to do something."

"Oh God, Ariana, what did you do?"

Her eyes got wild, and I was afraid she was going to pass out again. She reached for my hand and I gave it to her, but she squeezed it so hard I had to yank it back.

"I slept with Moses," Her voice was so low I barely heard her.

"What did you say?" I demanded. Obviously, I was the one who was having a problem because I could have sworn I had just heard her say that she slept with her boss, a black man.

"Moses and I slept together—no strings attached."

"Bitch, have you lost your damn mind?" I shouted and I didn't even realize it.

"I did it for Mike. You didn't have to see his face each time I told him that we weren't pregnant. He got so depressed because he wanted a baby so badly."

"News flash, he still ain't pregnant. You are and it ain't his. How the hell did you think you were going to pass this one off on him? For Christ's sake, Moses is black."

"I know. But if you saw his baby pictures, you couldn't tell it. He looked just like a Latino baby."

"I don't want to bust your bubble here, but I have to say this. In all my conversations with Mike, he appeared to have a problem with black people. So explain to me how the fuck you are going to explain to him that his child is black. He is either going to kill you or whip your ass so bad you are going to wish you were dead."

She was so serious, I started to wonder which one of us was bat-shit crazy.

"He will believe anything I say to him."

"Oh, man, I do not believe this shit. I just lost my mother and my sister is one twig short of the cuckoo's nest."

"It can work. Moses and I are about the same complexion. He said that he didn't get darker until he started working outdoors."

"And you believed that shit. What is wrong with you? You are going to mess up a perfectly good marriage over some bullshit."

"No, I'm not. I've given this a lot of thought. Moses is not going to be in the picture at all."

"If he is not going to be in the picture, why the hell was he the first name out of your lips before you passed out?"

She didn't have shit to say about that.

I got up and paced the room. I was trying to understand what could have possessed my sister to have sex with her boss, and I just couldn't get that working in my mind.

"Okay, I'll admit that I'm a little scared about who my child will look like, but that doesn't take anything from Mike. I did this for him."

"Bitch, please. You did this for your damn self, so stop lying to yourself and me. If you weren't attracted to Moses, this would have never happened in the first place."

"You don't know what you're talking about."

"And you are in denial. Your husband has said on numerous occasions that he can't stand black people. How are you going to justify your relationship with a black man and fucking him? You may not like what I'm about to say, but Mike is a racist and he is going to make you dead for trying to pass off a black child as his."

"What does race have to do with anything? I'll admit I probably shouldn't have slept with Moses, but I can't change that now."

"So what are you going to do when you have a black child? Do you think that Mike is going to stand by you?"

"Stop it. I don't want to talk about this now. We need to be focused on Madre."

She had a point. I had totally lost sight of what we were there for in the first place.

"How are you feeling?" I said, changing the subject.

"I'm ready to go. Can you see what I have to do to get out of here? We need to go to the house and call Padre."

I left her even though there were so many more questions swirling in my head, but she was right. We needed to start making preparations. The reality of losing my mother had not yet sunken in, and I was operating on auxiliary reserve. I went to the nurses' station and was told Ariana was free to go. The nurse said she would come to the room and remove her IV as soon as another nurse came back to relieve her.

I went back to the room. I still had some questions that I needed answered. "What would Moses have said if I called him?"

"Uh…I need to talk to him because now he wants to be a part of the baby's life."

"Oh, God. Are you out your fucking mind?" I was beginning to get light-headed.

"No, I told him that it wasn't possible and that I loved Mike, but he still needs to know what's going on."

"Girl, your ass is fucked-up. Not only is your husband gonna leave your ass bruised and busted up, our father is going to kill you."

She started to cry again and I could not help but to join her. I never felt so helpless in my entire life. I felt as if my life was spiraling out of control and there was nothing that I could do to stop it. "Maybe he won't come," she whispered.

"Oh, you have really bumped your head. His wife just died." Her comment irritated me because I had wished the same thing. I wasn't ready to deal with the drama a visit from my father would bring.

We were both talking about our parents as if we didn't even know them.

"Girl, I can't understand what you were thinking. Have you and Moses been hitting it all along and you just decided to tell me about it?"

"No, I promise you it was just that one time."

I couldn't tell if she were telling the truth or not. "So how did it happen? Because for the life of me, I can't even think about how that conversation went."

"We were working late one night and one thing led to another. I was under a lot of stress at home and he helped to make me feel better."

"Ha, I'd hate to be you."

She sat up in the bed like she was about to start trying to tear some things up but sat back when she realized she couldn't go anywhere. "I don't care what you say, it wasn't like that. Besides, it's too late to go back and try to undo it because it's done."

"You are right about that, but let me ask you one more question. What are you going to do when this baby is born?"

She stared at me but didn't utter a sound. I shook my head in disbelief. I tried to think of something that would make her feel better about the situation but I couldn't.

"Well, it is what it is. We'll just have to make the best of it," I told her, then said a silent prayer for us all.

CHAPTER NINE
ARIANA MENDOZA

Gabriela followed me in her car back to Madre Sita's house. We were going to break the news to Ramón and call Padre. I wasn't looking forward to making the call, but I knew we didn't have any other options.

The house looked different to me for some reason. It looked empty and abandoned from the outside. I knew I was being irrational, but I couldn't help it as a cold shudder moved up my spine. I struggled to open the car door because I didn't have the strength to open it. Lying back against the headrest, I waited till Gabriela approached the car.

"What's wrong?" she asked, her face barely inches from me.

"I'm tired. I just want to crawl up in a ball and go to sleep."

She unhooked my seatbelt and gently pulled me out the car. "You can't sleep in here. Let's go inside the house. You can nap in there."

My heart skipped a beat. Was she really going to let me rest while she took care of telling our family the news? "What about Padre?" I whispered.

"I'll handle that. Just come on." She led me to the front porch and propped me up against the doorframe while she searched in her pockets for the keys.

Ramón snatched open the door before she could get the key in the hole. "What's wrong? How is she?" Gabriela pushed me forward. I could not walk on my own and she allowed me to lean on her. Ramón took my other arm and led me to the sofa. I sat there with a stoic expression on my face while I cried on the inside.

"Madre didn't make it," Gabriela said as she wiped a tear from her face.

Ramón's eyes grew wide as he frantically searched both of our faces. I wanted to reach out to him but I just didn't have the strength. He fell forward into my lap, and I placed my trembling arm over his shoulders. His sobs were the only sounds coming from the house.

"I need to call Padre. Ariana, where is the number?"

At the mention of my father's name, Ramón sat up straight and dried away his tears. His eyes shot defiant daggers at Gabriela but before he could start complaining, she cut him off.

"He has to know."

I pointed to my purse and she brought it over to me. I tried to look for my address book but my tears made it difficult to see. She let me look for a few more seconds, then took the purse back and found it herself. She went into the kitchen to make the call. I was relieved.

"Did she suffer?" Ramón asked.

The question took me by surprise because I didn't get to see her and I didn't think to ask. The doctor was afraid that seeing Madra Sita would cause me to faint again and he didn't want to take that chance. However, I made a mental note to call the doctor find out. "No, baby, she didn't. She went in her sleep." I felt bad for lying. Even if it weren't true, what difference would it make for Ramón to know otherwise? It would not bring Madre back. I had too many images running around in my head and none of them were good. I imagined Madre lifeless on the hospital bed; my father's face when he learned of my deceit—the stress was too much.

"Where's Mike?" Ramón said.

"Uh…" I wasn't ready to go there. Having Mike around would have been more of a pain than a blessing. He tended to hover and I had too much on my mind at the moment to deal with him. "I haven't called him yet. I think I need to take a nap first." I put my feet up on the sofa and pretended to go to sleep, but inside my heart was racing. That last image scared me to death. What was I thinking when I slept with Moses?

I could hear Gabriela crying in the kitchen as her voice got louder on the phone. She was yelling at Padre. I wanted to go to her to see what the commotion was about, but I couldn't. I protectively placed my arms around my belly. Regardless of what happened, I would protect my child. The love I felt for my baby rose inside of me. "It will be okay," I whispered before I drifted off to sleep. I needed to believe that with all my heart.

I don't know how long they had let me sleep but when I woke up, all I could hear was yelling coming from the kitchen. Concerned, I gently rolled off the sofa and waddled my way into the kitchen.

Mike had his hands planted on the refrigerator, resting his head against the cool exterior. Gabriela was standing by the sink, and I didn't know where Ramón was.

"What's going on?" I asked them both as they turned to face me. The first thing I noticed was that Mike was not smiling. This was unusual because his face always lit up with a smile when I came into a room. Neither of them spoke for a moment, which caused me to take a step back.

Gabriela pushed away from the sink and came toward me. "How are you feeling?"

"I'm okay. I thought I heard yelling." I looked past Gabriela to my husband, but his eyes remained focused on the floor. The vibe in the kitchen just didn't feel right.

"Here, have a seat. The doctor told you to stay off your feet as much as possible." She pulled out a chair and started pulling me toward it.

I was still looking at Mike, waiting to hear what he had to say. I allowed myself to be pushed into the chair. "How long was I asleep?"

"For a couple of hours," Gabriela said, walking back to the other side of the kitchen.

The hairs were standing up on the back of my neck, and the baby had begun thumping against my stomach. I turned to Mike again. "I guess you heard the news."

He stood up straight but still didn't look anywhere near my face. His eyes were focused on my feet as if he couldn't stand looking at me. He acted as if he knew something that I didn't, and the guilt of my deception was eating me up inside. If someone didn't start talking soon, I was going to confess and let the chips fall where they may.

"Yeah, I heard." His voice had a bite to it and was not the normal tone he used when he talked to me.

"When did you get here?" I was still searching for his eyes.

"About an hour ago," he replied.

"Why didn't you wake me?"

He looked me in the face for the first time. I could have sworn I saw fire in his eyes. He nodded to Gabriela and I turned to her. My eyes were pleading with her to tell me what was going on. If I didn't know better, I could have sworn that she had told him my secret, but I knew my sister would not betray me like that.

"I called Mike," she said, "and told him what happened at the hospital. I told him you passed out and that the doctor wanted you to rest. He came over here to see you for himself."

"Oh, I'm sorry, baby, but I'm okay," I said, making light of the situation.

"Then why didn't you call me?" His voice was accusing. I drew back from the bass in his voice.

This was a side of my husband I'd never seen before. Normally, he was very laid back, timid almost.

"I—uh—there wasn't—" Shit, what was I supposed to say? At this point, the baby was kicking wildly, causing me to sit up straight in the chair.

"Why are you snapping at her?" Gabriela whirled around, causing her own eyes to glaze over. She stood there glaring at him with her hands on her hips.

"I'm not yelling. I just asked her a question," Mike said.

"What the hell is going on here? Why is everyone so upset?" I started to get up from the chair, but Gabriela forced me to sit back down.

"I told Mike that our father is coming this week and that you needed to be here with us. He's not happy about it."

I looked at Mike for confirmation. Surely, he understood my need to be with my family during this time.

"Mike?" I was so confused.

"I don't have a problem with you being with your family. The problem I have is that your sister said I can't be with you."

I slunk back in the chair in shock. He walked farther away and there was nothing I could do to ease his pain. My heart felt like it was breaking in two. Suddenly, all the lies and deception began to catch up with me. I had an overwhelming urge to vomit.

"This week? That can't be."

Gabriela sat in the chair across from me. "He is leaving tonight. I couldn't believe it, either, but that's what he said."

I needed some time to think. There had to be a way to fix this without hurting everyone I loved in the process. I got up from the chair to talk to Mike but he turned his back on me. "Sweetheart, it will only be for a few days."

"'Few days' hell. You are my wife and you belong home with me. I told you both the other night that I'm not about to hide the fact we are married or that you are carrying my child."

"Nobody is asking you to hide, baby. We just need to break this to Padre gently. He just lost our mother."

"Oh, so you agree with her?" He looked as if he wanted to punch me out.

I backed away from him. "It's the only right thing to do."

"No, the right thing to do was to be honest from the beginning. How the hell would you feel if I lied about you to my folks?"

"That's not fair. You don't even have any family." Those were not the best choice of words to come out my mouth, but it was too late to take them back.

"What kind of family is this?"

I didn't even dignify his question with a response.

"You've got to be kidding me. Your father lives in another damn country. You said yourself that you hardly see him, so how does that justify turning our lives upside down?" His breathing was deep and hard and his face had turned an unflattering shade of red.

I thought that he was on the brink of busting a blood vessel.

"Mike, calm down. All this damn yelling and stuff ain't going to change anything," Gabriela interjected.

"Excuse me, sister dear, but I was speaking to my wife." He looked at Gabriela as if he dared her to say something else.

"Well, she's my sister, so don't get it twisted. You can speak to her without yelling. I told you what the fuck the doctor said," Gabriela replied.

I knew I had to do something before words were said that couldn't be taken back. "Gabriela, I need to speak with Mike alone. Can you give us a minute?"

She looked at me as if I had three heads perched up on my neck. I met her gaze with a firm resolve of my own. She walked out of the kitchen without a backward glance.

I pulled out the chair directly across from me. Mike came over and took a seat, but his eyes were all over the room. I'd never seen him so agitated.

"Mike, I know how you're feeling, and I agree this situation sucks, but this is something I have to do. After the funeral, I promise you I will tell Padre."

"So that means I can't even come to the funeral? What kind of fucked-up shit is that?"

Oh, Lord, I hadn't even thought that far. But he was right. He would stick out like a sore thumb and cause all kinds of hell if Padre chose that moment to show his ass.

"Let's go outside." I got up from the chair and walked outside with Mick reluctantly following behind me. I took a seat on the bench chair and he sat beside me—his faced was knotted up and he was still an angry shade of red.

"I know that all of this sounds strange to you, but you have to understand where we come from. We grew up in a poor Columbian village separated by class. The more money you had, the better your living arrangements were. We lived in a one-room hovel, but we were happy. The only people we were exposed to were other people in our class. It's not that Padre hates all white people, he just doesn't know any. Everything he knows about any other race is what is portrayed on television. As a result, we were taught to stay with our own race."

"Okay, I can understand that, but if he was so hell-bent on you staying with your own kind, why did he bring your family to the states?"

"Is it wrong to want something better for your family?" I could tell that he was trying to understand and I appreciated it. That was one of the reasons I was drawn to him in the first place, his compassion for other people. He didn't say anything further, so I continued.

"I'm sure I can get Padre to understand, in time, how I feel about you and our baby, but the timing isn't right. It was never part of Padre's plan to leave us here alone. Had it not been for my grandparents' refusal to leave Bogota, he would have been here with us."

"So where does that leave us?" His voice trembled as he spoke.

"Let me get through this funeral as a family. I'm not sure who will accompany Padre. If I were to introduce you now, in front of his family, he would lose face. After things settle down, I will tell him about us...all of us." I rubbed my belly.

"How are you going to hide the baby from him?"

"I'll wear big clothes."

"And if something happens to you or the baby while you're pretending, what then?"

"Nothing will happen. I promise to take it easy, and if something happens, Gabriela will call you right away." I reached out and grabbed his hand. He didn't wrap his fingers around mine immediately, so I leaned over and gave him a soulful kiss, which he returned with a passion all his own.

"I'm sorry about your mother, baby," Mike said.

Once again, Madre's death had slipped from my focus. There was too much going on for any one person to take. Dealing with the pressure of losing Madre and Padre's upcoming visit was driving me insane. My shoulders hitched, but I refused to cry anymore right now.

"I hate to break up this little love fest, but time is running out," Gabriela said as she walked out on the porch.

I pushed away from Mike and stood up. It was time for me to take control as the eldest in the family. "Where's Ramón?"

"I don't know. He left right after you went to sleep." Gabriela stared at me.

"You let him leave?"

"What was I supposed to do? That boy has a mind of his own. I thought he needed some space." Gabriela seemed to become irritated.

I had forced her into an uncomfortable position, looking out for me and Ramón. "I'm sorry; I should not have said that to you. I'm going to go home and pack my things. I'll be back to help you prepare the house. I should be back in a couple of hours."

"Okay, don't overdo it," Gabriela responded, looking at both of us. She gave us a half-hearted grin and a wink.

I think she knew that I was going to take care of my husband before I made it back.

"Leave your car here. I'll help you pack and bring you back," Mike said, winking his eye.

"When Ramón comes back, tell him we need to have a meeting so stay put." I wobbled toward the door.

CHAPTER TEN
GABRIELA MENDOZA

If we were going to pull this off, I was going to have to run home and pack up a few things. It hadn't really sunk in yet that my madre was gone, and if I weren't so worried about seeing padre, I would have fallen apart. There would be enough of that over the coming days. For now, I had to get enough things to take back to Madre Sita's house to make it look like I still lived there.

I left a note for Ramón and headed home with my mind running a mile a minute. I mentally made a checklist of all the things I would need to bring back to the house with me. My padre said we would have the funeral in the house. It was an old custom, even though Madre had died in the hospital. Since she didn't have many friends, it would be a very small ceremony.

My thoughts wandered to Ariana and how she was going to handle the next few days. I didn't envy her position. Not only was she going to have to come clean about her husband, she was bearing another man's child.

I didn't see Tilo's car when I pulled up. I heaved a sigh of relief. If I were lucky, I would be able to get my things and bounce before she got home. Dealing with Tilo over the telephone would be a lot easier than in person.

When I went to my bedroom, the first thing I noticed was that Tilo had finished painting it and had put away all of the painting supplies. The room looked good. I could hardly wait to set up my desk and computer. I was going to start a home-based business doing taxes during tax season.

As much as I wanted to start unpacking my equipment, I knew I had to get moving if I wanted to beat Ariana back to the house. I grabbed my suitcase and started pulling things from my dresser drawers. I didn't know how long I would be gone, so I practically emptied my drawer of underwear and bras. From my closets, I took only my clothes I wore to work. My father hated seeing us in jeans and sneakers. He said it wasn't fitting for a girl. Humph, if he only knew. He had a lot of outdated thoughts, but he was my padre and I had to respect him.

Tilo stood in the threshold of my room. "Hey, what's up?" She was talking to me but she was looking at my suitcases.

"Thanks for finishing the room. It looks nice." I was nervous as hell.

"Uh, you going somewhere?" There was a hint of attitude in her words.

I sat down on the bed, rested my arms on my thighs. I felt like I was in the eye of a hurricane. Tilo moved farther into the room, looking around at the empty hangers in my closet and the half-closed drawers of my dresser.

"I got to go home for a minute. My mother didn't make it, and my family needs me."

Tilo's expression immediately softened as she approached the bed. "Sweetie, I'm so sorry." She rubbed her hands down my arms, kneeling before me. I wanted to cry, but I felt like I was all cried out. "Thanks."

She edged closer. I could feel the heat emanating from her skin.

"So how's everybody holding up?" Her hands were burning a trail up my arms and down my legs. I didn't want to feel anything, but she was too close.

"When we got the news, Ariana fainted. I thought they were going to keep her at the hospital, but they let her go. She's at her house now packing to go back to Madre's house. Ramón has shut down because he doesn't want my father to come home. Other than that, I guess we're okay."

Tilo stood up and climbed on the bed behind me. She pressed her knees against my back as she massaged my shoulders. I allowed my head to drift back. I wanted to just close my eyes and enjoy the moment, but I couldn't. I had to get back to my mother's. I tried to pull away, but Tilo held me tight.

"Can I go back to your mother's house with you?"

I stiffened. I did not want to have this conversation with her. Her fingers became more urgent as they slid down my arms. Her hands dangerously close to my breasts. Unconsciously, I arched my back, pressing my tiny boobs forward. She responded by boldly grabbing them and giving them a tight squeeze.

I exhaled.

I hadn't realized that I was holding my breath until I let it go. She dipped her head down and lightly kissed me on my forehead. She moved lower and kissed me on my cheeks. A low moan escaped my lips as she used her fingers to tease my nipples. Her dreads teased the side of my face, and I wanted nothing more than to run my fingers through them.

Turning, I pulled her around and onto my lap, deeply inhaling her scent. She filled my nose. I wanted her more than I'd ever wanted her before. I rocked back with my arms tightly around her waist. She twisted free and straddled me, stretching my arms out to the side. I understood what was about to happen. I welcomed it.

She pulled her tank top over her head and undid her bra. Her beautiful bronze boobs broke out of bondage, teasing me. I lifted my hands to touch them, but she quickly pushed them away. She wanted to be in control. I could feel the heat of her pussy through her jeans. She was driving me crazy. She knew it.

She unbuttoned my blouse. Her eyes never left my face. Her tongue moved seductively across her full lips. She nuzzled my breasts through my bra, and I thought I was going to lose my mind. I wanted to feel her hot mouth on my naked flesh. She was taking entirely too long to get us out of our clothes.

"Stop playing," I pleaded.

"Who's playing?" She laughed. She pulled down the straps of my bra and took my nipples in her mouth.

I bucked against her, but she tightly held me in place. "Shit." It came out more of a moan than a curse. She changed position, dipping her thigh between my legs. She grinded on me, kissing me deeply. I was on fire. Every inch of me wanted to touch her, to taste her. She pushed off of me and stood before me. She slowly slid her pants down. She was wearing a lime green thong that hugged her tiny waist.

"So, you were going to leave without saying goodbye to this?" She turned around so I could see that the material had slipped between the crack in her ass.

"Uh, nah, baby … I was about to hit you up on the cell."

She clinched her muscles, causing her ass to jiggle. I could feel the moisture gathering between my legs and my mouth felt dry as a dessert. I needed something to drink in the worse way, and I couldn't think of anything that I would have loved to drink more than her tangy juices.

"So, what'chu gonna do?" she said suggestively.

"I'm going to taste what is mine," I replied. I wagged my finger at her, urging her to come closer. I was in a playful mood despite all that was going on around me. When she got close enough for me to grab, I lifted her leg and placed it on the bed. With my hands around her waist to keep her steady, I moved in closer to smell her. "Umm, you smell good enough to eat."

She giggled this girlish laugh. My tongue struck the center of her clit. She moaned softly and arched her back, her grapefruit-sized breasts pointing toward the ceiling. Her nipples reminded me of twin pebbles, hard and swollen.

"Stop playing with it and eat it," Tilo demanded.

I licked her clit again, causing her body to jump. "Damn you taste good. Come sit on my face." I scooted back so that I could lie on the bed but still keep my feet on the floor. I wanted the leverage so I could flip her if she got too carried away while grinding on my face. The last time we did this, she damn near smothered me with her coochie.

"Aren't you going to finish taking your clothes off?"

I froze. I thought about telling her my plans, but that would certainly ruin the mood. "I will after I eat." I pulled her pussy closer to my face.

She signed as she lowered herself onto me. Using my tongue like a knife, I sliced into her and she started to cum. Instinctively, I wanted to push her away, but she was giving me exactly what I had asked for. Now the best I could hope for was not to drown in thc process. Eating pussy was a new thing for me. In fact, this whole lifestyle was new. I had never been intimate with anyone, let alone a woman. When we had first gotten together, it was all her idea.

I held Tilo in place, gently lapping at her swollen clit until her legs stopped shaking. When she was done, I rolled her on her side and cuddled up against her. I was content she didn't ask me if I wanted her to reciprocate, which was just as well because I needed to go. "Tilo?" I whispered in her ear.

"Huh." She sleepily answered.

"I've got to go. I should have been back at my madre's house by now."

She stiffened in my arms. "I don't understand this cloak and dagger shit. How come everything about you and your family is so secret? I take you around my folks all the time without all this drama."

"I know, but it's complicated. I promise I'll tell you about it when things get back to normal."

"So what am I supposed to do while you are gone?" She folded her arms and pouted like a little girl.

I didn't feel like answering that question. I wanted to say, the same damn thing you were doing before I got here, but I didn't. Our relationship was new, and I didn't want to say anything I would later regret just because I was under a whole lot of stress. "Please be patient, Tilo. I'll make this up to you after my father goes home."

As I left the house, I prayed that I would be able to live up to my promise because I honestly didn't know what was going to happen once our father got here. I turned once to see if Tilo was going to change her mind and give me a kiss, but she didn't even come to the window. Girlfriend was pissed.

CHAPTER ELEVEN
GABRIELA MENDOZA

Even with the delay of my unexpected sexual encounter, I managed to make it back to my madre's house before Ariana and Ramón. It felt funny coming into the house with no one to greet me. The house always had some sounds going on. Either it was the television, a radio, but never silence. This hurt my heart.

I dragged my suitcases up the stairs to my old room that I used to share with Ariana. The twin beds looked even smaller, although it hadn't been too long since I'd last slept in them.

"Humph, I never thought I would see this room again with suitcases in hand," I said, talking to myself, which I often did when I was alone. Shaking my head, I put away my clothes and stored the suitcases under the bed. After I put my toothbrush and deodorant in the bathroom, I was bored. I pulled out my cell and called Ramón. It was getting ready to get dark, and we hadn't seen him since noon. His phone rang three times before it went over to his voice mail. "Damn, where the hell is he at?" I was about to call Ariana but I heard a car pull up, so I decided to go out and help her with the bags.

***

"Took your ass long enough," I said as I went outside and grabbed one of her suitcases from the back seat. She pulled the lever for the trunk as I closed the car door. I walked around to the trunk, which was full as well. "Damn, girl, how the hell long do you think we are going to be here?" I looked at her, then Mike.

"Hush, you sound just like Mike. We stopped off at Walmart and bought some maternity clothes for me to wear to hide my stomach. You know how Padre feels about jeans so I had to pick up a few things."

We piled the bags on the curb and Mike pulled off without turning back.

"Shit, you should have asked him to tote this shit in the house." I watched his taillights fade away.

"Girl, you saw his mug. He wasn't happy—plus I would've had to say goodbye all over again. I've sucked enough dick tonight." She giggled when she said this, and I laughed with her.

"I feel ya."

She looked at me strangely, then I realized what I had said. She didn't know that Tilo and I were lovers, but I almost blew it. I started for the house, hoping she wouldn't notice my little slip of the tongue.

"So, you are dating? When did this happen?" She was walking so fast behind me that she stepped on the heel of my shoe.

"Damn, girl. You are scuffing up my new shoes."

"I don't want to talk about your shoes. I wanna hear about this man you are dating."

I winced at the mention of my dating a man, but I wasn't about to challenge her. "Shit, I wish Ramón was here to help with these bags. Why don't you go sit down while I get the rest of the bags in the house."

"Where's Ramón?" She looked around like he was hiding somewhere like he used to do when we were little kids.

"Hell if I know. It doesn't look like he's been here since we left."

"I sure hope he's not about to show his ass, because that's the last thing that we need right about now," Ariana said.

"I know that's right." I went back outside to get the rest of her things. I was thankful that I was able to derail her from asking anymore questions about my personal life. I was going to have to think before I spoke from now on, or at least until I could get back to my own house.

I had to make two trips to get all of her shit from the curb. She had packed everything but the kitchen sink.

"If Padre wasn't coming this week, I would leave all this shit right here in the living room floor."

"I'll help you get it upstairs," Ariana said.

"Like hell you will. Your husband ain't going to beat my ass because something happened to you. Just get upstairs so you can start unpacking. I've got to get me something to drink before I fall out." I went into the kitchen and noticed that the message light on the phone was flashing. I picked up the phone and put in the code to hear the message.

I pressed Replay several times before I hung up the phone. I was so pissed I didn't know whether to shit or go blind. Forgetting the water and the suitcases, I took the stairs two at a time and stormed into our bedroom. Ariana was sitting on the bed like she didn't have a care in the world.

"When the hell did you have time to call Moses?"

She looked like a mouse that had been cornered by a big cat. She started to get up from the bed, but I pushed her back.

"Answer me. When the hell did you have time to call him? Why is he calling this house?"

"Gabriela, you don't understand. He has a right to know what's going on with me. I won't be into work so I had to tell him."

"Don't play me, sis. If this was about work, then you would have called him in the morning during work hours!"

She looked around the room like she was trying to find a way to get out, but I wasn't about to let her out of my sight.

Suddenly, it occurred to me. "Oh snap! You're still fucking him, aren't you?"

"Uh—"

"Damn, girl, what are you thinking? Are you trying to fuck up your marriage?"

She started crying and rocking back and forth. Even though I was mad at her, I still couldn't stand to see her cry. I sat down next to her and put my arm around her shoulders. She leaned her head down and continued to cry.

"It wasn't supposed to be this way." Her voice was so low I had a hard time hearing her.

"Huh? What way?"

She pushed away from me and stood up and started pacing.

"We were only supposed to do it once."

I didn't know what to say to her. She acted as if just because she only intended for it to happen once, that would lessen the sin and the shame.

"So what are you saying?"

"I … uh … I don't know."

I threw my hands up in the air. "We don't have time to play these fucking games." I spun around and faced her. "Do you love Mike?"

"Yes, I love my husband. What kind of question is that to ask?" she shouted angrily at me.

"Oh, excuse me. You are fucking another man and carrying his baby, so forgive me for being so fucking confused about what's really going on." I was two seconds away from leaving the room.

"I didn't mean for this to happen. I told him that we couldn't keep seeing each other, but every time he calls, I make up some excuse to be with him. He got to me."

"So are you in love with him?"

She didn't answer. She didn't have to. It was written all over her face.

"You know there is not going to be a happy ending to this story. Somebody is going to get hurt, and I pray to God it ain't you." I fell back on the bed.

"Moses would never hurt me."

I could not believe the words that were coming out of her mouth. Why wasn't her first concern her husband? Or, better yet, our father? "Girl, you are seriously twisted. I'm going to get the rest of your suitcases." I left the room with her still standing in the middle of the room. It was ironic that both of our lovers were black, but I wasn't losing my fucking mind over my piece of ass.

Ramón came stumbling in the door as I grabbed the last two suitcases. He didn't even see me.

I watched him for several minutes before I spoke. "Where the hell you been?"

He practically jumped out of his skin. "Shit, you scared the hell out of me."

His eyes were red. At first I thought it was from crying, but as he tried to walk up the stairs, I knew the deal.

"Boy, are you drunk?" I could not believe what I was seeing. Ramón wasn't but seventeen years old and smelled like he had fallen in a vat full of booze.

"No, and why you got to be hollering and shit?"

"I ain't hollering. I just asked you a question." I put down the bag so I could have a better look at him.

He swayed before my eyes.

"If you ain't drunk, stand still."

He tried—bless his heart—but couldn't do it.

I wanted to be mad at him but if I had a bottle, I'd be drunk right about now too. "Take your stupid ass upstairs and sleep it off. You better pray that Padre don't get here and see you that way."

He looked like he was about to argue with me but instead he bumped and weaved his way up the stairs. I waited until he was all the way to the top before I tried to go up behind him with the last two bags. The last thing I needed was for him to tumble backwards and knock us both back down the steps.

I dropped the bags off at the door and went to make sure Ramón had made it to his room. Ariana was still standing in the middle of the floor looking crazy as hell.

Ramón was laid out on the bed, still in the clothes he had worn the day before. He didn't even bother to take off his shoes. I should have made his ass take a shower, but it was too late for that. I was about to go back and help Ariana when the phone rang.

"Hello," I said.

"Is Ariana there?"

"Who is this?" I asked, even though I knew who it was.

"Uh … Moses."

The brother had a lot of nerve. I dropped the phone back on the table and went into our bedroom. "Phone." I wanted to say so much more, but I decided to keep my mouth shut. I guess she could tell by the jut of my chin that it wasn't her husband.

She rushed pass me, grabbed the phone, and went downstairs so she could speak in private. As big as she was, she had no difficulty rushing down those steps to talk on the phone.

"Damn, he must have dicked you down good and proper," I said loud enough for her to hear, but she didn't acknowledge my comment.

CHAPTER TWELVE

ARIANA MENDOZA

Gabriela had absolutely no idea how good Moses' dick was. I plopped my fat butt on the couch, smiling from ear to ear, but calmed myself before I spoke into the phone so he wouldn't know how excited I was. "Hey, I got your message. How are you?"

"No, I'm one that should be asking the questions. How are you and my baby doing?"

"We're fine. Just a small scare."

"I want to come by and see for myself."

"Moses, you know that's not possible. Once Padre gets here, I'll try to sneak out to see you."

"Sneak out? You are a grown woman."

"A married, grown woman." I corrected him and I instantly regretted it. I didn't want to get him started on that you-have-got-to-get-a-divorce crusade that he had been talking about for the last few weeks.

"Don't remind me. I don't want to get into an argument with you tonight, especially since the doctor said you should take it easy, so I'll let that slide."

"Thank you, 'cause I really don't feel like arguing, either. This is hard enough as it is."

"Have you made any arrangements yet for the funeral?"

"No, we're waiting on Padre. He should be here tomorrow. I'm not even sure if they have any insurance to pay for all this."

"Wow, that's tough. Baby, if you need me, all you have to do is call me, okay?"

"Thanks, but according to my father, he has the money. We don't even know if he wants to bury her here or if he plans to take her back home."

"Do you think that's what he will do? I mean, that could be expensive. If he thinks like that, he might even expect you and your family to move back home with him?"

"Oh, God, don't even put that out in the universe."

"I'm sorry, baby. I didn't mean to be a fly in your ointment. How's your hubby handling all of this?"

I was surprised Moses even mentioned Mike, since I knew he didn't give a rat's ass about my husband. Moses was just making small talk, but I humored him anyway.

"He's not happy about me moving back home, but he's going along with it."

"Well, if you were my wife, I wouldn't be so agreeable. A wife's place is with her husband."

Sucking my teeth, I was tempted to say something smart, but I decided against it because in theory, I agreed with him. He just didn't know Padre.

"Hey, your sister sounds like a spitfire. Does she know about us?"

"Yeah, I had to tell her. She's afraid for me." I didn't tell him that she thought I was a silly bitch.

"Did you tell her that I loved you and would never hurt you?"

"Moses, stop saying that. You know I'm married and that what we have will never go anywhere."

He was quite for a few seconds, and I was afraid that he had hung up on me.

"Ariana, I can't help how I feel. If I could change it, I would. It's too late for that. I'm going to do my best to respect your relationship and your feelings, but I won't lie, even to myself, about how I feel about you."

Tears gathered in the back of my eyes. I closed them to keep them back. Moses had this rough-and-tough exterior but he could say the sweetest things to me that kept me coming back to him.

"Moses, we are going to have to be real careful with this. You can't call me on this phone anymore. If you want me, just call me on my cell. If I don't answer, leave a message and I will call you back the first chance I get."

"Why can't I call you?"

"Because I can't have Padre finding out about you right now. It would destroy him. He doesn't even know that I'm married. He's been away so long, it just wasn't something that I could tell him over the phone."

"Wow, that's deep. Still, if you were my woman, I would have taken you back home and done things right."

He was putting me on the defensive. I felt like I had to defend Mike because I had never given him the opportunity to speak to Padre. I wanted to explain all of this to Moses so he would understand, but I didn't have the time or the patience to go into it with him. "Moses, I have to go. I still have to unpack and try to get some rest before Padre gets here."

"Okay, baby girl. I won't hold you any longer. Call me tomorrow, okay?"

"I will." I carried the phone back up the stairs with me. Although I wasn't ready to go back in the room and face my sister, I still had things to do. I was out of breath by the time I got back to the room.

"Did you call your husband?" She raised a brow.

"Gabriela, don't start, okay? I know that you don't approve, but this is really none of your damn business." I started to unpack my things and did my best to ignore her.

"You're right: it's not. But when this blows up in your face, I want you to remember what the fuck you said to me."

I sank down on the bed because I felt like I was losing my mind. Gabriela was the only person in the world that I could depend on. "Gabriela, sit down please."

She didn't sit next to me but she did sit back on her old bed. "Seems like old times, don't it?" She chuckled, but it wasn't a merry chuckle; it was downright depressing.

"Yeah, I never thought we would wind up here again, especially under these circumstances."

"I know. It really hasn't sunk in yet that she's gone." She fluffed her pillow.

"It will hit us when Padre gets here. What if he wants us to move back to Columbia? Have you thought of that?"

"I'm trying not to. I really doubt if he would try that because he sent us here to have a better life," Gabriela said.

"Do you remember how we left?"

"What do you mean? We got on a plane, silly," I said with a smile.

She shook her head at my attempt of humor. Her face was very serious and she was scaring me.

"I was referring to what led to us leaving?"

"Oh, you mean Dezi and Fabio. I remember them dying, if that's what you're talking about."

"Not exactly. I remember hearing Madre Sita and Padre talking late one night in the kitchen. They said that if they didn't leave, we would all be taken away."

"Taken away? By who?" This was the first time that she had ever said anything like that. I was surprised she had kept such a secret from me.

"I don't know exactly, but Padre was real scared and he said that we had to leave right away."

"Well, if that's the case, then going back should not be an option we should have to worry about."

"Let's hope so."

I continued to unpack my things and put them away in the closets. In my head, I kept thinking of all those half-heard conversation that Madre Sita and Padre had had, and all the unanswered questions surrounding our brother's disappearances. Those thoughts caused a knot to well up in my. Gabriela noticed and came over and gave me a hug.

"It's going to be alright, Ariana, just wait till Padre gets here. He will fix things."

I hoped my sister was right, but I wasn't feeling as good about things as she was. There were a lot of decisions to make, and I wasn't sure Padre was the one to make them.

After I finished putting away my clothes, I lay down on the bed to take a little nap. The last few days had been murder on my body and mind. For a split second, I considered giving my husband a call, but I really didn't feel like hearing his mouth. Before I closed my eyes for the night, I looked over at Gabriela and she appeared to be sleeping as well.

CHAPTER THIRTEEN
GABRIELA MENDOZA

Being back in the room with my sister was going to be harder than I'd originally thought. I'd forgotten about her snoring. After a few minutes of sleep, she quickly reminded me of how much like a freight train she sounded. I don't know how Mike put up with that noise every night.

My thoughts went back to Tilo and I smiled. I wanted to confide in Ariana about my secret relationship with Tilo, but I was afraid of how she would react. I loved my sister and the last thing that I wanted to do was lose her respect.

The last thought I had before I blocked Ariana's snoring out and went to sleep was of my father. A part of me could not wait to see him again. He hadn't been home in over five years, and I missed him. He was a small man who I liked to think was trapped in the seventies. He was a simple man with no fashion sense. He didn't believe in wasting a lot of money on clothes and jewelry. In fact, he probably still had some of the same pants that his mother had bought him when he was a teenager.

Part of that came from the fact that we never had much money, but the other part was that he just didn't see the need. When we were little, I used to be embarrassed when he came home to visit in his old-fashioned clothes. I didn't remember which was worse, his homely clothes or the thick, coke-bottle styled glasses.

Something caused me to jump out of bed. Disoriented, it took me a few minutes to remember where I was. My heart was racing, but I didn't know what had caused me to feel this way. I looked at my sister and she was still sleeping. I looked at my watch and realized it was almost four in the morning. I had no intentions of sleeping that long. I had only meant to take a light nap then get up and clean the house in anticipation of my father's arrival.

I needed to go to the bathroom, so I quietly eased myself off the bed. I didn't want to wake up Ariana if I didn't have to. Going to the bathroom was another thing that I hated about living back at home. I had to share the bathroom with my brother and he was known to keep the lid up after he had used it. I can't tell you how many times my narrow behind had fallen into the water.

With my arms stretched out in front of me, I eased my way out of the darkened room. If I made it out of the room without tripping over anything, I had a good chance of making it to the bathroom without mishap. The hallway was darker than our room, so I felt along the walls, trying to find the light switch, but my fingers kept missing it. I didn't have time to search for it any longer, so I kept going forward, hoping that nothing new was placed in the hallway that would cause me to fall.

When I reached the bathroom, the door was closed. I tapped on it twice and waited to see if Ramón was in there. He didn't answer, so I turned the knob and went in. I flipped the light switch and the bright light practically blinded me. I hurried over to the toilet and quickly sank down on it. Luckily for me, the seat was down.

As I looked around the bathroom, I found it amazing that not many things had changed. Some things remained the same. The towels hanging in the bathroom were the same towels that had been hanging there ever since we had moved in. The shower curtain and the rugs were all the same. I felt like I had walked into some type of time warp. The only thing missing from our bathroom was Ariana's toothbrush and makeup that Ramón used to complain about littering the countertop.

I pulled back the shower curtain to see if the tub had a ring. Since this was Ramón's bathroom now, I was curious as to how well he kept it clean. Much to my surprise, it was spotless. I always thought that when he got the bathroom to himself, he would trash it just like he used to keep his room.

Getting up from the toilet, I washed my hands and decided to go down to the kitchen to find something to eat. I couldn't remember the last time that I had eaten anything with substance. I stepped out in the hallway and was reaching back to turn off the light when I noticed this strange man standing in front of me.

CHAPTER FOURTEEN
MOSES RAMSEY

I arrived at the office early today. Juggling a large cup of coffee, the *New York Times*, and my briefcase, I managed to unlock the doors to my office without spilling a single drop. I was feeling great and I attributed it all to Ariana, the future mother of my child. All I had to do was to convince her that we were meant to be, then everything else would work out as planned.

Pausing to retrieve my messages from the receptionist desk, I slipped them in the pocket of my suit jacket before I continued to my office. I loved coming into the office early. It gave me time to catch up on things without the constant ringing of the phone and periodic interruptions from the other members of my staff. Placing my coffee and briefcase on my desk, I took my messages out of my pocket and went to hang up my jacket, then closed my office door. With any luck, I would be able to get through my messages, read a few pages of the paper, and get a jump on my hectic schedule.

Shit, where the hell did spring go? I thought as I looked out my window. Although it was still early, I could tell that today was going to be another scorcher. It seemed like we had slipped right past those blissfully cool months and skipped straight to hot as hell. The walk from my car to the office was short but I had already worked up a sweat. I grabbed a tissue from the dispenser and wiped my brow as I sifted through my messages.

I did not expect to see a message from Ariana, but that didn't stop me from looking for one from her. As I flipped over the last pink message, I fought the urge to throw them all on the floor because none of them were from her. Pushing my messages to the side, I surveyed my office over the rim of my coffee cup. The love seat in the corner instantly brought a smile to my face because that was where I had first made love to her.

Placing my feet up on my desk, I reared back in my chair and traveled down memory lane. I remembered that day like it had happened twenty minutes ago.

A slight knock on my office door jolted me for a deep nod. I'd been reviewing surveillance tapes since four that morning in preparation for a final summation of an insurance fraud case I'd been working on for the last few weeks, so I was tired as hell. I glanced at my watch as I acknowledged the knock. "Come in."

Ariana peeked through the crack of the door with a slight smile on her lips. Her face refreshed me and I sat up straight in my chair.

"You okay in here? You've been mighty quiet," she remarked as she came in and shut the door behind her.

"Yeah, I'm alright, just finishing up this report." I turned around to my desk to pretend that I was typing but much to my chagrin, the screen was blank and she had seen it.

"Uh-hum." She started giggling.

"Okay, so I was sleeping. Can't a brother catch a few winks every now and then?" I laughed along with her.

"What you ought to be doing is going out and have you some fun. When's the last time that you just went out and did something spontaneous?"

"Uh—"

"Uh nothing. It's Friday. You should be out somewhere getting your drink on with some fine young honey."

Whoa, what was going on? This was time first time that Ariana had ever expressed an interest in my life outside of the office. Even though we had had some pretty deep conversations, she had never once inquired about what I did when I left the office. "Oh really? When did you become concerned about what I did outside of the office?" If she wanted to get all up in my business, than I was going to get in hers. "What are you doing here so late on a Friday evening? Shouldn't you be home tossing it up with your husband?" Even though I had meant to say it in a joking manner, it sounded sarcastic to my ears. I regretted the words the moment they were out my mouth. We were close, but I knew I had crossed over the line. A deep frown came over her face, and for a moment. I thought she was going to start crying.

"Well excuse me for caring." She got up and started walking to the door.

I rushed over to stop her. I had to let her know that I wasn't making fun of her. "Ariana, wait. I didn't mean that the way it sounded."

She snatched her arm from my fingers. "That's fine. I should be getting home anyway. Thanks for reminding me." She practically stomped to the door and snatched it open.

I couldn't blow it now. I had worked too hard to get close to her. I frantically thought of something to say that would cool her down. "I can't help it if I was feeling jealous." I stepped back, fully expecting her to take a swing at me.

"What did you say?" She shut the door.

I walked away from her and sat back down at my desk. My mind raced to think of something that would diffuse the situation. "I'm tired, Ariana, and not thinking clearly. Do you forgive me?" I sighed. Keeping my feelings in check was getting harder and harder.

She sat down on the love seat and continued to stare at me. She made me very uncomfortable, especially when she leaned back against the cushions and got comfortable. A sly smile crossed her lips. "Jealous about what?" She was not going to let this go.

My face started to heat up again. There was no way I was going to continue that conversation. I began packing up the files on my desk, hoping that she would get the hint and leave. She continued to watch me.

"Why are you staring at me?"

"'Cause I want to know why you won't answer the question."

"I told you I was talking out my head because I'm tired."

"Bullshit," she purred, causing me to blink rapidly.

I felt my dick lengthen, which only added to my embarrassment. I wanted to look at her, but I was afraid of what I would see. In my current state, I didn't trust myself. I leaned back in my chair and willed myself to relax. Ariana was playing a dangerous game and she didn't even know it. It had been several months since I'd been with a woman. Tonight it showed. Normally, I would not have lost my cool, but everything about her turned me on. I glanced at my watch again. "It's getting late." I still could not get up from my desk without her seeing my erection.

She stayed seated. "Did I tell you we're trying to have a baby?"

I felt like she had thrown a cold bucket of water in my face. "Say what?" I asked in disbelief.

"Mike. He wants to have a baby. We've been going at it for months."

"Don't you think that's a little personal to be sharing?" Not only was I shocked that she had said that to me, I was pissed because she planted an image in my head of her fucking someone else in my head. An image that I knew would hound me for days to come.

"No, we've shared so much more." Once again her voice held a seductive charm.

I felt like she was a snake charmer and she was drawing me in. I struggled to keep my eyes from her face. "Well, I guess you shouldn't keep your hubby waiting." This time I didn't bother to hide the jealousy that I felt.

"He couldn't hit my spot if he used your dick." There was no animosity in her voice.

"If it we're my dick driving, it would know exactly where to go."

"Show me…just this once…"

I looked up and she had taken off her shirt. Her bare breasts taunted me. Her tiny nipples were swollen with desire. Every rational thought left my big head and the little head took the lead. She stood up and unfastened her skirt, allowing it to drop to the floor. In a dreamlike trance, I stumbled to her and she quickly undressed me. We didn't speak. There was no need. Our bodies said everything there was to say. From that day forward, I've been torn between the lure of money and loving my client's daughter.

CHAPTER FIFTEEN

GABRIELA MENDOZA

My hand froze and my heart felt like it was about to leap out of my chest at any minute when I saw the intruder in our hallway. I opened my mouth to say something, but nothing came out. It was a good thing I had just peed, or I would have pissed all over the floor.

When the stranger took a step toward me, my vocal cords started to work. I let out a scream so loud, I could have raised the dead. The man took another step closer, but I was already retreating into the bathroom, trying to lock the door behind me. I expected him to reach out and grab me as I struggled with the door.

Ramón and Ariana came out in the hallway and we had the stranger cornered. He swung his head back and forth, not sure of who posed the worst threat, I suppose. Fearing he was a theft, I struck a pose to make him think I knew karate. Following my lead, Ramón did the same thing. If the stranger only knew how far from the truth that was.

Ariana stepped forward, pushing Ramón behind her. "What the hell are you doing in our house?"

While Ariana was talking, I was busy looking around the bathroom for a weapon. I was going to get the largest item in the bathroom and whack the hell out of this man.

"What, can't speak English?" Ramón jeered.

My hands closed around the plunger. It wasn't much, but I intended to use it as a baseball bat. I raised the plunger over my head and starting edging closer to him.

He took one step back. When he realized he was getting too close to Ramón and Ariana, he stopped his retreat. He threw his hands up in the air. "I just can't believe how big you have all have gotten," he said, chuckling.

"Who the hell are you, and what the fuck are you doing in our house?" I yelled.

"All right, little lady, I won't tolerate that type of language in my house." The smile slid off the man's face.

I was confused because I had never seen this man before in my life. He was Hispanic, but he spoke English as if it were a second language. In fact, he spoke it better than me, and I had been living in America for ten years.

"Excuse me?" Ariana said, taking a step forward.

"It's me," the man said.

"Me who?" I replied, lowering the plunger. It was clear to me that the man didn't have a weapon and wasn't going to hurt us or he would have used it by now.

"I know it's been a long time since I've been home, but surely it hasn't been that long that you don't even recognize your own father!"

"Oh hell to the no! You are not my father," Ramón screamed as he lunged at the man.

This was some type of sick joke. There was no way that this man standing before me could be my father.

First of all, my father did not speak English. The most he could say comfortably was yes and no. Other than that, he struggled. Secondly, where were his thick-ass glasses and those homely clothes? This man was dressed in an Armani suit with a diamond stud in his left ear. He had diamond rings on both of his hands and what appeared to be a Rolex watch on his wrist.

The stranger quickly grabbed Ramón's arms and held them to his side. Ramón was so mad, he was crying. I didn't blame him because I felt like crying too.

I was so stunned I could not move. I searched my mind for the last picture I had seen of my father and none of them looked even remotely like this man. He had to be lying. I raised the plunger up over my head, using it as a hammer, and I whacked him as hard as I could. The wood came down on his shoulder and split in two. The rubber bounced off the floor and rolled down the hall.

The man pushed Ramón away from him and reached up to grab his shoulder. I was ready to use the jagged edge to stab him when Ariana yelled out.

"Wait." She grabbed her stomach and fell back against the wall. She winced in pain, and I rushed to her side to support her. The fight went out of Ramón too, as he quickly moved over to aid Ariana. Ramón kept an eye on the stranger in case he wanted to nut up or something.

I led Ariana downstairs to the living room with Ramón right behind us. The stranger, who claimed to be our father, was right behind us. Once I got Ariana settled on the sofa with a pillow to place over her stomach, I went to my wallet to retrieve the last picture that I had of my father, which had been taken right before we left Columbia.

I studied the picture against the man before me. Although I could see some similarities, I still wasn't ready to believe that this distinguished man sitting in front of me was my father. I lowered my eyes to avoid upsetting Padre. It was disrespectful to stare.

Ariana recovered first. "When did you learn to speak English?"

"I've been speaking it for a few years now," he said. "I took some classes at the college."

"Fuck that! Where did you get all that bling?" Ramón asked.

"I have told you about using that type of language in this house. Now I know this is a shock to all of you, but I won't tolerate that type of disrespect."

"Humph!" Ramón was cruising for a bruising, but I could understand how he felt.

For years, we barely had enough food to eat so it was a bitter blow to find out that my father was living large. We always assumed his conditions were worse than ours and a knot of resentment rose in my throat.

"What about your glasses? How can you see?" Ariana asked. She was being very calm, but I knew her well enough to know this was just the calm before the storm.

"Oh, those." He reached up to touch his face as if he had just realized that he wasn't wearing them.

"I had that laser surgery several years ago."

That was the final straw for me. I jumped up from the sofa and started pacing the floor. I didn't want to be the one to tell this man that he could kiss my entire ass, but just looking at him made me want to kill him. I could not believe he would do this to us. I thought about all the years we had prayed for him, believing he was living in squalor when that was obviously not the case. In fact, from the looks of him, he was living better than us.

For a few moments none of us spoke. I guess we were all trying to process the information we were just given. This reunion was not going exactly how I had expected it to go, and I was sure my siblings echoed my feelings.

"I'm sorry to hear about your mother."

"Our mother? You say that like she wasn't your wife! Who the hell are you?" I screamed. I had had enough. I wasn't going to stand there making small talk with this virtual stranger for another second. I was going home. If he were lucky, I might come back in the morning, but I had to get out of that house before I said something I would truly regret. I started going up the steps and he stopped me.

"Where do you think you are going?" My father was on his feet and staring at me as if he could hear what I was thinking inside my head.

"I've got to go out to get some air," I replied.

"It's four in the morning. I will not have one of my daughters out roaming the streets like some hooker at this time in the morning," he said and sat back down as if that would be the end of it.

Well, he didn't know me.

"I'm a grown-ass woman. I'll go out if I want to." I headed toward the stairs. I was so mad I didn't try to hide it from him or anybody else. I mean, just who the fuck did he think he was?

I went upstairs and grabbed my purse. I thought about throwing my things in a suitcase and calling it a wrap, but I wasn't that damn crazy. By the time my foot reached the bottom step, my padre was out his seat and in my personal space. Our lips were so close, we should have been kissing.

"I said you are not leaving this house. Now sit your ass down!" This time he spoke in Spanish.

I didn't understand everything he had said, but I clearly understood the *ass down* part. He turned and walked away from me and took a seat on the sofa. Ariana's eyes were as wide as saucers. Ramón looked like he was about to run up to our father and punch him in his face.

I continued to stand, debating what I should do. The inner conflict was killing me. On one hand, I felt like I owed this man my respect, because he was my father. On the other hand, I couldn't ignore how he had deserted our family. When Ariana started to get up from the couch, I knew that I needed to sit down. I didn't want to upset her any more than she already was, so I went to sit down next to her. Ramón came over and sat next to us too. We stared at our father.

He pressed the crease in his pants as he sat back in the chair. He clasped his hands in front of his face and rested his elbows on his thighs. He gave each of us a thorough look before he began speaking. "I know this is a difficult time for you all, but you have nothing to worry about now. I'm here."

I looked at Ariana to see if she was going to say anything, but she had her lips firmly clamped together. Angry words threatened to erupt from my mouth, and I fought real hard to keep them in.

"Once we have buried your madre, we will all sit down to discuss your futures."

"Our futures? What are you talking about?" I demanded.

"I've had enough of your insolence, Gabriela, for one night. Now I am trying real hard not to go off on your ass, but you are making this most difficult. For right now, it's late. I want you all to go back to bed. We will talk again in the morning after everyone is rested."

He got up from the chair and climbed the stairs leading to our mother's room. We heard him shut the door. I could not believe he had just dismissed us. I was furious.

"Ariana, what the hell just happened?" I asked.

She was fighting back tears and I felt sorry for her. Out of all of us, she knew and loved our padre the most. She was his little princess. She remembered the gentler times with my father that I had long since forgotten.

"Let's not make any rash decisions tonight. He's right about one thing: It is late and we are all working under a lot of stress."

"Are you defending him?" I asked, incredibly.

"No, Gabriela, I'm not defending him. I'm just saying that we shouldn't form any opinions one way or the other until we have all had some more sleep."

"I don't need no sleep. I hate that motherfucker," Ramón replied.

"Ramón, I've told you before that regardless of how you feel, he's still your father." Ariana got up as if she too were going to dismiss us.

"He didn't act like my father to me. Shit, did you get a hug and a kiss? Because I damn sure didn't get one?" I said.

"At least you got the chance to hit him. I'm glad he didn't try to hug me. I'm just waiting for a reason to knock the shit out of him," Ramón replied.

"Please, I can't do any more tonight," Ariana said as she slowly walked up the steps. She walked like she carried the weight of the world on her shoulders.

"She's right, Ramón. Come on and let's try to get some sleep. We'll figure out who that motherfucker is in the morning," I whispered the last part of my statement so Ariana wouldn't hear me. We both followed her up the stairs and went to our rooms. For the first time, I locked our door.

Ariana and I changed our clothes and got into bed, neither of us bothering to hang them up. I waited till Ariana was in the bed before I turned out the light.

"He doesn't look like use." I had expected her to say something to refute what I said but she didn't.

"Goodnight, Ariana."

"Night."

CHAPTER SIXTEEN
GABRIELA MENDOZA

The sun had barely begun to peek through the blinds and already our father was up, starting shit.

"Why is this door locked?" he asked, banging on our bedroom door.

Not only did he not look like himself, he didn't even sound like himself. Kicking our clothes underneath the bed, I went to open the door.

"Where's Ariana? She should be downstairs cooking breakfast," he said.

"Ariana's not feeling well. I can fix breakfast," I said, turning around to get my robe.

"What's wrong with her?"

"She has a bad headache." I lied because I didn't want to cause any unnecessary attention to her stomach.

"What she needs to do is start getting some exercise. That girl is getting fat."

He spoke about my sister as if she wasn't even in the room. Part of me wanted to punch him in the mouth. The other part of me wanted to go to Ariana to console her because I knew she had heard what he said. I said a prayer as I tightened the belt on my robe. I was not going to start my day off arguing with that man. I stood there waiting for him to get out the way so I could go fix breakfast.

"What, no hug?"

He had to be kidding. I just stood there looking at him as if he had lost his happy fucking mind. There was no way I was going to willingly hug this man. I gave him the eat-shit-and-die look. He backed out of the doorway. I wasn't even going answer his stupid question. I feel like I went to bed living a nightmare and woke up still in the twilight zone.

Next my father went and knocked on Ramón's door. "Ramón, it's time to get up. There are some deliveries to be made." He didn't even wait for Ramón to respond and he came down the steps behind me.

I wondered how he knew what deliveries needed to be done since he had just arrived, but I allowed the thought to slip away.

Last night I convinced myself that we were being too hard on our father. After all, I probably scared the shit out of him when I had screamed when I saw him. I tried to put myself in his shoes when he came in and nobody knew who he was. That had to hurt his feelings and that was probably why he acted like such a jerk. But in the cold daylight, I realized that what I saw last night was a good as it got.

The only thing I could hope for was that he finished his business here at the house and got the hell on back to Columbia. If necessary, Ramón could live with either me or Ariana. As far as I was concerned, my father could sell the house and we would never have to see him again. In fact, I was going to suggest that when we had our meeting to discuss our futures.

Ramón came in the kitchen as I finished frying the bacon.

I could tell by the look on his face that not only was he suffering from a massive hangover, he was pissed off as well. "Ramón, I hate to admit this, but you were right about him all along."

"I told you something wasn't right about him. Did you see him last night?"

"Yeah, I'm still shocked. You know what he asked me for today?" I put my hands on my hips and worked my neck like I'd seen Tilo do when she was angry.

"Nah, what?" Ramón watched me.

"He wanted a hug."

"You have got to be kidding. Ooh wee, I hate that dude." Ramón's voice was getting loud.

I had to grab his arm to reel him back in. I didn't want his voice to carry into the next room. "Just play along. Once we get Madre settled, we will be making some moves on our own. The way I see it, you can come to live with either me or Ariana, and he can sell this place for all I care."

"I can get my own place," Ramón replied.

"No, you can't. You're still too young. If you move in with me for a year, you will be old enough to get your own place. But we still have got to get through this with padre, so please, try to keep a civil tongue in your head because if he puts his hands on any of us, I'm going to jail."

"Yeah, you and me both." Ramón went to the cabinet and got glasses for everyone. "Where's Ariana?"

"She's still up in the room. I told padre that she had a bad headache." I kept the part about her being fat to myself because I knew that would just make him go off again. As hard as I tried, I couldn't get those words out of my mind. I could only imagine how Ariana was taking it. Knowing her, she was probably upstairs in the room crying.

I finished making eggs and toast and called everyone for breakfast. We all stood around the table for prayer. Normally, we would hold hands and say the prayer as a family, but all that went out the window when padre sat down and started piling food on his plate.

I felt like we were starring in the movie *Body Snatchers* because nothing about this man was familiar. There was no way in hell he would have allowed us to touch a meal without saying grace. It was a tradition that had stuck with us long after he had returned home, and one I practiced at my house with Tilo.

"What are y'all standing there gaping at? The food is getting cold," Padre snapped. If he had remembered the tradition that he had started, he gave no indication of it. I looked to Ariana for guidance, but she bowed her head. I tried to catch her eye, but she refused to look at any of us.

I poured juice for all of us before I sat down. There was no conversation and the tension in the room could be cut with a knife. I tried to eat but my appetite failed me. The only person who didn't seem to have a problem eating was my father.

"This is the first time that we have ever sat down to a family meal without Madre Sita." The words just slipped out my mouth. It was just a thought I had but, I surely didn't mean to say it out loud. When I did, three heads swung in the direction of her now empty chair.

Carlos Mendoza, our padre, pushed his empty plate away as he studied each of us carefully. I don't know about my sister and brother, but I needed to hear him say something that would make everything better.

"We got off on the wrong foot this morning and I'm sorry. I should not have come so late, probably should have checked into a hotel until the morning, but I was eager to see you all," Carlos said as he threw his napkin on his plate.

I sat there waiting for him to continue. He was off to a fairly decent start, but he had a lot more explaining to do. I guess my siblings felt the same way because they didn't respond either.

He stood up and pushed his chair up to the table. My eyes were pleading with him to continue, to show us some form of affection, to be our father instead of "the man."

"I'm about to go make the arrangements for your mother. I figure we will have a small ceremony followed by the burial. There is no sense prolonging it since she didn't have any friends or no other family here."

"How would you know if she had friends? What about what we want?" Ramón was on his feet.

Carlos took a deep breath before he answered. "Son, despite what you may think, I loved your mother. We communicated on regular basis. If she had any friends, she would have told me."

As much as I hated to admit it, he was right. She did not have any friends. In fact, she rarely left the house unless one of us was with her. Up until that moment, I never questioned whether or not she was happy.

"Does anyone want to come with me to make the arrangements?" He looked around the table at each of us.

I could not return his stare. As much as I wanted to make sure that he did right by my mother, I was not ready to go anywhere with him. I needed time away from him.

"I see. When I get back, we will talk." Carlos grabbed his keys and black briefcase off the coffee table and left the house.

When the door had closed behind him, it seemed as if we all exhaled. I had so many questions running through my mind, I didn't know where to start.

I got up from the table and started clearing the dishes. I needed to get out of the house for a while, and I was going to use his leaving as the perfect time to do it. Ramón dried as I washed the dishes. Ariana remained seated at the table. Her eyes were bloodshot and she had dark circles underneath them.

"Ariana, do you think you should go and see your doctor? You don't look good."

"I know, I'm fat," she replied and burst into tears.

I had hoped that she didn't hear that nasty comment Carlos had made, but it was obvious she had.

"Girl, you ain't fat. You are having a baby." I smiled when I said it, but I knew that it would do nothing to help her feel any better.

"I still don't like that motherfucker," Ramón replied.

If he expected us to chastise him, he was wrong because I believed he spoke for all of us.

"Look, I'm going to run home for a while. I need to clear my head while he's gone," I said.

"I think I will go and see if I can see the doctor. This baby has been kicking my ass all night, and I haven't gotten any sleep. If I have time, I may even run by and see Mike. Ramón can you go with me?"

"Yeah, I don't want to be here with him by myself if you two don't get back before he comes home."

Ariana said, "Good."

I ran upstairs, changed my clothes, grabbed my purse, and started out the door. "If anything happens, hit me on my cell, okay?"

"Yeah, I'm going to charge mine while we are in the car. I forgot to do it last night."

"Okay, cool." I practically ran to my car. I needed to speak with someone objectively about what was going on in my mother's house and the first person who came to mind was Tilo. At first I wasn't going to confide in her, but

I needed someone who wasn't connected to the situation to hear me out.

Tilo was still sleep when I got to the house. She had recently changed her work schedule and was working four days a week, ten hour shifts. I sat down on her side of the bed and gently rubbed her face. She was so beautiful it took my breath away. I just loved her honey-brown skin and the way her nose flared while she slept. I thought it was because of the earring that she wore in her nose. She tried to convince me to get one, but I wasn't having that. It took me forever to get my ears pierced.

"Baby," I said, not wanting to scare her. She was naked underneath the sheet, but I didn't want to think about that right now. I just needed to talk.

"Huh?" Tilo peeked up at me and smiled. She brought her arms up around my neck and pulled me closer as her lips sought mine. Her breath was a little rank, but I didn't mind. I didn't take the time to brush my teeth either, so I'm sure mine wasn't minty fresh either.

I gently pushed her away. "I need to talk with you. Can you get dressed and come into the living room?"

"This sound serious. Are you okay?"

"Yeah, I'm okay. I just need to talk and I don't have much time."

"Okay, give me a few minutes and I will be right there."

I could see the worry lines that were etched on her forehead, but she did as I asked and got out of the bed. I could not help but to admire her firm ass. I wished my ass looked that good. I stifled the urge to grab it and pull her back to me but I knew if I did that, we would wind up in bed. I went into the kitchen and put on some coffee. I wasn't used to starting my day without it, but my madre didn't even have any in the house.

Tilo came into the room as I was finished making us both a cup and sat down on the sofa. "What's up?"

"Uh…this isn't going to be easy for me, but I need you to hear me out. There are some things happening at my mother's house that I don't understand and I need your advice."

"Okay." She started to get up to sit closer to me, but I push her back in her seat.

"No, you sit over there. I ain't going to be able to concentrate with you all close to me."

She smiled and for a few seconds. I did too.

"How's everybody doing?" she asked.

"It's crazy over there."

"I told you I would come with you if you wanted me to."

"I know, baby, and I appreciate that but you see…uh…that won't be a good thing. My father is there and he's real strict."

"Strict? What's that supposed to mean? You're a grown-ass woman."

"I know that and you know that, but he apparently didn't get the telegram. I tried to come back here last night and we almost got into a fight."

"A fight? Come on now, you can't be serious," Tilo said.

"You don't understand. Where we come from, the man is always right. We were taught at a very young age not to question our elders. My father ruled our family, even though he didn't live with us for most of our lives. My mother was nothing more than a puppet when he was around."

"That doesn't sound like much of a relationship to me," Tilo replied.

"That's just it, I never thought about it—I don't think any of us did. It was just the way things were. He had these strict rules about us not dating, who we were allowed to play with, and we weren't allowed company at our house."

"That's barbaric."

"I guess it was. But until I moved out on my own, I didn't know any differently. Did you know you were the first person that I have ever kissed?"

"Girl, stop playing. I may have been the first *woman* that you have kissed, but I don't believe that I'm the *first* person," she said, laughing.

"It's true," I said sadly.

"You mean you have never been with a man?"

The look on her face told me she didn't believe a word that I had said, but it was important to me that she understood that.

"I promise you I'm telling the truth. My mother kept us all at the house until we started working. We were allowed to go to school, but we had to come right home. Since we couldn't bring anyone to the house, I never had the chance to get with anybody else. My sister was my closest friend until I met you."

"So what are you trying to say? You met a man and now you don't want to chill with me?" She started squirming in her seat.

Tilo was bisexual, but I didn't really know what I was. She was getting me off track. I wasn't trying to talk about us.

"No, baby, this ain't about us at all. I'm just trying to get you to understand my upbringing."

"Okay, I'll be quiet."

"My father is a bigot…there, I've said it."

"And."

"Well that's one of the reasons you can't come to the house. He would not understand me having a black friend, and he really wouldn't understand if I told him that I loved you."

"That's none of his business, but I can respect your wishes for me to stay away while he is here. My folks are cool, but what I do in my private life is none of their concern."

She was right, her parents were cool. I had met them before and they were so nice to me. Never once did they make me feel out of place because of the color of my skin or where I was born. They treated me like I was one of the family. "It goes deeper than that. Right now we are all living a lie. Well, all of us except Ramón. He's the only one of us still living at home. Ariana is even pretending not to be married and pregnant."

"How can you pretend not to be pregnant? Is she showing?"

"Yeah, but she's wearing bigger clothes, trying to hid it. This morning my father called her fat and it really hurt her feelings."

"Then why don't you say something? What's he going to do, beat y'all?" She started laughing at the idea, but I found nothing funny about the situation. She didn't see the look on my father's face last night when I had told him I was leaving.

"Girl, I don't know how to explain this all to you without sounding like I'm crazy or something. But this…man, we don't even know who he is."

"What man, honey?"

"My father." I let out a big sigh. There was so much going through my mind that I couldn't get the words out fast enough.

"Boo, you are not making any sense." She started to get up but I shook my head *no*.

"Okay. Give me a second."

I took a few sips from my coffee cup, even though it had grown cold. Tilo got up and refreshed our cups. Once again, I could not help but to look at the way her ass bounced in her boy shorts.

When she sat back down, I drank half the cup before I started again. "The man that I remember was small. I guess he appears bigger to me now that I've grown up. We haven't seen him in years. I remember being ashamed of him as a child."

"Why's that?

"He's so old-fashioned! You don't understand, Tilo, what it's like being a foreigner in another country and trying to fit it." She raised her eyebrows at me like I had said something totally stupid.

"Baby, I was born here, and I still feel like I'm trying to fit in, so don't talk to me about that," she said with attitude.

"Damn, that didn't come out right. I'm sorry." I finished the rest of my coffee and allowed her to calm down.

"We wanted to be just like the rest of the kids around us, but he wouldn't let us. We wanted to wear the fly gear and shit, but he had us looking like poster children for the underprivileged."

"Aw, poor baby."

Tilo wasn't understanding how much this had scarred us.

"Tilo, he used to come see us with his high-water pants, rice sneakers, and these thick-ass glasses. He looked like one of the actors from *Nerds*. I used to hate it when he came to our school. The other children would tease us for weeks behind those visits."

"Kids can be ruthless."

This time I felt like she could understand where I was coming from.

"Over the years, he came to see us less and less. He stayed in Columbia to take care of his mother and father, who had simply refused to move to the states. We were always told that he didn't have the money to come see about us, but we never got the feeling that he didn't love us. We thought he was doing the right thing."

"Okay, but you've obviously changed your mind. What happened?"

"You should see him. He looks like he's stepped out of the pages of some fashion magazine. He's gotten rid of glasses, had his hair styled, and wears more bling that P. Diddy. He looked so different, I didn't even know who he was. I thought he was a robber!"

"You have been watching way too much television." She laughed at me.

"It's not funny, Tilo. It's like having a stranger in the house."

"Gabriela, you've changed. Ariana has changed. Why is it so difficult to accept that your father has changed?"

"I don't give a damn about the fact that he's changed. That's not the point I'm trying to make."

"Well, what is the point, sweetie?"

Was she patronizing me? "The point is, Tilo, we have always been dirt-poor. There was no money for that extra stuff. Hell, this man has even learned how to speak English. He went to college, for Christ's sake. None of us went to college. He had enough money to have laser surgery on his eyes while we were struggling to keep the heat on in our house. Ariana and I started working when we were sixteen just to help my mother make ends meet! That's my point."

"Oh, I feel where you are coming from."

"Can you imagine how different our lives would have been if he had allowed my mother to go to school? She didn't even graduate from high school. They had gotten married when she was just sixteen. She had her first child that same year, and he kept her bare foot and pregnant until we moved here."

"And you feel like he abandoned you and your family?"

"You damn right I do." I jumped up and started walking the floor. All those emotions that I had pent up from the last few days came crashing down on me at the same time. I was hurting so badly, I just wanted to scream.

Tilo came over and held me in her arms. "What can I do, baby?" She was kissing me on my neck and arms as I shed tears that felt like they were coming from the soles of my feet. I thought about what she had said before I answered her: "I just need you to be here for me. I'm a mess right now and the rest of my family is no better. I just need to get through these next couple of days, and I might have to move Ramón in here with us when it's all over with."

"Sure, baby, I'm down for you. Ramón can use your room and you can sleep with me."

I tensed inside the circle of her arms. I appreciated her understanding and her willingness to help, but I wasn't quite ready to expose my sexuality to my family. I gently pulled away from her. I would have to think about this a little more. When I had originally suggested it, I was thinking that Ramón would sleep on the couch. I didn't even consider the fact that he would have to find out about my love life at the same time. "Thanks, baby."

I looked at my watch. I had been gone for over two hours. I needed to get back just in case my father had returned. "I've got to go. He said he was going to talk to us about our future when he got back, but I have my own ideas. I want him to sell the house and take his narrow ass back to Columbia. That is why I asked if Ramón could stay with us. He's not old enough to get his own place yet. I figured between me and Ariana he would have somewhere safe to stay."

"If he's under eighteen, won't your mother want him to go back with him?"

"Girl, don't even put that shit out in the universe. Ramón hates him, has for years. And this new crap is making it even worse. I can't tell you how tight it is up in that house right about now."

"I'll bet. How's your sister?"

"She's taking it hard. Won't even speak about it, to be honest. She's supposed to be going to the doctor's now, so I really got to get going."

"Alright, baby. If you need me, just call, and please try to hold it together. Your family is depending on you."

"I know, thanks." I kissed her gently on the lips.

She moved in closer and started grinding against me. She felt so good, but I knew I didn't have time for any more than what we had already shared. I pulled away from her and started walking toward the door.

"If you can get out later, stop by. I'll keep it hot for you." She had dipped her hand in her shorts and was stroking her cat just to entice me.

"Damn, you are wrong for that." I closed the door before I could get sucked back into her arms and, ultimately, her bed.

CHAPTER SEVENTEEN

ARIANA MENDOZA

"How is Padre going to plan a funeral for Madre Sita when she didn't even go to church?" Ramón asked.

"I don't know. I thought he wanted to have a private ceremony for her at the house, but who knows what is going on in his head."

"You ain't even lying about that. Gabriela said she wanted him to sell the house and that I could come to live with either you or her."

"She did? Well, we'll cross that bridge when we come to it. If he does sell the house, I think he should give us the money because we have been the ones who have had keep things going."

"I don't care what he does. I just want him to leave us alone."

I did too, but I was not about to admit that to Ramón. I was still having a hard time getting the image of Padre's face out of my mind when he had gone off on Gabriela. It was a face that I had seen before and that I had hoped to never see again.

■■■

It happened a few months after my older brothers were abducted. I never knew the exact details of their disappearances. It wasn't something my parents discussed openly in front of us children, but late at night, I could hear them whispering about it. Padre said they were in the wrong place at the wrong time. I was only four. I didn't know what that meant, but I always remembered the phrase.

My parents got into a terrible argument the night Dezi and Fabio disappeared. This was the first time that I'd heard Padre yell at Madre Sita. I remembered him saying he knew who had taken his sons and he was going to take care of them himself. Madre said that he would bring *them* down on our house, but I had no clue who *them* was. He said he was not about to sit back and let them pick us off one by one. She begged him to stay in the house but he pushed her out of the way, causing her to fall on the floor. I ran into the room as he was leaving and that's when I saw that look. He had looked at right me, but I doubt if he even saw me.

Madre made me go back to bed. We never talked about that night again. We left Columbia shortly after that. After that, Padre was never the same.

■■■

The doctor said everything was okay with the baby. He said I needed to get more rest and to take it easy. I lied and said I would. I was relieved to find out that we were okay, which took a load off my mind.

"Everything okay?" Ramón asked.

I had left him in the waiting room while I went back to see the doctor, and he wasn't too happy about sitting in the waiting room with all those pregnant women.

"Yeah, we're okay. I just got to continue to take it easy."

"So, where are we headed now?"

I wanted to stop by and see Moses before going to the house. I knew that if I showed up at work, he would keep the visit very professional. Although I knew that this attraction I had for him was wrong, I could not control how I felt about him. Moses excited me in ways that my husband never could and it wasn't just the physical aspects of our relationship.

"I just got to stop by my job for a hot minute. Stay in the car, okay?"

"Yeah, I'm good. Just don't be too long, 'cause it's hot as a motherfucker out here."

I struggled to keep from smiling. Hearing Ramón cuss was funny to me. He had such a sweet face and the words just didn't fit his demeanor. It was like he was trying to be all hard but inside he was as soft as a marshmallow.

"Boy, you have got a trashy mouth."

"I got it from my sister," he said, hiding his smile.

He didn't lie about that. Gabriela was the queen of cussing. She didn't even realize she was doing it most of the time.

"Don't be blasting no loud music in front of my job either, you hear?"

"All right, just don't be all day." He sunk down in the seat and starting playing with the radio.

He was a good kid. I only hoped that he would continue to stay out of trouble. He scared me the other night when he came home drunk. He was too young to be out there experimenting. Gabriela might be on the right tract by letting Ramón come live with one of us. My only problem was which one of us it was going to be.

■■■

I got in the elevator and pushed the button for the fourth floor. In my haste to see Moses, I didn't even stop to think about what I was wearing. I had on this oversized shirt, which did nothing for my figure, and I didn't have on a stitch of makeup. I was about to change my mind and go back to the car when the doors opened and in stepped Moses.

"Hey beautiful! What are you doing here?" He walked up to me and hugged me just as the doors closed behind him.

I lost myself in his kiss. My hands were everywhere, feeling on him. He felt so damn good to me. If the ride were longer, I would have jumped on his dick right there in the elevator. He pushed away just as the door opened. We stepped away from one another.

He walked out of the elevator with me and we went over in the corner to talk, away from the security guard's prying ears.

"I just went to the doctor and I had to stop by and see you."

"Doctor? Is my baby okay?" He moved his hand to touch my stomach, but I step away.

This was not the place for us to be displaying our affection for one another. Some of the people who I worked with knew my husband and probably wouldn't hesitate to rat me out. "We're fine. I just wanted to reassure myself. I haven't been sleeping well and the baby has been restless."

"Only a few more months to go, sweetheart, and it will all be over."

Moses was so sure of himself. Nothing rattled his cage and I admired that trait. I loved the way he walked into a room and took control. He would never allow anyone to disrespect hi, unlike my husband. When I was with him, nothing else in the world mattered. It was the time that I was away from him that was kicking my ass. I still didn't know what I was going to do about my marriage. Part of me still loved Mike, but I wasn't in love with him. He didn't excite me like Moses did.

"I can't stay. My brother is in the car."

"Oh, for real? Can I meet him?"

"Uh, he doesn't know about us."

"That's cool. I won't say nothing, I just want to meet my future family is all."

I just looked at him. Moses said things like that all the time, but I didn't know if he was serious or not. I wondered what he would do if I actually filed for a divorce. Would he step up to the plate and take care of me and the baby or was he just talking smack to get in my panties? "Okay, we have to get back to the house anyway. I'm not sure what time my father will be back."

"Oh, he made it in?"

"Yeah, he got in early this morning. He is making arrangements for Madre right now."

He walked with me to the car. I wanted to tell him about the rest of the stuff that was going on at the house but there wasn't time.

"'Sup?" Moses nodded to Ramón.

Ramón looked between me and Moses and smiled.

"Ramón, this is my boss, Moses. He wanted to come out and meet you."

"I'm good. Hey, you got any job in there that I can do?"

Moses threw his head back and laughed. It was a deep, belly laugh that made us all laugh with him.

"Oh, so you ready to work now?" Moses asked.

Ramón nodded. "I've been ready, but my mother wouldn't let me get a job until I finished school."

"Well, she was right. School is very important. Without that high school diploma your life won't be worth two nickels."

"Oh, I'm going to finish. I just wanted something that I could do after school or on the weekends."

Moses reached into his pocket and pulled out his business card. "I like the way you think, young man. Give me a call so we can talk about it. I'm sure we can work something out if your sister agrees with it." He turned and smiled at me.

I had tears shinning in my eyes. I had never expected Moses to be so nice to my brother. "Thanks. We'll see. I've got to get back to the house. I just wanted to thank you for allowing me time off so that I could be with my family."

"No problem. Ariana, if you need anything, anything at all, call me." He turned and started walking down the street. He must have been on his way to a meeting.

"Nice guy," Ramón said when I got back into the car.

"Yeah, he's cool." I was so excited about seeing him, I didn't even ask him where he was going.

"I can tell he likes you too," he said with a smile.

His comment caused me to tap on the brakes a little bit harder than I intended to, jerking us forward in our seats.

"Put your seatbelt on," I advised. I didn't want to participate in any more conversation about Moses. I took the time to put my own seat belt on as well.

"Do you think he meant it?"

"Huh?" I wasn't sure what Ramón was talking about. All I could hear was his saying that Moses liked me.

"About the job. Do you think he meant it?"

"Oh, that. Yeah, he rarely says anything he doesn't mean." I really hoped that that was true.

"Oh, it's like that?" He had this sneaky smile on his face.

I searched for something to say that would get him off the subject of Moses. "What are you going to wear to the funeral?"

The smile instantly disappeared from his face. "I don't know."

"Maybe I'll ask Padre to get you a suit."

"Thanks, but no thanks. I don't want anything from that man."

I started to press the issue but I really didn't want to think about our father either. "Do you have somewhere that you want to go before we go back to the house?"

"Nah, I'm good."

We drove the rest of the way in silence.

■■■

As we pulled up to the house, I scanned the street to see if I noticed any unfamiliar cars. "Did you happen to see what type of car Padre was driving?"

"No, I didn't even think about it when he left. I just wanted him gone."

"Yeah, it didn't even cross my mind about how he got to the house. Hell, I didn't even know that he could drive." From what I could tell, Gabriela wasn't back either. I parked and we went inside.

Dinner time was approaching, so I needed to figure out what to cook. "What do you want to have for dinner?"

"I don't care."

"Gee thanks. I was looking for suggestions."

"I'd be happy with a pizza."

My baby starting kicking like he was up for pizza as well, but I knew Padre would shit a brick if I tried to do that.

"I know, right? I say we go for it. If the fucker doesn't like it, he can take his happy ass in the kitchen and fix something else."

We burst out laughing.

I ran my fingers through his hair before I could stop myself. I had forgotten that he didn't like it when I did that anymore.

"Damn, sis, stay out of my hair."

"Oops, my bad. I keep forgetting you don't like that."

"I'm going upstairs to play on my *Wii*."

I smiled. The *Wii* was a Christmas gift from me and Gabriela.

"You better not let padre catch you. You know how he feels about video games."

"Fuck him." He went up the steps, leaving me alone with my fears.

I started to go into the kitchen but all of a sudden I got so tired, all I wanted to do was take a nap. The pregnancy was taking its toll on me. My ankles were swollen and my lower back hurt all the time. The doctor said it was because of the way the baby was sitting. I sat down on the sofa and began rubbing my belly. "All this room you got in there and you want to hide out in one spot."

The baby pushed back on my hand in acknowledgment that it knew I was speaking to it.

Before my eyes could close, my cell phone rang. I reached over to the table to dig my cell from out of my purse. "Hello?"

"Hey baby, I've been waiting to hear from you all day. How are you?" Mike asked.

My heart sank deep in my chest. I knew I had forgotten something. Every time I thought about calling him, something made me push the thought aside. Or maybe it was because my thoughts stayed with Moses. "I'm good. Things have been hectic, that's all. I was about to take a nap before I started dinner."

There were a few seconds of uncomfortable silence.

"Did your father ever get in?"

"Yeah, he got here around four this morning."

"Oh, wow, how did that go?"

I didn't really want to rehash everything that had happened, so I kept my answer short: "It was okay. He's changed."

"How so?"

"Look, babe, can I call you back later? I really need to take a nap before I fix dinner."

"Why can't Gabriela fix dinner? She said she was going to help you." His voice was filled with accusation.

"She is helping me. She fixed breakfast this morning. I can't expect her to do everything around here."

"Well, she ain't pregnant." He was bound and determined to keep me on the phone even after I had told him that I needed to get some rest.

I knew I was being unreasonable, but I got an attitude. "No, she's not pregnant. That doesn't mean I have the right to take advantage of her." My voice was as cold as I felt inside. I couldn't remember when my feelings for Mike had changed, but it was becoming very clear that they had. Besides, the baby ain't his no way.

"Look, I'm not trying to make you mad. I just miss you, that's all."

My heart softened for a second.

"I know, baby. Just let me get a nap and I'll call you later, okay?" I should have waited for him to say something before I hung up, but I didn't. It didn't take long before I drifted off to sleep. I was in the middle of a very good nap when I heard the front door close. I sat up and looked at my watch at the same time. What had started out as a fifteen minute power napped turned into over an hour-and-a-half slumber.

"What's for dinner?" Padre came in the house and before he even said hello, he was already asking me about dinner.

I knew he had spoken to Madre like that, but I wasn't his wife. "I haven't started it yet. I was waiting till you came home to see what you wanted to eat." I was lying my ass off and I believed he knew it.

His look told me that he was disgusted with me. I braced myself for what I thought would be coming next. Instead he surprised me.

"Don't worry about it. Let's order a pizza."

My mouth fell open as I looked back at him. This man masquerading as my father continued to surprises me, and I didn't know how to take him. "Are you serious?"

"Yeah. By the time you get something ready, it will be eight o'clock. I don't like to eat my food that late. Maybe you should change your eating habits too. I see you have picked up a little weight." He sat in the easy chair and opened up the paper.

If he realized that he had hurt my feelings for the second time in one day, he did nothing to acknowledge it. I pulled out the phone book and found the number to the nearest Pizza Hut that would deliver. I placed an order for two large pizzas with the works. If he wanted something special, he should have ordered himself.

"Where is everybody?" He looked up from the newspaper.

"Gabriela had to run a few errands, but Ramón is upstairs."

"What kind of errands?"

"I don't know. I didn't ask her."

Gabriela walked through the front door—perfect timing. I tried to warn her with my eyes that he had been asking about her, but she wasn't looking at me.

"Where have you been?"

"Out."

He folded the paper and put it down on his lap. I could see a vein bulging out the side of his neck.

"I'm trying to be nice and you keep pushing my buttons. I don't know what kind of household your mother ran around here, but when I ask you a question, I expect a decent answer."

The air in the room instantly heated. If I didn't know better, I would have sworn the air condition had quit working. Sweat appeared on my forehead and everything. I got up off the sofa just in case I had to step in between them. "I ordered pizza," I announced. Gabriela looked at me like I had lost my damn mind. I wanted her to just leave the room but our padre had other ideas.

"Sir, I'm not trying to be disrespectful. I wasn't aware that I needed to provide a detailed account of my activities to you," she said, gritting her teeth.

I was proud of her for standing up to him without losing her cool. He didn't know Gabriela like I did. She would rather cuss someone out than to explain herself.

"Good. From now on, you know the rules." He unfolded his paper.

My eyes pleaded with Gabriela to let it go. I waited for the explosion that I felt was coming, but she surprised me and held her peace. She started to go upstairs.

"Where are you going?" Padre asked.

Damn, why was he fucking with her like that? It was like he was trying to provoke her into a fight.

"I would like to go to the bathroom. Do I need permission to piss too?"

"Of course not. Don't be ridiculous," he responded as he returned his attention to the paper.

She stuck out her tongue as she went up the stairs.

CHAPTER EIGHTEEN
GABRIELA MENDOZA

I locked myself in the bathroom. Tears of anger streamed down my face. In all my years on this earth, I have never wanted to hit someone as badly as I wanted to hit my father. Any love that I might have felt for him was officially gone. He managed to kill—in a single night—the twenty years of love that I held for him in my heart.

I washed my face and went to my room. I wanted to just lie down for a while. That, however, would have been asking for more trouble. When I had come home, I was so deep in thought I didn't even realize that he had gotten there already until I heard him mention my name.

I went back downstairs and peeked out the front door. I was looking for the car he was using so I would not make the same mistake again. It didn't take me long to spot it, because it sat out like a sore thumb amongst the other battered vehicles that littered our block. He was driving a white, convertible Benz. I wanted to go see if it had rental tags on it, but I was afraid. If it didn't, that would mean he was planning on staying. I shut the door and went back in the living room and took a seat next to my sister. "Did you make the funeral arrangements?" I boldly asked.

For a few minutes he didn't answer me. I was about to repeat the question when he folded his paper back onto his knees.

"Yes, it is done. We will have a small service in the morning. Do you think you can find something suitable to wear?"

The man's tongue was sharper than barbed wire. He had no regards for our feelings. I wondered what it was like for our mother while loving this man. Was he like this with her or did he reserve these hateful things just for us?

"If you are suggesting that I wear a dress, I don't own one." If he wanted to fight me with words, we were about to get it on.

"Figures. If there was more time, I would take you shopping. You will just have to do your best. Luckily, there won't be many people here for you to embarrass me."

"Figures? What does that supposed to mean?" I was ready for a fistfight now. If he said anything bad about my mother, we were going to thump.

"I didn't mean anything bad, but I know how your mother was about spending money."

"That's because we didn't have any money to spare." I kept the *unlike you* comment that was itching the back of my throat to myself.

He turned his nose up and said, "There was plenty of money."

His arrogance pushed me closer to the brink of no return. Ariana placed her hand over mine and squeezed. I knew she wanted me to shut the fuck up, but enough was enough. I was trying to get to my feet but Ariana was now using her fingernails to cut into my flesh. If she didn't stop, she was going to draw blood.

The doorbell rang and I was thankful for the interruption. I waited to see if he was going to get up an answer it, but he acted like he didn't even hear it.

"I guess that's the pizza man," Ariana announced. She looked around for her purse.

I didn't want her to pay for it. She needed to save her money for her baby. I got up and went in my pocket for my wallet. As I walked to the door, my padre called me back. He gave me thirty dollars. The doorbell chimed again and Ramón came down the stairs.

I opened the door and took the two boxes from the delivery girl. She was cute in a roughneck sort of way. I could not imagine delivering pizza for a living—it was just too dangerous. I gave her the money and waited while she counted out our change.

"Tell her to keep the change," my father said.

The delivery girl looked at me in shock. He had just given her an eighteen-dollar tip. She yelled her thanks over my shoulder and quickly left as if I were going to try to take it back. I took the boxes into the kitchen and Ariana came in to help me set the table.

She walked up close beside me. "Did you see that knot of money in his pocket?"

"No, I wasn't paying attention, but I did notice that he is pushing a new Benz."

"Where did he get all this money?"

"I don't know but we need to find out."

She shook her head in agreement. I had a bad feeling about all of this.

My father took his place at the head of the table. "Did you wash your hands?" he asked Ramón.

Ramón looked like he was about to argue with the man until I discretely kicked his leg under the table. He got my point and, went back upstairs to wash his hands.

My father was eating before Ramón's foot had hit the first step. I shook my head as I bowed it to say my prayers.

If Ramón was as surprised by the pizza as I was, he didn't show it when he came back to the table. He just grabbed a few slices and began to eat. I was determined that I was not going to allow this stranger to spoil another meal for me as he had done the last one.

We ate in silence, each of us lost in our thoughts. When we were finished, we gathered the dishes and washed them. My father retired to our mother's room. It was seven o'clock at night and we had the whole evening before us with nothing to do.

"That man obviously has some plans for us, and I—for one—don't want any parts of them," I said.

"I agree. He's been very secretive," Ariana added.

"So, what do we do about it?" Ramón asked.

I got up and went in the dining room to where Madre wrote out the bills and kept her records. If my so-called father really was in contact with our mother over the years, the letters would either be in there or somewhere in her room.

"What are you about to do?" Ariana whispered.

"Bear with me. I'll be right back." The desk Madre used was set off in the corner. It was an old desk, quite possibly an antique, with a roll top that she normally kept closed unless she was working. Up until this point, I had never touched it. In fact, I didn't believe any of us had ever wondered what she kept closed up in that desk.

I pulled out the small chair that she used while she worked and sat down. I know it was just my imagination, but I felt like the warmth of her body still warmed the chair. I gently pulled up the top. The hinges squeaked as I did. I hoped it wasn't loud enough to draw attention to what I was doing. I felt like I was invading her privacy. If we were going to find some answers to the questions that were plaguing us, a little snooping was in order.

The first thing I noticed when I opened the desk was a worn picture of our family before my brothers' disappearance marred our happiness. In the back row, my brothers stood next to my father. He had his arms around their shoulders. My mother stood in front of our father with Ramón in her arms. Ariana was standing beside her. We were standing in front of a hut that was our home, and, even though our clothes were tattered and our feet were bare, we looked happy.

The picture had creases in it as if she had handled it often. I slid it into my pocket to examine at a later time. The desk had several slotted compartments built inside. The first slot contained nothing but bills. They were sealed with stamps already on them. I put them in my pocket as well to be mailed at the first opportunity. The book that she kept all her delivery information in was in the next to the last slot. I pulled it open. Save for the addresses, I could not make out what it said. In the final slot, there was a bunch of letters held together with a big rubber band. From looking at the postmarks, it appeared as if they were in date order.

I pulled the most recent letter out of the stack. Much to my chagrin, it was written in Spanish and I could not read it. I took them too just in case they held some hidden clues. I was sure that I would find someone who could translate them for me. The rest of the desktop was empty. I opened the center drawer and it was empty save for some pens, pencils, a few paper clips, and a small key.

I examined the key. It was too small to open any door in the house that I knew of. I pocketed the key to see if Ramón knew what it went to. The other drawers in the desk only contained blank paper. I pulled the top closed and went back in the living room.

"What did you find?" Ariana asked.

"Nothing much but some letters that I can't read, some bills that need to be mailed, and this key." I held the key up for their inspection.

"What does it fit?" Ariana asked.

"Beats the shit out of me. Ramón, do you know?"

He barely looked at me as I continued to hold up the key. His eyes had begun to water again, so I let him off the hook.

"It's probably for the cash box that she keeps in her room," he said. When she gets paid, she puts the money in there. When she had enough, she would send me to the store to get her some money orders to pay the bills."

"She didn't have a checking account?" Ariana looked at him.

"No, she didn't believe in them. She was afraid that someone would try to steal her money," Ramón replied.

"I wish I knew that. I would have convinced her to get one, even if I had to manage it myself," I said and sat down.

"Why? It was never a lot. She worked weeks to get up enough money to pay one bill. All those deliveries I made, the packages I picked up…it just wasn't worth it to me. She worked herself to death."

"Yeah, if this house wasn't paid for, I don't know how we would have made it this long," Ariana replied.

"Then why does our so-called father keep saying that there's plenty of money?" I looked around the room and neither of them had any answers. "Do you all get the feeling that we don't know either of our parents very well?"

They both nodded their heads in agreement. This was a sobering thought since I had always believed we were such a close family.

"What did you do today?" Ariana asked out of the blue.

"Uh…I went home and talked to Tilo. I had to let somebody know what was going on over here in case I needed bail money to get out of jail for killing that motherfucker upstairs."

We all laughed, but I was as serious as a heart attack.

"What did the doctor say?" I realized that I had forgotten to ask her earlier.

"He said that I should continue to take it easy at least until next month. After that, if the baby comes early, there is a good chance that he will be able to survive."

"He? You know the sex of the baby," I asked. I was thrilled because we needed more boys in the family.

"Yeah, it's a boy. I've known for a minute. It's Mike who wants to be surprised. I told him that this wasn't a Christmas gift, but he still doesn't want to know."

"Oh, I think I have a good lead on a job," Ramón announced happily.

"A job? Where at? I thought you went with Ariana to the doctor's." I looked from him to her.

"I did go with her. After we left we stopped by her job and I met her boss. He gave me his card and told me to call him about a job working with him some evenings and on the weekends."

I shot Ariana a nasty look to let her know that I knew what that shit was about. We were going to have to have a serious talk when we were alone. It was time she told me the real real deal with her and Moses. "Oh, that's nice. I've been hearing a lot about this guy, Moses, lately." If Ramón had noticed the tension in my voice, he did not acknowledge it. Ariana knew exactly where I was coming from, though.

"He's real cool for a black guy."

Those words sank in the room like a leaded weight.

I chose my words carefully: "Ramón, it isn't proper to say things like that."

"What did I say?"

From the look on his face, I could tell that he didn't mean anything by his statement. He was obviously repeating something he had heard many times before.

"You said 'for a black guy.' It is not necessary to make the distinction that he is black. Either he's cool or he's not."

"Oh, my bad. I really didn't mean any disrespect."

"I know you didn't. I just wanted you to be aware of how negative that may sound to someone else. You wouldn't want them to say that you were cool for a spic, would you?"

"Okay, I got it. You don't have to beat it like a dirty rug."

He was sulking now but the point I was trying to make was too important to ignore, especially since I was involved with a black woman and my sister was obviously involved with a black man.

"So, what do we do now?" Ariana asked, trying to change the subject.

"We don't have a choice but to wait and see what Mr. Man has in store for us. Let's just try to get through the service tomorrow without any more arguments. We owe that to Madre," I said.

Ariana stood up first. "I need to find something to wear for the funeral."

"Yeah, me too," Ramón said.

I watched my siblings walk away in silence. I could not help but wonder how well I knew them. I turned out the lights, made sure the door was locked, and went upstairs to our room.

CHAPTER NINETEEN
GABRIELA MENDOZA

I woke up in a very foul mood. I was horny as hell and tired of sleeping in a tiny bed in a room that I shared with my sister. It had been over a month since the funeral and our padre was still here. I didn't know how much longer I would be able to stand living this way.

Ariana and I were still in our room, but it wouldn't be long before we were expected to go downstairs to fix his breakfast. "Ariana, I'm done. This is the last day that I'm going to spend in this house living a lie. What is he waiting around for?"

"I don't know, but I'm sick and tired of this too." She rolled over on her side and faced me.

Her belly was so big, it appeared to be hanging over the side of the bed. Her face and legs were as bloated as her stomach. If I didn't know better, I would have sworn she was having twins.

"Girl, I can't believe that you've been able to hide this baby from him for so long."

"I know. But if he doesn't leave soon, I won't have a choice but to tell him. I only have a few outfits left that will fit me. I can't keep wearing the same thing every day."

"I know. Yesterday I tried to sneak out to the store and get you something but he called right before I could go in and demanded to know where I was. The last thing I needed was for him to hear the greeter at Wal-Mart welcome me to the store. That would have led to more questions that I didn't want to answer."

"At least you and Ramón get to leave the house. He expects me to be here twenty-four-seven to wait on him and his friends."

"Have you found out who they are yet?" I was referring to the two men who had come to our house a few weeks after the funeral. We were introduced to them but their relationship was never explained. We were waiting for our padre to tell us of his plans, but he seemed content to feed us information on a need-to-know basis.

"Not yet. When I'm around, they only speak in Spanish. I don't remember enough about it to understand what they are saying. Now I wish we would've paid more attention to it while we were growing up," Ariana said.

"You and me both. What about Ramón? He knows more Spanish than both of us put together. Have you asked him yet?"

"No, he spends a lot of time with that guy named Chico Velasquez when he gets home from school. Haven't you noticed that?"

"Yeah, what's up with that?"

"I'm not sure, but he talks like him and now he's even started dressing like him. Ramón is turning into a thug right before our very eyes."

It was sad, but it was true. Although he still acted like he could not stand our father, he appeared to be fascinated with the younger of the two men who traveled with my father every time he left the house.

"He's going to have to let me out of the house today," Ariana said. "There is practically nothing left in the cabinets to eat. I'm going to have to go to the grocery store, and he's going to have to give me the money to do it. If I'm lucky, I'll be able to pick up a few things to wear while I'm out."

"Do you want me to stay home from work to help you?"

"No, I'll be alright."

She answered too quickly, so I knew she had more up her sleeve than she was willing to admit.

"Have you spoken to Mike?"

Her face morphed. Her tiny eyes appeared to get smaller. Her whole body tensed.

"Yes. He said if I didn't come home soon, he would file for divorce," she whispered.

"He said what?" I didn't realize how loud I was until the sound ricochet back at me.

"Keep your voice down," she admonished.

"When did this happen? How come you didn't say anything before?"

"I'm still trying to wrap my arms around it myself. If you want to know the truth, that would suit me just fine."

"What?" Once again my voice rose.

"If you're not going to keep your voice down, I'm not going to tell you anything else."

"I'm sorry, but you can't just drop a bombshell on me like that and expect me not to react."

She got up and started to gather her clothes. I decided to keep quiet and let her tell her story in her own way.

"I came to the realization that while I love Mike, I'm not in love with him. This situation with Padre has forced me to look at that. He deserves so much more than I'm willing to give him."

"Have you told Mike this?"

"Hell no, he would be over here on a silver bullet. I'm surprised he's stayed away this long."

"And what about the baby? Are you planning to raise it all on your own?"

"What choice do I have? I'm not giving him up."

"That's not what I meant, girl, and you know it. I was speaking about Moses."

"We'll see. He says he wants to be in our life, but I'm not going to hold him to anything just because I'm pregnant."

I got up and started to get dressed as well. I didn't envy the position that Ariana was in. It was going to be hard raising a child alone. She knew it, because she watched our mother do it for years.

"I said it before and I'll say it again. I got your back no matter what happens."

"Thanks, Gabriela, that means a lot to us." She patted her belly as she went to the bathroom to take her shower.

Since I had taken my shower last night, I got dressed for work. I was surprised that I was allowed to keep my job and to be honest, it was the only thing that kept me sane. At least with work, I could still see Tilo and keep her informed with what was going on.

She, however, was also losing patience with the whole situation. She could not understand why I continued to allow my father to control me, but I had an ulterior motive for sticking it out, which I had given her all the details that I knew about the money. My father had mentioned money too many times for me not to stick around to find out what it was all about. If there was some money around, we were entitled to some of it. Even though Tilo was pissed with the whole situation, she said she would help me get it if I needed her. I still had the key to the money box but haven't been able to get in my madre's room long enough to find it.

I noticed the *For Sale* sign in the yard on the way to my car. Although I was not surprised by his decision to sell the house, it still hurt to actually see it happen. Briefly I entertained the thought of buying it from him, but I quickly dismissed the idea. That house held too many memories for me, and I was ready for a change. My biggest concern now was where Ariana and Ramón would live.

With Ariana's potential divorce, her place was out. The apartment Tilo and I shared wasn't big enough to take on Ramón, my sister, and the baby. I felt like I was trying to complete a difficult balancing act with the scales weighted against me.

I had made strides in unraveling the mystery of my parents but it was slow going. I had Tilo take the letters that my mother had received from my father to a translator to see if they would shed some light on my parents' relationship. For some reason, I knew that the letters held the key to solving the mystery.

It was Monday, which meant Tilo would not be at work today. We were planning on getting together for lunch but that just seemed too long away. She told me that she would bring the letters back to me when she came. I had her copy them so I could return the originals just in case my father knew about them and went looking for them.

In the weeks since he had been in the house, we still didn't know him any better than we did the day he had got there. He basically kept to himself and only spent time with us during meals. Under his leadership, the laundry business thrived. He shipped out more shirts than Madre had ever done. Frankly, I didn't see when he had the time, but I wasn't there with him during the day. I made a mental note to ask Ariana how he did it.

This increased business kept Ramón busy as well. He spent so much time making deliveries, I had begun to worry about his schoolwork. He was so close to finishing his senior year, I didn't want him to mess up and not be able to graduate with the rest of his class. He told me he had it all under control and when I saw his progress report, I so proud of him that I almost cried. I assumed our father paid Ramón for his services since he always had money. When Madre ran the business, everything she made went into the house. I prayed Ramón would not be fooled by the money and convince himself that he didn't need an education. If that happened, I would kill my father.

I met Tilo at the Taco Mac on East Ponce De Leon for lunch. She was already seated in a booth in the back of the room when I arrived. I was glad she chose to sit in the back so we could have a little privacy. I wanted to slide in the seat with her but I knew that if I did, that would call more attention to us. I wasn't ready for all that drama.

"Hey baby. Damn, you look good."

She did too. She was wearing a cute little halter dress that displayed her twins nicely. Her nipples were erect and pointing in my direction. I wanted to stick one in my mouth and suck on it just like a brand new baby.

"You like this, Mommy?" She batted her eyes at me.

"Yeah, if I had a dick, it would be hard right about now."

"You are so funny. I can't wait for us to be alone so you can show me how much you like it." She blushed.

"Girl, stop it. Don't remind me. I woke up this morning so horny just thinking about seeing you today. If I could have gotten away with it, I would have called off work and spent the day lying in your arms."

"Dag, why didn't you do it?"

"'Cause, man, my father is tripping. I wouldn't put it past him to show up on the job. He is looking for a reason to make me quit, so I'm just biding my time until he's gone. He put the house up for sale so that must mean he's ready to go."

"How do you feel about that?"

"Honestly? It hurts a little bit. But if it means that he will leave us alone, than I say let it go. I hope it sells quickly. Since it's so close to the college, I think it might. But, with this economy, who knows. People aren't buying houses like they used to and those that have homes are losing them to foreclosure."

"He should give the money from the house to y'all."

"Yeah, he should but I ain't gonna hold my breath. Do you have the letters?"

She pulled a large envelope off the seat next to her and handed them to me.

"Thanks, baby. I don't know what I would do without you."

She was saved from responding when the waitress came and took our orders. Since it was so early in the day, we decided to split a taco salad. They gave out way too much of it anyway, and I could never eat the whole thing.

"So do you know anything else about those two guys who hang around with your father?"

"No. It's creepy having them around all the time. Every time I look up, one of them is staring at me. If I didn't know better, I would think we were under some type of surveillance."

"I don't mean to put this thought in your head, but do you think your father would stoop that low and do that?"

"For what? I just said it because that's how it feels. None of us do anything worthy of being watched."

"Oh, honey, I beg to differ because when you slip between my thighs, it's something to behold."

"You are so nasty but I love it," I replied with a wink.

"I do have another question to ask you, though," she said in between forks full of lettuce and chili sauce.

"What's that?"

"How come your father allowed you to work and not your sister?"

"Ariana's boss gave her time off to have the baby. I guess that's one of the perks from sleeping with the boss. As far as my father is concerned, he never knew she had a job. He thinks she stays at home by choice and that's the reason why she's so fat."

"Does he still say that to her face?"

"Yeah, every chance he gets. He even offered to get her a membership at a gym."

"She should do it just to get out the house for a while. I'm sure the exercise won't hurt the baby."

"Believe me, she thought about it. That shit can backfire because he will be expecting to see results. The only result he's liable to see is her getting bigger before the baby is born. I'll be so glad when she drops that baby."

"Well, I hope this shit is resolved soon. I still don't know what your sister intends to do with that baby if your father is still living with y'all when she goes into labor."

"I know. That's why I need to find out what's in these letters so we can tell him to leave sooner." I looked at my watch and realized that if I didn't leave then, I was going to be late to work. "Baby, I got to go. If I can call you later tonight, I will." I sat there for a few minutes just staring at her. I wanted to lean over the table to give her a kiss but there were way too many people in the restaurant for that. I reached in my wallet and put a twenty on the table. Since we weren't drinking, that would be more than enough to cover the meal and the ice teas we had drunk.

"Love you," Tilo mouthed.

I nodded my head, indicating that I had heard her. I would show her how much I loved her later. When I got to the door, I turned around for one last look and blew her kiss.

CHAPTER TWENTY
ARIANA MENDOZA

It was slightly after three when I got back from the grocery store. I was gone longer than I originally planned, but I had enough groceries in my car to justify my lengthy trip. I unlocked the door before I started carrying the bags inside. It would have been nice if my father or one of his sidekicks would have offered to help, but it was just as well that they didn't. Had they been up close to me, they would have heard how difficult it was for me to get around with the added weight of the baby. Plus, I needed to be able to get my outfits in the house and into my room without detection.

The clothes were the last bag that I brought in the house and left setting on a kitchen chair while I put away the rest of the groceries. I really wanted to sit down and rest for a minute, but Jesus Ortega was staring at me as usual. I was really beginning to hate his sneaky ass.

I was bent over putting fruit in the bin when he came into the kitchen behind me. He was so light on his feet, I didn't know he had crossed the room until I saw his feet in between mine. I stood up so quick it caused me to get light-headed. When I started to swoon, he grabbed me. His arms formed a circle around my waist as he helped me to a chair. For once, I was grateful that he was there. If I had fallen, I could have hurt the baby.

"I knew it," Jesus hissed as he pointed his finger at me.

"Huh?" I was still seeing little spots before my eyes.

"I fucking knew it." He spun around in a circle.

His face was so contorted, I couldn't tell if he was happy or mad. Since this was the first time he had said more than two words to me, I didn't know what to think.

"Thank you." Even if he was a dick, he still helped me.

"I told that shithead that you were pregnant!"

Suddenly my chest got tight. I felt like I couldn't get enough air. He was making so much noise, I knew it was only a matter of time before his outburst alerted my father.

"Shush, please don't tell my father," I pleaded.

"Bitch, please. It's too late for that shit." He looked at me as if he wanted to spit in my face. He left me in the kitchen.

I was so scared, I didn't know what to do. Gabriela was at work and Ramón was probably out running errands. I couldn't allow Jesus to tell my father about the baby. I would much rather it come from me and my confession was long overdue. He would be hurt and angry that I had deceived him but he was still my father.

Frantically, I looked around the kitchen for my keys. I was going to leave the house for a while to give my father a chance to cool down before I confronted him. In a way, I was relieved that the secret was out, but I still wanted to put some distance between me and my father.

I was almost out the door when someone yanked me back by the roots of my hair. "Yowl!" My hasty departure was temporarily halted. I used my arms to keep my body from being dragged back in the house, but the force holding my hair was too strong.

"Where the hell do you think you're going?" Jesus asked as he dragged me into the living room and tossed me on the sofa. He kneeled over me with his knee pinning me down.

"You son of a bitch, get off of me."

"Or what…slut?" Jesus snarled at me.

Chico stood next to him, egging him on.

"Chico, if you don't believe me, pull up her shirt. I told you the bitch is pregnant," Jesus shouted.

My mind was still reeling from being called a slut and the brutal way I was being manhandled. When my brain registered the last comment, my eyes bucked. Surely they would not be so bold as to lift up my shirt.

"Oh, hell no!" I yelled.

"And the bitch has a mouth on her too, Jesus." Chico complained.

This time, Jesus did spit in the middle of the floor. Saliva dribbled off of his thin lips. This situation went from bad to very bad to worse when I heard my father came downstairs. Instinctively, I wrapped my arms around my stomach. Bile came bubbling up my throat. I started to gag but neither of the two men made a move to help me.

"What in the hell is going on in here?" Padre yelled.

Chico backed away from me but not far enough for me to make a run for the door. "Tell him," Chico said as he pointed to Jesus.

My eyes widened in fear. I felt like a little girl waiting for my father to come rescue me, but those thoughts flew right out of the window the second he had put his hands on me.

"Your bitch here is pregnant," Jesus said. A look, closely resembling glee, crossed his face.

I looked and saw a boner in his pants. That motherfucker was getting pure satisfaction from my situation.

"What are you talking about? Ariana, is this true?"

I felt like I was five years old all over again instead of twenty-two. Hot tears streamed down my face. My father's face turned red as he looked at his friends for confirmation.

"Tell the slut to lift up her shirt," Jesus said.

I made a mental note to myself to kick that motherfucker in the nuts at my first opportunity. My father marched over to me and pushed me back against the sofa and snatched up my blouse for the whole room to see. I was beyond humiliated. My eyes begged him to be understanding, but his face harden like granite. My father slapped me hard across the face. I was stunned. He'd never laid a hand on me before. If I didn't hate him before, I hated him now.

"Who did this to you?" he bellowed.

The same crazy look that I'd seen in his eyes the night my brothers were taken was back—this time it was directed at me. I opened my mouth but nothing came out. Not that I was going to confess or anything, I just needed a place for some air to go because I had been holding it ever since he had struck me.

"And you said she was fat—" Jesus would've gone on but my father silenced him with a menacing stare.

"Shut up?" He directed his attention back to me. "I asked you who did this to you and don't lie." He smacked me again and busted my lip. He hit me like I was a man instead of his child.

"Padre, don't!" I was trembling.

"Don't you *Padre me*, you slut. Answer the question."

I hung my head. If he would do this to me, his own child, I could only imagine what he would do to Moses if he found out about us. I did the only thing that made sense. "My husband," I whispered.

"Liar." He raised his arm again and I tried to prepare myself for the blow.

"What kind of game are you playing here?" Jesus' nostrils flared. He seemed to be madder than my father.

This situation was playing out like a bad movie. I could not tell who the actors were and what role they were playing.

My father and Jesus started yelling at each other in Spanish. It looked as if both Jesus and Chico were very angry at my father. Jesus got up in my father's face and started pointing his finger at him. When my father pushed him back, Chico grabbed his arms and held them behind his back while Jesus punched him in the stomach repeatedly.

I should have been happy that the focus was off of me, but I knew things would only get worse. While they were fighting, I slipped off the sofa, hoping to make it to my car before they even noticed I was gone. I moved slowly, trying not to draw attention to myself. My heart beat so loud I was sure that they could hear it. Jesus was right behind me. Ooh wee, if the Lord ever blessed me with the opportunity to shove my foot up his ass, I would give 20 percent of my check instead of 10 to the church.

"Where the fuck do you think you're going?" Padre shoved me back in the direction of the sofa.

I faked right and ran left but—because of my advanced pregnancy—I wasn't as nimble on my feet as I was in my mind.

"Sit your slutty ass down."

I fell onto the sofa, rolling to my side so that all of my weight wasn't on my stomach. My father's face was red from the exertion, but the focus was back on me.

"I'm going to ask you one more time, who did this to you?"

"My husband, Mike. If you don't believe I'm married, ask my husband."

"Fine, tie her ass up," my own father said.

"Huh?" Obviously I didn't hear him correctly. I know Padre didn't instruct these goons to tie me up. What the hell kind of shit was this? If this was a bad dream, I wanted to wake up.

Rough hands hauled me off the sofa and forced me into the dining room. They used some towels from the kitchen to tie my arms to the dining room chair. I watched my father go up the stairs. I was praying he was going to get a gun and shoot these fools. That prayer quickly died when I saw him return with three pillowcases. He used to ties to bind my feet to the legs of the chair and the other was rudely stuffed in my mouth.

I searched father's face for any form of remorse. His eyes were like empty sockets. If he even recognized me, I couldn't tell. He was off in a land where family doesn't exist. Tears continued to stream down my face, but they didn't have any effect. They left me in the dining room, but they didn't go far. I could hear them talking in the living room.

I couldn't imagine what they were saying. I had a harder time trying to figure out how this whole day had turned out so wrong. I knew that Padre would be upset when he found out I was pregnant, but I had no idea that he would lose his fucking mind. My only hope of salvation was Mike. He would just tell Padre that we were married and expecting a child and that would be that. I tried to work the pillowcase out my mouth so I could tell them I needed to go to the bathroom, but Jesus had shoved it so far in my mouth I couldn't get my tongue behind it to push it out.

Jesus was a mystery to me. He acted as if he hated me and didn't even know me. I hadn't said more than ten words to him the entire time that he had been around the house. Why were his actions toward me so vicious? Perhaps he had me confused with his baby's momma or something. I was snatched from my thoughts when I heard the front door slam.

Ramón had made it home.

I couldn't see him, but I could hear him kidding around with that bastard Chico. When I got out of this, I was going to make sure my brother knew exactly what Chico had done to me.

"Did you make those deliveries, boy?" I heard my father ask him.

I knew that pissed Ramón off because he hated to be called "boy," especially in front of his newfound hero.

"Yeah, I made 'em." I could hear the attitude dripping from Ramón's voice. Despite how he felt about Chico, he still wasn't feeling our father.

"You better watch that tone of voice with me, boy."

I started praying that Ramón would hold on to his temper until he was able to clear my name.

"Come over here, boy." My father was really being an ass. "When did your sister get married?"

The question was thrown out there casually as if it were a common known fact.

"Huh?"

"You heard me. How long has your sister been married?"

"Ariana is not married."

"Who said I was talking about Ariana?" There was a brief pause.

"All right, let's try a different approach: When's the baby due?"

"Uh—"

"I'm warning you, don't lie to me." Padre's voice dropped down to a deep baritone.

"What baby?"

Padre let out a laugh that scared the shit out of me. I wanted to call out to Ramón, but that wasn't happening. I needed him to come and untie me so we could get the hell out of there. Then, I wished that Moses were here to help me awaken from this terrible dream. The baby was in hyper drive, kicking against my uterus, intensifying my need to pee.

I struggled against my restraints. Short of toppling the chair over, I gave up. I was tied too tight. As I was trying to catch my breath, I heard Padre tell Ramón, "I need you to make another delivery."

"I just got back. Can't it wait until I make the deliveries tomorrow?"

"Don't question me, boy."

I heard Ramón sigh.

"The package is on top of the television. The address is on the package."

The front door slammed and I knew I was all alone.

Then Padre said, "Bring the bitch in here."

I pissed on myself.

His two goons walked into the dining room with big smiles on their faces. If there was one thing that I was sure of, they were enjoying this. They picked up the chair and carried me to the living room. I struggled again to get free, but it was pointless. I could feel my left eye beginning to close.

Padre snatched the pillowcase out my mouth and threw it at me.

"Why are you doing this to me, Padre?"

"Shut up! You speak when you are spoken to," Padre growled. "I could kill you for disgracing me this way!"

"I'm telling you the truth. Call my house and ask to speak to my husband. He will tell you the truth. Ramón was just trying to protect my secret because I told him not to tell you." Tears continued to stream out of my eyes.

"You lying, conniving slut!" He spat in my face.

Chico and Jesus had smirks on their faces that made me and the baby sick.

"Padre, please stop this. Call Mike, he will clear this up. His number is 555-321-4356."

"I have grown weary of this game." He took off his belt, wrapped it around his fist, then struck across my legs.

I screamed then said, "Please." I didn't mind begging, it was all I had left. I screamed again as the leather strap made contact again.

Padre nodded to Jesus who then made the call using the speaker phone in the living room. I used to love that phone and the memories it represented. We used it to speak with my padre on it during a time when he could be considered a father, but today I hated it. The phone rang several times before Mike picked up. I had never been so happy to hear his voice than I was today.

"Hello," Mike said.

"Michael?"

"Yeah, this is him."

"I'm Carlos Mendoza, Ariana's father."

"Hello, nice to finally have the opportunity to speak with you. I can't wait to meet you."

"Oh, you know about me?" Padre was acting so nice.

I wanted him to cut to the chase so they could untie me and I could go to the bathroom and clean myself up.

"Uh...yes, sir—she's mentioned you." Mike was stumbling over his words.

"How well do you know her?"

Oh shit, I could tell where he was going with this line of questioning. It didn't look good for me. Chico must have sensed I was going to scream again because he wrapped his hands around my throat. My eyes bucked in fear. The only thing that escaped my mouth was a soft whimper.

"Uh...we went to school together," Mike replied.

Another dose of hot urine ran down the seat of the chair and pooled on the floor. Mike wasn't going to be able to help me now.

"Oh, that's nice. What about the baby?"

There was a pause that lasted entirely too long. The only thing I could hear was a loud silence.

"What baby?" Mike was playing along with my ruse.

When he said that, I knew I was going to die. There was no way they were going to let me live with the things that they had done to me tonight. They would have to spend the rest of their lives looking over their shoulders if they did, especially Jesus!

"I see. Sorry to have bothered you." Padre disconnected the call. He turned to Jesus. "Find out where he lives and get rid of him."

The room started to get dark. I could still see their faces, but I couldn't hear what they were saying. Padre just stood there looking at me. If he was bothered by the fact that Chico had his hand wrapped around my neck, I couldn't tell.

"What about her?" Chico asked.

"I want that child gone. Take her to the place and handle it."

Chico dragged my limp body out the room, still tied to the chair. He took the throw off the sofa and placed it over my head. He then lifted the chair and carried me out to the car.

"What do you want done?" Chico asked

"Don't ask me any more stupid questions, handle it."

The last thing I heard before I passed out was my screams.

CHAPTER TWENTY-ONE

GABRIELA MENDOZA

As luck would have it, I had to work late. I was closing on a deal that our firm had been working on for months. I called Ariana to let her know I would be late, but she didn't answer the phone. I was going to call the house number, but I didn't want to speak to my father if I didn't have to.

"She's probably asleep and didn't hear it," I said to myself as I closed my flip phone.

Living at home with my father was like living in a library. The only time we gathered as a family was for meals. There was no conversation, just the sound of forks hitting plates and ice tinkling in glasses. When we would finish eating, Ramón and I would clear the table. He helped me with the dishes because Ariana prepared the meals.

My father didn't like Ramón helping with dishes. He claimed that it was woman's work. I wanted to tell him that he needed to step all the way into the twenty-first century. Many of his thoughts were archaic. For the most part, we allowed him to say what was on his mind and went on about our business. The things that he should have been talking to us about, he didn't—like when the hell he was going home.

The house was dark when I got home. I wasn't surprised because I didn't expect them to stall dinner for me. I looked around for my father's car and was happy to see that it wasn't there. As I turned my key in the door, I prayed that he had finally left us alone.

I turned on the light by the door. Ariana's purse was setting right by the door. This was unusual for her. Normally, she would take her purse to our room just in case our so-called father got nosey and decided to go in it. I picked it up and slung it over my shoulder.

"No wonder she didn't hear me calling her," I said as I went into the kitchen to see if they left anything for me on the stove. I wasn't really hungry, but I would eat if there was something there. I froze and turned up my nose. A strong urine stench hung in the air.

The next thing that struck me odd was all the groceries were still in bags waiting to be put away. Ariana had told me she was going to the store, so I was surprised that she would leave things this way. Fear invaded my heart.

"What if it's the baby?" Stifling a cry, I raced through the living room and up the stairs.

Upstairs was just as dark. One thing that I hated about older houses was the light switch was at the bottom of the stairs and I would have to go back down in order to turn on the light. Not wanting to waste any more time, I continued to feel my way.

I flipped on the upstairs' light. I thought the light would give me comfort; instead it made me realize just how alone I was in the house. My heart pitched in my chest when I realized her bed was empty. I dumped our purses on the bed, then sat down and tried to think logically.

Perhaps my so-called father decided to take the family out to dinner. In my wildest dreams, I could not see that situation playing out. If Ariana did go somewhere with him, she would have left a note. I ran into Ramón's room. It was empty as well. It didn't look like he had been at home since leaving for school this morning. Normally, he would turn his *Wii* on mute and play games until dinner. His controllers were not even connected to the television, which was a sure indicator that he hadn't been home.

"Where the hell is everyone?" I yelled at the walls. Even the goons were gone. I fought the urge to panic because that would not help the situation. I called Tilo to take my mind off the situation and to see if she had any luck with the letters. I closed and locked our bedroom door. The last thing I needed was for my so-called father to come upstairs and catch me on the phone. "Hey baby," I crooned into the phone. I needed to hear her voice in the worst way.

"Gabriela, I'm so glad you called. I really need to talk to you."

I was so befuddled over the empty house, I wasn't really paying any attention to what Tilo was saying. I thought she was just telling me that she missed me.

"It's real import—"

"When I got home, the house was all dark and nobody is here."

"You and your sister could be in—"

"She didn't even put the groceries away," I continued, thinking maybe she would shut up if I kept on talking at the same time she was. I didn't know what Tilo was rambling on about, but I needed her to know something strange was going on.

"—great danger," Tilo shouted.

"Huh?" She had finally gotten my attention.

"Haven't you been listening to me?"

"I'm sorry, I guess we both were talking at the same time." I started walking down the stairs. I had forgotten all about trying to keep my phone hidden.

"Listen to me: I think you and your sister are in great danger," she repeated.

"Why? What's wrong?" That strange feeling that I had felt when I walked into the house got worse. Tiny beads of sweat started to trickle down my back. I walked over to the living room window and peeked through the curtains. I wanted to make sure my father didn't creep up behind me and hear my conversation.

"I got the letters back from the translator. She asked me if this was for a book you were writing."

"Why would she say that?" I started to get irritated. To me the comment was trivial and nothing compared to the fact that my whole family was missing.

"She said it read like a movie. She wanted to know if it was for a book. That got me curious so I started reading it. I think your parents owe all of you some explanations."

I took a seat on the sofa. "What kind of explanations, and what do you mean that we are in danger?"

"Wait, let me go get it," she replied.

"Hurry up. I don't know how long I have before they came back."

She must have put down the phone because I could hear her running through our apartment.

"Hold on," she yelled.

I stared at the clock, wondering how much time I had to myself. Part of me wanted to jump in the car and ride over there so I could see for myself what she was talking about. The other part of me prayed that she didn't come back to the phone and tell me some jacked-up shit that was going to piss me off.

"Okay, I'm back."

I could hear her fumbling through some pages, obviously looking for the part that worried her most.

"I haven't finished reading it, but from what I gather, your parents used you and your sister to barter passage to the United States."

"Barter? What does that mean?"

"He called it an arrangement where you two married someone they chose. I don't know all the details yet, but obviously your mother regretted that decision," Tilo replied. "Your parents got rich on the *arrangement* too."

"Tilo, stop playing. My parents wouldn't do that," I exclaimed. Even as I said those words, a smidgen of doubt crept into my thoughts. After all, who was I to say what my father was capable of doing since he was nothing like the man I remembered from my childhood.

Tilo continued, "From what I read in the letters, your mother was pleading with your father to cancel the arrangement and to separate himself from the cartel and the money."

"Cartel? What cartel? Girl, you have been watching too much television 'cause you are on some real CSI shit now." I was joking around but the more I heard, the harder it was for me to refute what she had said.

"Your mother was worried because your father was accepting money from them. He sent her most of it. She was afraid of the long-term implications. Where's the money, Gabriela. You must know something."

"See, Tilo, that's where everything you have said falls apart. There never was any money. Our family was less than one paycheck from poverty." Even as the words left my mouth, I thought about my father's sudden wealth. Doubt began to tug at the outer recesses of my mind and a seed was planted.

"Baby, you must read these letters and decide for yourself. I have a feeling that the answers to all these questions are in here. Why don't you come by now since no one is there? Maybe we can pinpoint the whereabouts of your mother's money before it falls into the wrong hands."

"I can't. I have such a bad feeling about this. Ariana's purse and car are here, but she isn't. It's not like her to just leave the house without her purse. And I seriously doubt if she would go anywhere with my father, especially without calling me and telling me something."

"Well, she must have?" Tilo responded.

I was about to say something about the groceries sitting in the middle of the floor and the urine stench when I heard a car door slam. Rushing to the window, I peeled back the curtain to peek without being seen. My heart was slamming inside of chest. "Tilo, someone's coming."

THE PLOT THICKENS

CHAPTER TWENTY-TWO
MOSES RAMSEY

My friendship with Ariana's grew with the passage of time. She shared her fears, hopes and aspirations with me, and I gained a new respect for her. I remember asking her why she had married so young and her answer shocked the shit out of me: She said "because he loved me." She never confessed to loving her husband—and that's all my silly heart needed to hear. I fell in love right then and there.

Shaking my head, I threw my empty coffee container in the trash. Sitting there daydreaming totally defeated my purpose for coming to the office early. Placing my feet on the floor, I turned around to power up my laptop. I wanted to draft a few letters before my temporary secretary, Ara, came in.

Allowing myself one last trip down memory lane, I reread the letter Ariana had sent me the night after we had first made love:

> *Have you ever felt like you have spent your whole life merely reacting to stimuli? Raising your hand at the appropriate time and nodding* yes *when you really meant* no*? Have you ever lived just for the sake of something to do? Well, I have spent my whole life that way and then came you.*

You once asked me why I had married so young, and seemed surprised by my response. I did not realize how silly I had sounded until I saw your face. I had never been asked that question before, so I said the first thing that came to mind. Often times people emulate what they see. Now that I have had a moment to think about my reasons, I guess that was my excuse. I did what I was trained to do, I pleased my man. Never once did it occur to me that I should have been pleasing myself. That is until I met you.

When I married my husband, I emulated the only relationship I knew, that of my parents. My father loves my mother and that's what matters. I can't remember the last time I saw her smile, I never expected her to. I became her and didn't even realize it. Then came you.

In a very short amount of time you have become my stimuli—my reason to say what I feel instead of what's expected. And even though I know this can never be more than what it is, you have given me reason to love. For that, I will forever be grateful. I never knew it could be like this. In my dreams you will always be mine. And while it will be difficult to continue to pretend to be happy with my lot in life, I shall because I know a part of you will be with me forever.

Thanks for opening me up—in more ways than one.

Always, Ariana

My eyes were torn from my screen when the phone rang. My gut instinct told me to ignore it, but curiosity got the better of me. My heart rate soared as I reached for the phone. The only person that I knew who would call me at this time of the morning was Ariana. She knew my routine. "Moses Ramsey," I answered in my best Barry White voice. My dick thickened in anticipation.

"Hey baby," my mother crooned.

Shame raced through my veins as I pushed my dick back in between my legs. I felt like my mother could see my dick as it strained against my zipper.

"Mommy?" I was stunned. I moved my hand away from my dick. Moms had a sixth sense about their children, and I immediately felt guilty about sleeping with a married woman.

"What's wrong, sugar?" Concern dripped from off her tongue.

"Huh?" I stalled. I didn't want to lie to her, but I damn sure wasn't going to tell her the truth.

"You don't sound like yourself," she replied.

"Uh, I'm sorry, Mom, I was just preoccupied. How are you?"

"I'm good. Your dad and I were just talking about you, so I thought I would give you a call."

A feeling of dread came over me because I knew what her next statement was going to be. "Wow, you must have felt me thinking of you too. If I wasn't so busy with this big case I'm working on, I would hop on a plane and come down to visit you," I lied. It wasn't that I didn't love my parents, I just didn't want to get into the inevitable discussion about my marital status. They thought because I was a single, black male—living in Atlanta—I had to be gay, and they felt obligated to save my soul from eternal damnation.

"Another one? Honey, you work too hard," Mom said.

"Hey, somebody got to work in this family since you and dad both retired," I said, laughing.

"Your dad and I are not retired, we just don't work anymore. We want to enjoy our life."

Damn. I had made her mad and wasn't even trying. I was trying to be funny, not insulting. But she took it the wrong way. It was just like my mom to take my words and twist them all around.

"Mom, chill out. I wasn't throwing shade, I was making a joke. I mean, you know I love you, right?"

"Of course I do, honey, but your dad and I worry about you all alone in Atlanta."

Here we go. She made it to her favorite topic of conversation in record time.

"Mom, I'm a grown-ass man." I had taken leave of my senses when I cussed at my mom.

"Moses Ramsey, watch your mouth. You may be grown, but I can still take a switch to your behind if you don't mind your manners."

"I'm sorry, that slipped out. I wasn't trying to be disrespectful." I ate a huge slice of humble pie with that slip of the tongue.

"Humph! That's what I was telling your dad. Those people in Atlanta are just running wild. What you need to do is find yourself a nice young woman and settle down."

"Mom, let's not go there again. Please." She was ruining my good mood, and I wanted to get off the phone before we started to argue again.

"What, you don't like women all of a sudden?" She threw that jab so fast, I didn't have a chance to duck.

"I love women. For your information, I have one. In fact, we're having a baby…" Oh shit, I had let her push me straight up to the cliff, and I hurled myself over it. I got up from my desk and started pacing the floor.

"What…honey, come here…Moses—"

I heard the phone hit the floor. My mom was ranting in the background. She was calling for my father. I considered disconnecting the call, but I knew they would be on the first thing smoking if I had done that. My mind started working overtime. I was trying to figure out something to say before my dad got on the phone. I could hear my mom praising God in the background.

"Moses, what's going on? Your mom is going to church in here, talking gibberish, and I can't make heads or tails out of what she's saying."

"Hey, Dad," I replied, hoping he would just let it go.

He knew better than anyone how my mom could go on and on about nothing. Over the years, he had learned to tune her out.

"Dad my ass. What's this about? And please don't tell me you done gone gay on us," he shouted.

"For crying out loud, Dad, let me say this for the last time: I'm not gay. I get so tired of both of you saying that to me. That's like saying if you are a rooster and you live around hens, you are gonna lay an egg."

"Well, if you are not gay, then why is your mother over here acting like a damn fool?" All of a sudden it got real quite on his end of the phone, but I knew it was the calm before the storm. Like clockwork, my mom recovered her voice. I could hear her in the background fussing at my dad. I let out a sigh of relief because I was off the hot seat. She didn't take too kindly to my dad saying she was acting like a fool.

"Son, I'll call you back later, perhaps when you get home from work." He rushed off the phone.

Relieved, I replaced the receiver on the base. Before I could walk away from it, it rung again. I snatched my hand away from the phone, praying that it would stop ringing before I was forced to answer it. Defeated, I answered it ready to fight with my mom and dad again.

"Moses Ramsay," I said just in case it was actually a business call.

"Hi, Mr. Ramsay, this is Ramón."

Relief washed over me but that feeling quickly turned to dread. If he was calling me, something had to be wrong. He had been doing odd jobs for me for the last two weeks but he rarely called me.

"Ramón, what's wrong?" My fingers gripped the edge of my desk so hard, my knuckles were white.

"Wrong? Nothing's wrong. I just wanted to let you know I would be late coming in this afternoon. I have to stay at school to make up a test."

Relief washed over me like a mini-wave. Releasing the desk, I sank down in the chair. I exhaled a big sigh.

"Mr. Ramsay, are you there?"

"I'm sorry, Ramón. I thought you were calling to tell me something was wrong with your sister."

"No, she's fine—just big as a damn house," he said, laughing.

I wanted to tell him that she looked absolutely beautiful to me but didn't know how he would react to that. "Good, tell her I asked about her, okay?" What I really wanted to say was put her on the phone, because I missed hearing her voice. She normally called me each night from her cell right before going to bed. She had been very quiet the last few weeks. She did tell me that things around her house were crazy so I tried to understand. Secretly, I was happy that she was living at home and not with her husband.

"I'll tell her for you when I get home. I'm at school."

"Okay, I'll see you when you get here. Getting your education comes first, right?"

"Yes, sir."

"Hey, what did I tell you about calling me sir? I know I'm older than you, but I ain't that old. I thought you were going to call me Moses?"

"Sure, sir—uh—I mean Moses. I'll see you later." He hung up the phone.

We went through that ritual every day. It seemed like overnight he would forget that it was okay to call me by my first name, but I was determined to break that habit.

CHAPTER TWENTY-THREE
MOSES RAMSEY

When I hung up the phone, I made up my mind that I was done with work for the morning. My concentration was gone. I was supposed to be working on some paperwork but I was feeling too fidgety and it wasn't from the coffee. Speaking to my parents always did this to me. They made me feel inadequate, even though I considered myself a successful man. They, however, thought something had to be wrong with me because I hadn't found a wife and settled down. They didn't understand the drive and determination that I used to push myself through school and start my own practice.

Grabbing my jacket from behind the door, I put it on and left the office. I needed to feel the sunshine on my face and clear my head. I decided to take a walk down the block and get another cup of coffee. I know I didn't need it, but any old excuse would have done right about then.

I couldn't get mad at my folks for wanting me to settle down. At this point in my life, I was ready, but as luck would have it, the woman I fell in love with was married. The situation was further complicated because I had been paid to keep close tabs on her and her family. I took a seat in the coffeehouse, hoping that the change of scenery would be good for me.

Almost immediately every female eye, black and white, turned to me. Although none of them came over to my table, I could see the change in their demeanor. Eyes batted, legs crossed, lips were seductively licked. Each one tried to get me to notice them, but they just appeared to be thirsty to me. Pulling out my phone, I dialed Ariana's cell because I really needed to hear her voice.

The ladies who were trying to get my attention rolled their eyes at my blatant lack of interest. I wanted to snicker but that would only antagonize them. The phone rang four times before it went to voice mail, taking my heart with it. "Hey baby, I just wanted to hear your voice. Call me when you get a chance, okay." I disconnected the call. I tried to sit there and finish my coffee, but I felt like a fish in a clear blue pond with the ladies still vying for my attention. Slowly, I got to my feet and headed for the door.

"Leaving so soon?" one brazen woman asked. She was a slender black woman with a short haircut and a cute smile.

"Yeah, got to get back to the office," I lied.

"You work around here?" She reached for the door, held it open for me, then followed me out to the sidewalk.

"Not far from here," I replied. I did not want to encourage the conversation so I started walking toward my office.

But the chick had balls. She wasn't going to allow me to dismiss her like that.

"My name is Tammi." She extended her hand and practically forced me to take it. After she shook my hand, she continued to hold on to it. She ran her finger around my ring finger and smiled.

I assumed she was looking for the telltale ring that some brothers mistakenly display when they tried to hide their marital status.

"I'm Moses," I said as I gently pulled my hand away from her.

Another lady, who was in the shop with us, walked by and shot daggers at Tammi with her eyes. In fact, if looks could kill, Tammi would have gone up in a puff of putrid smoke. A smile tugged at the corners of my lips as I captured the visual in my head.

"You have a beautiful smile," Tammi said.

"Thanks, so do you." I turned to allow her to walk in front of me so I could check her out. I told myself it wouldn't hurt to look. She was about five feet five and had a banging body, but she didn't hold a candle to Ariana. I was tempted by the gentle sway of her ass, but I could tell Tammi had all the characteristics of a stalker written all over her face.

"So, are you from here?" She fell back into step beside me. Her legs were long so she easily matched my pace.

"No." I kept my answer short and sweet. I thought that if I didn't ask her any questions about herself, she would get the hint that I wasn't interested. I was wrong.

"I just moved here from Baltimore and, boy, is it different." She had piqued my curiosity with that one.

"Different, how so?"

"The pace is different, number one. And the men, they are different too." She chuckled when she said that as if she knew something I didn't know. It was almost as if she were baiting me.

"I don't see how Atlanta's pace would be any different from Baltimore's. It's a big city too." I wasn't going to touch that part about the men with a ten-foot pole, because she might have misconstrued it as interest.

"Oh, that's not the pace that I'm talking about. See, back home, when a man saw a beautiful lady sitting by herself, he would not hesitate to come over to the lady and introduce himself." She dropped that statement like a fart in a small room as she turned to face me.

Now I could have been an asshole and said something to the effect of, "If I saw a beautiful woman, then I would step to her," but I didn't. Instead, I let it go. We walked on as I deliberately passed my office. Something told me not to let her see where I worked or she would be camped at the doorway every day.

"You don't have anything to say?"

I could feel the attitude brewing, and it confirmed my suspicions about her—another angry black woman.

"I didn't realize I was supposed to comment on that. I thought you were telling me your observations."

She stumbled in her step. I instinctively reached for her, but she snatched her arm away. I held up my hands to show her I didn't mean her any harm. I stopped walking and so did she.

"I wasn't asking your opinion," she said with a huff.

"Good. That's why I didn't offer it." If she wanted to act like an ass, she could do it by her damn self because I wasn't taking that trip with her.

"Are you one of those down-low brothers?" She was rocking her head when she said that, causing a vein to pop out in her neck. It wasn't a good look for her at all.

"Why do I have to be on the low, 'cause I didn't step to you?" Now I was mad as well. It was the second time today that I had to defend my masculinity.

"I'm just asking, that's all. Don't get all bent out of shape about it." She smiled sweetly as if she hadn't tried to call me out.

"Frankly, it's none of your business. But on the real, that's not my problem. I'm just not interested in whatever you have to offer."

"I wasn't offering you a damn thing. See, that's another difference between the North and the South. Y'all are so full of yourselves."

"Look, you obviously have me confused with someone else, so I'm going to leave you now before I say something that I would normally not say to a lady. Have a nice day." I turned around and started walking back down the block. I wanted to turn around to see if she was still standing there, but I wouldn't give her the satisfaction. I honestly thought she was going to take off her shoe and wing it at my head. So, to be on the safe side, I walked past my office again just to make sure she didn't see where I worked.

Glancing at my watch, I realized that I had wasted a good hour, but I still wasn't in the mood to work. I called my good friend, Gerard, to see if he was down for a game of racquet ball at the gym.

Gerald had kicked my ass again. I was going to have to tighten my game up before I called him out again. "Good game," I said in between breaths.

Gerard made me sick because he didn't even appear to be winded. He was in good shape, but so was I. I worked out at least three times a week and run five out of seven days a week.

"Man, you got to get you some pussy before you fall out." Gerard laughed as he headed for the showers.

"Damn, so that's the secret?" I was dumbfounded at the simplicity of his assessment.

"Yeah, you got your balls all locked up all the time. It clogs the veins. You need something to get the old blood flowing, you know what I mean?"

As much as I hated to admit it, he might have had a point. Prior to my relationship with Ariana, I was practically celibate. Casual sex had never appealed to me. Relationships required too much of my time, and I didn't have it to spare.

"Can I tell you a secret?" I asked as I followed him to the showers. So far, I had not confided in anyone about my relationship with Ariana. Not that I was hiding it, it was just complicated.

"Yeah, bro, you know how we do." He turned to look at me.

"I'm involved with someone."

He clutched his heart and stumbled back.

"See, that's why I didn't tell your ass in the first place. Always with the jokes." I was getting angry.

"Man, lighten up. You just shocked me, that's all." He punched me lightly on the shoulder, and I kind of relaxed a little bit.

"I'm serious about her, so I'm real sensitive about it," I admitted.

"That's cool. I feel the same way about my boo. So who is she? Do I know her?"

"Yeah, you've seen her around." I started to get nervous again because he was waiting for me to tell him who she was. Now I felt like kicking myself for opening up my big mouth.

"Are you going to tell me this year, nigga?" he said, joking again.

"Ariana, from my office."

"The Columbian girl? I thought she was married."

"That's only part of the problem."

He whistled through his lips and shook his head. "My mother always said you can't choose who you love." He put his hand out for me to give him dap.

"Thanks for listening. It's been tough because she's really going through it right now with her family. Her mother died and she's caught up in that. It doesn't help that I was hired to investigate her and she's carrying my baby, too." I dropped that little nugget and hopped in the shower.

"She's what?" he yelled, stepping into the stall with me.

"Nigga, get your ass out of here before someone walks in here and starts some shit and I have to bust them in the mouth."

He looked down and realized what the hell he had done. He quickly walked out, muttering under his breath, "Stupid ass."

CHAPTER TWENTY-FOUR

TILO ADAMS

"Shit!" I groaned when I opened my eyes and saw the clock. I was going to be late for work if I didn't move my ass immediately. The fact that I had been able to sleep at all was surprising to me because I had spent most of the night reading the letters Gabriela had given me. Throwing back the covers, I raced into the shower with thoughts of the letters running through my head. I wanted to get my hands on that money. Of course I would have had a better idea of where it was hidden if I had read the letters from her madre, but I had enough information to let me know that I was barking up the right tree. For now, I would play Gabriela closer and when the opportunity presented itself, pounce on it.

Gabriela had a very colorful family history. The letters had proven to be enlightening. From what I had read, Gabriela's father was a dictator who used the fear of the past to control their future. He was a manipulator playing silly mind games to make sure his wishes were carried out.

"He obviously hadn't heard of the woman's liberation movement," I muttered to myself. But apparently, Gabriela's mother had never heard of it either, or she would have kicked his egotistical ass to the curb many years ago. It's one thing to be in a domineering relationship when the man is there twenty-four hours a day, but it's whole different ballgame when he is thousands of miles away. If it were me, one of two things would have happened: I would have pretended to agree to do whatever he said and lived my life, or I would have told him to kiss my natural black ass and went about my business. Knowing me, it would have been the latter.

I grabbed the letters and my keys and raced out the door. I didn't want to hear my supervisor's mouth about being late. She was a nice enough lady, but she didn't tolerate tardiness or unexcused absences, and, in this Post-Bush economy, I needed my job—for now.

As I drove, I continued going over what I had read and those thoughts both chilled and excited me. If Gabriela's father was that controlling, then nothing would stop him from demanding that his family return to Columbia with him

I worked as an abstractor for the Title Guarantee Company. It was my job to search property titles for new loans to make sure they were free and clear of liens before a new mortgage was taken out on the property. It wasn't the most glamorous of jobs, but it paid the rent and allowed me to be out of the office for extended periods of time without anyone looking for me.

Gabriela's job was to transcribe my notes, and she prepared the title policies for the properties. That's how we became friends in the first place. I remembered the first time we had gone out together. We went to a popular night spot that catered to a mixed crowd. I wasn't present to witness all the drinks that were given to her or her subsequent erratic behavior, but I had heard enough rumors. The first person I ran into told me that Gabriela was drunk. I didn't believe them. When I heard it again, I went looking for her. I searched the entire club and couldn't find her. I don't know what had made me check outside, but I'm glad I did.

Back in the day, a person could leave the club and come back in. That shit wasn't happening these days. Supposedly, Gabriela had left the club to get some air. I found her buck naked in the backseat of her car, knocked out with the doors unlocked. That was a sight I don't ever want to see again. I immediately feared the worst. I thought she had been raped and left for dead.

"What the fuck?" I screamed as I looked around to see who might have harmed her. Terror gripped my heart as I pulled open the door.

"Hey, Tilo! I got hot in there, so I took off my clothes." She burped loudly.

"Hot hell! Put your damn clothes on. Why the fuck didn't you roll down the windows? It's December for Christ's sake!" I was beyond pissed.

"I can't. I threw up on them."

I stood dumbfounded staring at her. "What you can't do is sit in the damn car butterball naked. Are you trying to go to jail?" She had worn a jumpsuit so when she took off the top, she took off everything. Not knowing whether she had stripped in public or waited until she had gotten to the car, I felt the need to get the hell out of that parking lot. Since she was in no condition to drive, I took her keys. Although I had been drinking too, I at least knew enough not to take off my clothes.

Gabriela struggled to put her jumpsuit back on as I backed out of the parking space. I wanted to get as far away from the spot before someone noticed I was sitting in the car with a half-naked Latino woman.

I wasn't used to driving Gabriela's car and wasn't good at shifting the gears. We had traveled about a mile before I got the hang of it. Just as I got comfortable, I came to a slight incline in the road. I immediately started to panic, and the car started sputtering.

"Shit, what do I do?" I yelled, but Gabriela had nodded off. I wanted to reach across the seat and smack the hell out of her, but I needed both hands and my feet to keep the car moving. As I went up the hill, the car died. I tried several times to get the car going again but it refused to cooperate.

"Gabriela, either you get up and drive this bitch or we are going to have to get out the car because we are sitting in the middle of the fuck—"

Before I could finish my sentence, we were struck from behind. The car began to spin in circles. I had my foot pressed firmly on the brake, but it did nothing to stop the car from spinning. We were hit so hard, I was afraid her tiny car was going to flip over. Luckily, it didn't.

"Switch seats with me," she said.

I looked at her like she was crazy. My head was pounding, and I wasn't thinking straight.

"Switch seats with me or your ass is going to wind up in jail."

She didn't have to say it again. The last thing I needed was to be picked up for a DUI. We quickly changed seats and Gabriela pretended to be unconscious when the police arrived. I was so scared. I could have shit a brick. To this day, I don't understand why the police didn't haul her drunken ass away. In fact, she didn't even get a ticket.

CHAPTER TWENTY-FIVE
TILO ADAMS

I hadn't been to work for an hour yet and already my phone was ringing off the damn hook. "Tilo Adams, how may I help you?" It was my boss, Tanya, calling. I started to get nervous. She never called unless she was about to chew on my ass about something.

"Can I see you in my office?"

I glanced at my watch. Mentally, I ran through all the things that I could have done to land myself in trouble. Since I made it to work on time, I couldn't think of any reason for her to want to see me. "Sure, I'll be right there." Without wasting any time, I grabbed a pad from my desk and rushed to Tanya's office.

"Close the door," she instructed.

A wave of anxiety spread through my mind. Nothing good could come of a closed-door session.

"What did I do?" I said.

"Relax. It has nothing to do with you."

I exhaled a sigh of relief. I couldn't lose this job yet. But if things worked out the way I planned, Tanya and this job could kiss my ass.

"It's about Gabriela. I know that the two of you are friends, and I'm worried about her."

I was surprised to learn that Gabriela even made it onto Tanya's radar. She didn't fraternize with peons like us. "She's been going through a lot, but she'll be okay." I wasn't about to get into a detailed discussion with Tanya about Gabriela's personal life. Gabriela would have to do that herself.

"She didn't show up for work today and to my knowledge, she hasn't called in."

It didn't even occur to me that Gabriela wasn't in her office. "What? That's not like Gabriela. Something must have happened." If Gabriela did a no-show, something major must have happened and I intended to find out what was going on. I fidgeted in my chair, waiting to be dismissed.

"Company policy states that failure to call in is grounds for automatic termination."

"Come on, Tanya, have a heart. You know Gabriela doesn't operate like this. Something must have happened."

"I understand. That's why I called you in. If you speak to Gabriela, have her call me immediately. I'll see what I can do to keep this between us, but I won't cover for her for long. I will not risk my job for her or anybody else for that matter."

"Thanks, Tanya." I stood up. I really wanted to tell her to take a large, juicy bite out my ass, but I kept the thought to myself.

I pulled my cell from my hip and called Gabriela's number, but it immediately went to voice mail. My mind drifted back to the letters and I couldn't help but to think that her absence and the letters were somehow connected. I grabbed my purse and decided to head over to the courthouse so I could plot without someone looking over my shoulder. I also wanted to be someplace where I could speak with Gabriela in private when she called back.

It was time for me to do a little investigating on my own and searching the title to Gabriela's parents' home would be a great place to start.

According to the letters, the Mendoza family owned several properties. Some of them were in the more affluent areas of Buckhead, Midtown, and Alpharetta. If this were true, it meant that their family had more money than I originally thought.

Gabriela's father wrote at length about proposed marriages that he had arranged for Gabriela and Ariana. Gabriela's mother must have had second thoughts about it and that upset their father. His letters contained tirades in which he denounced his wife and her loyalty to their family. He was bitter about the disappearance of his sons and blamed his wife for having girl children. I needed Gabriela to shed some light on this because it was difficult to fully understand what he was venting about when I was only reading his side of the story.

I called Gabriela again and left her an urgent voice message. "Call the job! Tanya's acting like an ass. Then call me. I've got to talk to you."

I pulled out the letters and began my research. I logged into the computer that I used to conduct title searches in the courthouse. I typed the address of Gabriela's house and waited for it to pull up the information. I wanted to know when the house was bought and how much money was owed on the property. If Gabriela's claims of poverty were true, they would still owe a sizable balance on the loan. To my surprise, the deed to the property was not in the Mendoza name, it was titled to a corporation called Nosotros Properties, which I remembered from a *60*

Minutes episode. Nosotros was allegedly controlled by a Columbian criminal organization called the Cali Cartel.

"Interesting," I muttered. Switching screens, I retyped the address to see if the house was mortgaged, but none were listed. If the Mendoza's were leasing the property, that would make sense, but it did raise a red flag inside my head. I recalled Gabriela telling me that her father had put the house up for sale, but I was baffled as to how he could do that if he didn't own the property.

"Who are these people?" Talking aloud was customary for me and those around me knew it, so they didn't bother to look up from their computer screens. For some people, searching titles was boring, but I found it very interested. To me, it was like putting together the pieces of puzzle. I loved puzzles. The only boring titles were single-family ones that required little or no research. I liked having to dig deeper to find the true ownership of properties.

I logged onto the Internet and did a Google search for Nosotros Properties. I was beginning to feel like Inspector Gadget without his newfangled toys. Nosotros was listed several times, but the corporate office was not in Atlanta. So why would a corporation that specialized in commercial and industrial properties hold the title on the Mendoza properties?

"Hmm, the plot thickens." I read the company's mission statement but could not find a listing of its partners. If Mr. Mendoza was a partner, it would explain why their house was held by a corporation. But it wouldn't explain the other properties. I went back to the title search screen and did a search of all properties owned by the corporation.

The Atlanta listings were all in the areas mentioned in Mendoza's letters to his wife, but they were designated as either commercial or industrial. There was only one sure way to find out what those properties were.

I jotted down those addresses and logged off the computer. "Road trip," I whispered. I tried Gabriela again but continued to get her voice mail. I could only assume she was around her father and could not risk using her phone. My plan was to visit each of the locations after I got off work. Content that I was doing something constructive, I went back to the office to see if I had any assignments.

I sat in my car in front of the last property on my list. I was tripping. All seven locations of the Nosotros properties all claimed to be adult care facilities. All but five were in residential neighborhoods and none, as far as I could tell, were handicap accessible.

"Where's the freaking ramp?" Warning lights were going off in my head. I drove away deep in thought. After spending the last three hours driving around Atlanta, I had more questions than answers. Although each property displayed a sign offering assistance for elderly patients, none of them were wheelchair accessible.

"Why would these neighborhood associations allow a home to be placed in their gated communities? Why weren't they stopped when they applied for a business license?" I wasn't up on all the zoning rules and regulations, but it didn't take a rocket scientist to figure out that something wasn't right with this whole situation, and if it would get me closer to the money, I was determined to find out what was really going on. I could not shake the feeling of doom that followed me around all day.

I was almost home when I decided to make one last trip for the evening. I wanted to drive by Gabriela's mother's house just to make sure things were okay, even if I was on the outside looking in.

CHAPTER TWENTY-SIX
MOSES RAMSEY

Ramón was acting strange today. Normally, he would come in and out of my office during the three hours he spent with me each night. Today, however, he stayed at his desk working on the files I had left out for him. It was grunt work with no urgency so I was surprised by his dedication to the task.

I stared at him from my doorway. He was so intent, he didn't even notice me standing there. His young features were balled up in a frown as if he were concentrating very hard. The task was menial and did not deserve the attention he was giving it. Something was not right with him today.

"Ramón, you don't have to finish those files today," I said, laughing to ease the tension.

He practically jumped two inches up out of the chair. "Huh?" He blinked at me as if he couldn't see me clearly.

"I said, you don't have to finish those files today."

"It's okay, unless you have something else you would like for me to do."

He was so proper sometimes I just wanted to shake him to tell him it was okay to cut the fool with me. Even though I hadn't known him long, I took a liking to the boy from the first day we had met. I admired his enthusiasm for such a menial job as filing. He never once complained, even if I asked him to empty the trash cans or fill the copier with paper.

"I'm about to make a run. Can you hang out for a few more hours or do you have to go home and do your homework?"

At the mention of home, his face scrunched up even more, piquing my curiosity. If school wasn't bothering him, it had to be something going on at home.

"I'm good. You want me to stay here and answer the phones?"

"Actually, I want you to go with me and keep me company."

His face brightened immediately.

"Are you taking me on assignment with you?" He grinned, showing all of his teeth in the process.

I couldn't help but smile with him. "Yeah, but if you tell your sister, I'm gonna have to box your ears," I said, chuckling.

He started at me in total confusion.

"It's a joke, Ramón. An old-fashion saying…sort of like saying, I'm gonna bop you upside the head," I said, smiling.

Once again, his smile brightened his entire face. "If you want to know the truth, they don't know that I work with you."

"That's actually good news, since the work we are doing is confidential. Come on, then. I won't have you out too late since it's a school night."

Another frown attempted to mar his face, but he made an effort to hide it. I went back to my office and logged off my computer and grabbed my car keys. I also grabbed the binoculars that I kept hanging behind my door for surveillance purposes.

"Can I carry those?" Ramón asked, pointing to the binoculars when I came out of my office.

"Sure, but be careful with them. These bad boys cost more than you make in a month."

"Then maybe you should give me a raise."

I could see the smile dancing around the corners of his lips. He finally started to loosen up, and I was glad I had suggested the outing. I didn't really need him to ride shotgun with me but seeing him excited pleased me.

"I'll see what I can do about that, Mr. Smarty Pants."

His look told me that he was unsure of my reaction to his joke, but I ruffled his hair to show I meant no harm.

"Cut that out. Did you get that from my sister?" He started fussing with his hair to slick it back again.

I wiped my hand on my slacks to get rid of whatever chemical he used to slick it back that way. "What you got on your hair, butter?" If he were black, I would have said *lard.* He probably wouldn't have known what the hell I was talking about.

"Mousse," he replied, sulking.

"Sorry. I promise not to put my hands in that shit again." I laughed when I saw the hurtful expression on his face, but his frown turned into a smile as we got closer to my car. I had just bought a new Jeep Wrangler and I was itching to take her for a spin. It was a metallic green Rubicon complete with its own navigation system.

"Wow, is this you?" Ramón said, pointing toward the jeep.

"Yeah, you like it? I just picked it up today."

"It's hot. How much did it set you back?"

Only a young person would ask someone how much they paid for their whip. It was almost as taboo as asking a woman how old she was. "A lot, but I've wanted one since I graduated from college, so I decided to treat myself. Hop in." I could tell he wanted to do just that, but he opened the door and climbed in while I attempted to hop in but didn't quite make it. Falling in would have been more accurate. Ramón struggled to keep from laughing but it was so comical to me, I couldn't help it.

"I'll have to practice that some more," I mumbled.

"You sure do," he said and nodded his head in agreement.

"Hey, that wasn't open for comment," I said with a smile.

He took his hand and wiped the smile off his face but it lingered in his eyes. They actually twinkled.

"Where we going?" He tried to change the subject.

"We got a new client. The husband thinks his wife is cheating on him. She should be getting off work soon. We are going to follow her to see where she goes."

"What if she goes to meet another man?" Ramón said as he bounced in his seat.

"We take notes. When we have the evidence that we need, we present it to the husband."

"But what if she just goes home?"

"Then we come back and try to catch her another day. A lot of times I don't catch people doing wrong the first time out, but you can best believe if someone comes into the office and is willing to pay our fee they probably have a valid reason for their suspicion."

"Is this what you do with your day while I'm at school, follow people around?"

"That's part of it. Sometimes people hire me to check out information and I can do that without even leaving the office." I immediately felt like an asshole for betraying the relationship I had with his sister and the friendship I was building with him.

"You mean like search for it on the Internet?"

"Yeah, something like that."

"Why are they hiring you when they can do it themselves?" Ramón made a very astute comment, and I smiled at him to acknowledge it.

"If everybody thought like you, I would be out of a work."

"Good point," he admitted.

"Besides, everybody doesn't know how to search for things on the Internet. Sometimes the Internet can be used to create a smoke screen. It takes a trained individual such as myself to see through the smoke and report the facts."

"Smoke screen? I don't understand."

I had driven about three blocks from the office and parked the car. Ramón looked like another question was brewing in his inquisitive mind.

"Okay, say, for example, you owned a nightclub and you wanted to attract a young crowd. You could create a website with pictures of all these people going in and out of the club, take pictures of the inside with some people you hired standing around for effect, and have these words coming across the screen telling you how great the place is. You have built up the hype and hopefully people will come to the club. But, when they get there, it's deserted because the place closed down three months before, but the website is still there. You won't know the real deal until you go check it out for yourself."

"Damn, ain't that false advertisement?"

I wanted to tell him to watch his mouth, but I decided against it. I had worked hard to make him to feel comfortable around me and I wanted to keep it that way.

"People do it all the time. Everything isn't always the way it seems."

"So, is this where she works?" He pointed at the building we were sitting closest too.

"Yeah," I said as I took the binoculars from Ramón.

"How do you know what she looks like?" He was eagerly looking out the window.

"She shouldn't be too hard to spot." As I answered him, the doors to the three story building were opened and several women came out at once.

"Who? They all look alike to me," Ramón said.

There was something about the way he said it that sounded funny to me and I burst out laughing. The tips of Ramón's ears started to turn red. He had to know that I wasn't laughing at him but with him because he had said the same thing black people always said about whites, they all look alike.

"Sorry, side joke. That was before your time."

He shook his head like he didn't understand and kept watching through the window.

"Our target has a small dog that she takes with her everywhere. When our girl comes out, she will let the dog out as well."

"Are you just messing with me or are you for real?"

"I promise you I didn't make it up, so we are looking for a small dog." We didn't have to wait long before the same woman who had tried to throw herself at me earlier came out the office carrying a large purse. She pulled the dog out of the purse and sat him on the ground. He immediately started dancing around her feet as if it were glad to finally be free.

"That's sick!" Ramón said.

"Her husband said the same thing. He said she doesn't go anywhere without that damn dog, and those were his words."

Ramón shook his head as we watched the dog pee against the side of the building. "If I owned that building, I would make her clean that shit up. Doesn't she know that it's going to start to stink in a few hours?"

"Obviously she doesn't care. Don't do anything to draw attention to us. We will just follow behind her to see where she goes."

Ramón sat back in his seat. The accused's name is Tammi Sykes, and she works as a nurse in a clinic.

"How is she going to work in a doctor's office and bring a dog to work? Isn't that unsanitary?"

"I would say so. The husband thinks she is having an affair with someone on staff because they are not complaining about the dog. He said she was either sleeping with the boss or she wasn't really working at all. That's what we are here to find out."

"Man, this is so cool," Ramón replied, jumping up and down in his seat as he spoke.

We watched Tammi walk her dog several feet before she scooped him up and put him back in her bag.

"It's not all fun and glory, Ramón. Sometimes I sit for hours and never see my suspect. We got lucky today."

"I'll say. If I was that dog, I would have bit her before I let her put me back in her purse."

"Yeah, me too," I said, smiling.

Ramón wore all of his emotions on his face. If he was happy you knew it. "She's getting into her car. We have got to follow her!"

I thought he was going to jump out of the jeep and start running after her.

"Calm down, son, if we pull out right behind her, she might become suspicious. We don't want to blow our cover, remember?"

"Oh yeah, sorry. I got caught up in the game."

"It's no game, Ramón. Being a private investigator is dangerous work because you never know how someone will react to being followed. I have had some pretty bad scares since I have been in the business." I stopped speaking while I maneuvered out of my parking spot. Tammi's car was about three car lengths ahead of us, and I wanted to keep it that way. Getting too close could spell disaster.

"Wow, I didn't know you were a P.I."

"You weren't supposed to. What I do for a living is on a need to know basis."

"So, what happened?" He switched gears on me and for a second, I almost forget what Ramón was talking about.

"Oh, now it's a funny story but at the time, that shit was not funny." I was so comfortable with Ramón, I kept forgetting he was still a minor.

Ramón divided his attention between me and the road, trying to decide which one was going to provide more excitement. "Tell me. I could use a good laugh."

"I was following this guy because his wife was convinced he was cheating on her. I followed him to a park. Can't remember the name, but it was in Baltimore. Anyway, he was fishing with a group of friends and I got careless and fell asleep. When I woke up, I panicked and turned on my headlights—"

Tammi made an illegal lane change and turned right. I had to quickly switch lanes without alerting any attention to myself so I could make the turn. I didn't want to lose her, especially since Ramón was with me. Once I had the car back in my sights, I resumed my story. "Those fools were standing in the middle of the beach butt ass naked with some sheets covering their heads. The headlights scared the shit out of them. When they realized I was black, they started charging the car." I took my eyes off the road long enough to look at Ramón. I could tell he was having a hard time holding in his laughter.

"Are you saying that the Klan is gay?"

"I don't know about the Klan, but those guys were obviously doing something other than burning crosses."

"What did you do?"

"Put my shit in reverse, trying to get the hell out of there."

"Did they catch you?" Merriment was dancing in Ramón's eyes as a smile tugged at my lips.

"One of them suckers leaped on my hood. His naked ass was hanging on to the windshield as I sped away. I slammed on the brakes, but he didn't let go. I ain't gonna lie, I was scared that night. If those crackers would have caught me, I would have just been another missing black man."

"How did you get away?" Ramón asked, his eyes were wide as quarters.

"He finally fell off when I got to about eighty miles an hour and turned a corner practically on two wheels. I'll bet he'll never jump on another nigga's car like that!" Tears came out the corners of my eyes as I remembered the day.

"Serves the fucker right," Ramón said, holding his hand out for a pound.

Suddenly, it wasn't funny anymore. I wasn't being a good role model to Ramón and it was obvious to me that he needed one. "I've got to stop cussing around you. I'm going to work on me, but I'm going to need you to work on you. If you start talking like a sailor, your sister is going to kill me. We can't have that."

"I don't cuss around her," he said, shooting me an eye.

I knew that wasn't true because Ariana and I had talked about it. I stared at him for a few seconds and he lowered his gaze.

"All right, I'll work on it," he said.

I fought the urge to mess up his hair again, but I was glad I had set the record straight. In the meantime, Tammi led us through downtown Atlanta to Lithonia as the sun set. Rather than take the expressway, she rode the streets.

"What she doing here? There ain't any hotels on this strip," Ramón said.

"I don't know. Let's pull over here and wait."

Tammi got out of her car and went into the adult day care center she had parked in front of. Given the fact that she worked in a doctor's office, it wasn't inconceivable for her to visit another care facility.

"I want to see what she's doing," Ramón said. His fingers were snaking toward the door handle.

We had been in the car for over thirty minutes, and I was losing my patience. I was ready to leave. I would follow up on Tammi at another time. "I think we should wrap this up. It's dark, and I need to get you home."

"We can't leave now! What will you tell our client?" He was clearly excited and dedicated.

"There's nothing to tell him. She's a nurse and she went to a clinic." I started the car ready to pull off.

"Or it could be a smoke screen."

Realizing that he had thrown my own words back at me, I was curious about how he came to his assumption. "Why do you say that?"

"If this is an adult day care center, why is the parking lot full at night?"

"Well I'll be damned. Whoops," I said as I realized that I had cussed again. I raised my hand to toss his hair but he quickly moved his head out the way.

"I might be right," Ramón said.

"Son, you made a good observation. Jot down the name of this place and let's get out of here. We'll check out the place tomorrow." I waited until he wrote down the name and the address and I drove him home.

During the drive, my mind was going a thousand miles an hour. Ramón had gotten me thinking about the possibilities. What could be going on at the center at that time of night?

As I pulled up in front of his house, I started to get nervous. "Ramón, are you going to get into any trouble?"

"Nah, my father probably doesn't even know I'm not at home. I can pretty much come and go as I please. He got my sisters on lockdown, but he don't care about me." He was out the car and up the sidewalk before his comment registered with me.

"What the hell did he mean by that?"

CHAPTER TWENTY-SEVEN

TILO ADAMS

Gabriela's car was parked in front the house right behind her sister's car. Seeing Gabriela's car made me feel better, but I still couldn't figure out why she had not called me back. More important, why she didn't come to work today? On the outside, the house looked peaceful, but I would have given my left tit to be a fly on the wall inside. I could not imagine what it must be like to live with a virtual stranger, even though they called themselves family.

There was a light on in the living room and two upstairs, but the house didn't have a warm and inviting atmosphere. I didn't know what I had expected to learn by coming here, and I was about to leave when I noticed a green jeep slowly coming down the street. The driver appeared to be uncertain as to where they were going. I scooted down in my seat as the Jeep approached my car. Since I didn't know what kind of car their father drove, I didn't want to get caught peeping at their house.

As the Jeep came up alongside my car, I noticed the driver was black. It surprised me when he stopped directly in front of Gabriela's house and Ramón jumped out. I was completely outdone because I assumed that all members of the Mendoza family, with the exception of Gabriela, didn't fuck with black people. Gabriela never came right out and said it, but she hedged around enough to let me know that I wouldn't be welcomed at their dinner table.

Ramón leaned into the open passenger window of the jeep and spoke with the driver, then went and into the house. The driver waited until Ramón had closed the door before he pulled off.

"Very interesting," I said out loud. All of a sudden it became more important to me to find out who was this handsome stranger was who Ramón seemed so comfortable with.

I followed the jeep.

Since I couldn't milk Gabriela for any information at the moment, following the stranger was the wisest choice. I maintained a discreet distance. The driver didn't appear to be in any hurry and that suited me just fine. Rush hour was over so we had the streets to ourselves. I enjoyed the leisurely pace. I even rolled down the window to enjoy the rare breeze that was flowing.

My mind drifted back to the letters and Gabriela's strange absence. She didn't call me back and I was getting pissed. I saw conspiracy in just about everything so I was trying very hard not to rush to judgment. However, remaining objective was difficult to do with so much money on the line.

"She could at least call and say I'm alive, dammit!" I pounded the steering wheel in frustration. Dividing my attention from the Jeep in front of me and my purse, I looked for my phone and ran across the handle of my gun. Out the corner of my eye, I noticed that the Jeep had turned on its turn signal and was making a right-handed turn into a subdivision. I paused for a several seconds before I followed his vehicle.

As I completed my turn, I was blinded by high beams. I had driven into a trap—a dead-end street. I jammed on the brakes. As I stopped my car, another vehicle sped past me and blocked me from behind. I stuck my hand in my purse and gripped the handle of my gun. Before I could decide what to do, he had reached my car and swung open my door.

"Why are you following me?" the stranger demanded.

"Uh…" *Thinking.*

"Uh hell. I want to know why you were following me."

I was trying to think. I couldn't figure out if he was a threat or not yet. I weighed my options. I couldn't go straight unless I wanted to drive into someone's living room and backing up was out of the question. So I did the next best thing—act my ass off until I could peep his game. The tears began.

"Who are you?" he demanded. His handsome face broke down into a menacing glare.

I helplessly cringed with one hand in front of my face, the other safely in my purse. Waiting.

"What are you crying for?" His voice was gentler this time.

Wiping my eyes, I looked up at him hoping for some compassion. He was even cuter up close than he was from a distance.

More thinking.

"I saw you drop off a friend of mine, and I wanted to make sure you weren't a drug dealer or some kind of a pervert," I whined. I told the truth so one of two things were about to happen. Either he was going to laugh at my stupidity, or I was going to shoot his stupid ass. It made no difference to me.

"You are a friend of Ramón's?"

The familiar way he had pronounced Ramón's name caused me to relax. My gut told me I had nothing to fear from the handsome stranger.

I released the handle of my gun. "Yes, his sister and I are friends and roommates." I still had one hand up in the air, the other I used to wipe my face. Even though I felt safe, I kept the tears flowing from my eyes. I learned as a little girl that tears were good leverage.

"Stop crying. I'm not going to hurt you."

"Thank you," I replied. I was going to turn it up some more, but I could tell he was soft.

"Would you like to go get an ice cream cone with me?" His offer was unusual, to say the least.

I had expected him to tell me to get lost and leave him alone, but he was offering me an olive branch. "Huh?"

"If we stay in the street like this too much longer, someone is bound to call the police. It seems like we have something in common. I would like to speak with you some more."

He had a point. We clearly had something in common, the Mendozas.

"Can we just get some coffee from the Waffle House instead?" I wanted to speak with him as well, but I preferred to do it in a public place.

CHAPTER TWENTY-EIGHT
TILO ADAMS

Moses waited until after we had ordered our coffee before he started questioning me again. I wanted him to drive this conversation so I could assess what he actually knew and his usefulness through his line of questioning.

"Do you make a habit out of stalking your roommate?" He smiled when he said it so it didn't sting as bad.

"I wasn't stalking her…I just did a drive by to make sure she was okay?"

"Why didn't you go inside and ask her?"

Damn, I fell into that one with both feet. I threw a question back at him. "Who are you, and how do you know Ramón?"

"Ramón works for me part-time. I also know his sister Ariana. She works for me as well."

"Oh…I heard about you." Now my wheels were really spinning.

"All good I hope," Moses said. He smiled.

"I don't know about all that," I said. I did hear good things about him, but I wasn't about to blow up his head.

"So, are you going to tell me your name?"

"I'm sorry, it's Tilo."

"Hey Tilo, nice to meet you. I'm Moses."

"Whoever heard of a black man named Moses?"

"My father." He wasn't smiling when he answered this time.

"Hey, I didn't mean it in a negative way. I was trying to be funny."

"No, it's cool. At least you didn't ask me to part the Red Seas."

I nodded my head in agreement as a smile crossed my face. "You're lucky I'm afraid of water or I would have."

"Thank God for small favors. I wish I had fifty cents for every time someone has said that to me. I would quit my job and live like a fat rat."

"I'll bet."

We settled into a comfortable silence, even though I had a million questions I wanted to ask him. I wanted to know what he knew about what was happening in the house.

"If you are Gabriela's roommate, why didn't you wait for her at the house?"

This man was sharp. The average man would have missed that tiny detail.

I leaned forward. "Ah, you were paying attention." I laughed to ease the discomfort that had snuck up on me. Even though we were in a public place, he was still a stranger.

"I get paid to pay attention to details," he smugly replied.

"Oh yeah, what do you do?"

"I own a private investigation firm."

"And the plot thickens. Were you acting in your professional capacity tonight?"

"Actually, I did take Ramón with me on assignment today. I was dropping him off because we were out later than expected."

"Is that wise taking someone so young with you?" I was thinking of all the bad things that could have happened if things went bad.

"Oh, it was harmless enough. I was following a woman suspected of cheating on her husband. I wasn't doing a full-fledged surveillance. I just took a look-see before the actual investigation starts." He sipped his coffee. His eyes appeared to bore a hole into my brain.

"I'm a nosy heifer. Was she cheating?"

He let out a rich and hearty laugh. "It's too early to tell. She works as a nurse. We followed her to an adult day care center. Unless she's dating one of the physicians, I think she's clear."

"Where did you say she went?" Moses had my complete and undivided attention.

"A care facility for adults on Covington Highway."

Stunned by the coincidence, I tried to remember the names of the properties that were being controlled by the Cali cartel through the guise of Nosotros Properties. I mentally went through my list of adult centers, trying to associate the names with the locations. "WeKare," I mumbled.

Moses' head snapped up at the mention of the name.

"Damn, were you following us all that time? I must be slipping," he admitted, shaking his head.

"You are not going to believe this, but I was looking into some day care centers earlier today and that was one of them that I checked out."

"Do you have someone in your family that needs their services?" Moses asked.

I didn't answer him right away, because I was struggling with how much information I was going to reveal. I cocked my head and gazed at him intently. My gut told me that he was useful and my gut was normally right. "No, the name popped up while I was doing some research. I'm a title abstractor."

"And super sleuth by night?" He cracked himself up.

I didn't find shit funny, but I laughed with him. "Hey, I didn't laugh at your profession. What if I called you Inspector Gadget?"

"I'd be flattered. Gadget was the man. Too bad he doesn't come on television anymore because I loved that cartoon."

"Is that why you went into the business?" I was intrigued by Moses. He was the first PI that I had meet and I was curious about what made him tick.

"Naw, I'm a nosey bastard too."

We both laughed. The waitress came over and filled our cups. I didn't know if she was being a really good waitress or if she was trying to tell us to keep the noise level down.

"Excuse me, I need to go to the restroom." I really did need to use the restroom but that wasn't the only reason why I had left the table. I wanted to phone Gabriela one last time before I reeled Moses all the way in. If she answered the phone and eased my suspicious nature, fine. If not, I was moving on to plan B. Once again, the phone went directly to voice mail. This time the box was full so I couldn't leave a message.

Something was definitely wrong. Gabriela would never allow her phone to get locked up like that. My mind was made up. I headed back to the table to share with Moses. He stood as I approached the table. Moses was about to be my new partner in crime. He just didn't know it yet.

"A gentleman too? My heart can't take it," I said with a smile, knowing full well the opportunity had just knocked.

"Blame it on my mom." He returned the smile.

"How well do you know the Mendoza's?"

His head snapped up as if my question had caught him off guard. Once again, his eyes seemed to bore a hole inside of me. I got the feeling that he wanted to trust me as badly as I needed him.

"Can I be honest with you?" He looked at me with pleading eyes.

"I hope you would because I have a feeling that you and I are going to need each other."

He continued to study me, but I didn't back down from the challenge.

"I'm in love with one of them," he said.

Fear gripped my heart. I knew that there would be a strong chance that Gabriela would meet a man and fall in love, but I never thought it would happen so soon. Ever since she had admitted to me that I was her first, I felt it would only be a matter of time before she decided she didn't want to be with a woman anymore. Well, I had a trick up my sleeve for both of them.

"Holy shit, I was not expecting that answer." My heart felt so heavy but I had resigned myself to the fact that I was losing her to a very nice man.

"You asked me to be honest."

I was pissed with myself for missing the fact that Gabriela was a two-timing bitch. "My mother always told me to be careful of what I asked for." I tried to make light of his confession. I abruptly decided that I didn't need him anymore and wanted to get as far away from him as humanly possible. I grabbed my purse to pay my share of the check.

"It wasn't supposed to be this way. She wanted to see what it was like to be with someone other than her husband, and I was honored she had chosen me. But now, with the baby and all, I can't let her go."

"Gabriela is pregnant?" This conversation had gone to hell in a hand basket. It was hard enough envisioning Gabriela laying under this beefy man but to learn that she was about to have his baby was too much. I got up, ready to flee, until Moses stopped me with his answer.

"Gabriela? No, not her. Ariana is pregnant." My mouth gapped open as I fell back in my seat. It took me a few seconds for my breathing to return to normal.

"But Ariana's married." As soon as the words tumbled out my mouth, I knew that I had made a mistake. I didn't intend to sound judgmental.

"I know. It wasn't supposed to happen, but it did."

"Wow, I don't know what to say."

"So what's your story?" He drained his cup.

I looked down at the remaining coffee in my cup and suddenly wanted something stronger to drink. "What do you say we go get something stronger to drink? I don't live far from here, you could follow me."

"I think that's a great idea."

"I believe it's your turn to play true confessions," Moses said as he raised his glass in mock salute.

We were drinking rum straight with no chaser. He had lain out on my sofa as if he were in a psychologist's chair.

"So how does Ariana feel?" I was going to tell him about my relationship with Gabriela but I still had a few other questions I wanted to ask.

"She told me that she loved me, but it's real complicated because of her family and her husband. I don't like standing on the sidelines, but I have to respect whatever decision she makes. I can only pray that she makes up her mind before the baby is born."

"I don't think you have much to worry about because if that is your baby, the shit will hit the fan then. Are you prepared to step in and be that baby's father?"

"I'm ready to do that and then some. I want to marry her."

"Really? I'm surprised."

He sat up on his elbows. "Why? You think all brothers are dogs?"

"No, I wasn't implying that, but you are in for a fight. I admire the fact that you aren't running away. But it's not just the fact that she's married, it's that whole family thing. I've never met a family with some many hang-ups about race."

"Ariana is not a racist." He sat up all the way, obviously angry at my comment.

"Hey, calm down. I'm just saying that the whole family has been raised to stay inside their own race. Gabriela told me that her father doesn't even know Ariana is married, let alone pregnant. She's at the house right now, trying to hide her big belly."

"Are you serious? He doesn't know?"

"That's what Gabriela said. We laughed about it, but I could tell she was worried about what was going to happen once her father found out."

"Damn, now I really feel bad because I can't be with her."

"Trust me, you would just make the situation worse. He will be mad that she deceived him, but he will get over it a lot quicker knowing that it was a white man who took his little girl instead of a black man."

"Well, I'm just going to have to convince them that I'm the better man." He lay back on the sofa.

"When's the last time you spoke to her?"

He didn't answer right away, and I could tell he didn't want to.

"Uh…it's been a few days."

I let that statement settle in the room. "Gabriela and I are lovers." I took a long swallow of my drink and got up to get the bottle.

He held out his glass before he spoke. "Wow—you don't look—wow!"

I was glad he didn't finish his sentence. That last thing I wanted to hear was that I didn't look like a lesbian. I really didn't consider myself as one either since I also enjoyed being with men. I liked to think of myself as *sexually diverse.* I could love anyone, for the right reason. "Damn, if this wasn't our lives, it might have been funny."

"Yeah, tell me about it," he said.

"We should both go over to the house and ring the bell and say *Guess Who's Coming to Dinner.*" I laughed, but it was sad to think it would never be that simple for either of us. "I have not spoken to her either, and I'm worried."

"Is that why you were parked out in front of the house?"

"Yeah."

He sat up and placed his feet on the floor. With his hands on his knees, he looked at me. He had a faraway look in his eyes. I got up from my chair and started pacing. Even though I had told him a lot, I wanted—no I needed—to be able to tell him the rest of it.

"Come here for a minute," I instructed. I went to the dining room and retrieved my briefcase with the letters in them and sat down at the table. Opening the case, I pulled out the transcription of the notes.

"What's all this?" He stood over my shoulder, which made me very uncomfortable. The scent of his cologne was playing with the hairs in my nose. I waved my hand, indicating that he should take a seat. I may have been hustling the lesbian game right now, but I loved a hard dick, especially on a man who smelled so good.

"Sit down. I need to speak to your alter ego, Gadget," I said with a smile as I pushed a pad and pen to him. I was sure I had found my mark who would help me find the Mendozas' fortune.

"Go, go, Gadget," he replied glumly.

CHAPTER TWENTY-NINE
MOSES RAMSEY

"Speak to me." I looked up from the letters.

"I'm no detective," Tilo said, "but I watch enough television to know that something ain't right. When I talked to Gabriela a few days ago, she was upset. She tried to tell me something, but I was too busy trying to be heard. I didn't let her finish what she was saying. I expected to see her at work, but she didn't show up and that's not like Gabriela at all."

"Okay, let's start with the facts. What is all this!" I picked up the pages and started flipping through them.

"Gabriela's mother kept all the letters that her husband wrote her."

"It's in Spanish, though."

"I know. Gabriela asked me to find someone to unscramble them because she couldn't read them. I found a lady at Clayton State College who used to live in South America for several years. She translated them for me."

I took the papers Tilo handed to me and started reading them. "Can I get the *Reader's Digest* version?" I felt like an invisible clock was ticking and we were running out of time.

"Okay, based on the notes, Gabriela's father, Carlos Mendoza, arranged marriages for both his daughters with high-ranking Cali cartel members in exchange for passage to the United States. I believe he will try to make them marry while he is here. He also sent his wife over a million dollars of untraceable barrier bonds, which belong to the Cali cartel."

"Are you fucking kidding me?"

"I also believe his wife didn't agree with him and was trying to stop him."

"Tilo, if what you are saying is true, then things could get ugly real fast. How in the hell does he think he is going to force two grown women to do some barbaric shit like that?"

"That's part of the problem. I don't think they know what he's up to or that their mother has the bonds hidden. Gabriela hung up before I could tell her. A million dollars is a lot of money."

My eyes lit up at the mention of money—real money. I could do a lot with a million dollars. It must be nice. "Let's just take a ride over there and stop this nonsense." I jumped up and headed to the door. I wasn't thinking very clearly. I was ready to march in the house like an avenging crusader and snatch my woman out of the jaws of insanity.

"Wait. We can't do that. First of all, we don't have any proof—this is all speculation. If our black asses show up at their house at this time of night, we would either get shot or find ourselves in jail," Tilo explained.

As much as I hated to admit it, she had a good point. I slowly sat back down. I felt defeated and I didn't like the feeling. I envied Tilo's objectivity because she was using her head.

"You've got to stop thinking with your emotions. If my gut instincts are correct, they are in serious trouble. If we are going to be able to help, I've got to count on you to keep a level head."

Wow, she just read my ass. I was not acting like the trained professional that I was. Tilo was right, I needed to get my heart out of the situation and listen to the facts as we knew them. "Damn, you are right. I allowed my heart to get in the way of my good judgment. I'm okay now. What else you got?"

She studied me for a moment before she continued. "Some of the things Gabriela told me about her folks aren't adding up. She said her family was poor and that they were barely making ends meet. I know for a fact that Gabriela gave her mother money every week to keep a roof over her head. She also said Ariana contributed to the house because their laundry business was a joke. So what did their mother do with the bonds?"

"Ariana's mother worked in a laundry? I never knew that about her." Listening to Tilo talk, I wondered if I really knew Ariana at all. She had never led me to believe that her family had money.

"Don't take it personal. I get the impression they don't talk much, even among themselves."

That statement made me feel a little better, but I still couldn't get the image of my baby being in danger out of my mind. "What exactly are you telling me?" I was growing impatient. I felt like Tilo was spooning me bite-size chucks of information instead of coming out and saying exactly what was on her mind.

"I did a little snooping of my own today. Gabriela told me that her father put their house up for sale. When she didn't show up for work today, I went looking to see who held the mortgage on the house."

Tilo was confusing me. I didn't see what one thing had to do with the other. My mind was racing trying to fit the puzzle pieces together. "Tilo, it's late and I'm not thinking straight. Spell it out for me because I can't see the connection."

"Okay, let me break it down. Who knows, I might be jumping to conclusions too. That's why I'm glad I ran into you." She stopped mid-sentence. It took everything in me not to reach across the table and shake the information out of her.

"The house doesn't have a mortgage," she said. "The deed to the house is in the name of a corporation called Nosotros Properties, which is run by the Cali cartel, and Gabriela's father signed the deed."

"He could have borrowed the money from them. Is Nosotros Properties a lending institution or something?"

"I don't think so. According to what I found on the Internet, they are an investment company, but for the most part, they only buy big commercial properties, which is how the cartel washes their money."

"So they gave him the money to start the laundry. Big deal."

"No, Moses, I said *big* commercial properties. According to Gabriela, their business barely turned a profit."

"Then it was a bad investment." I pulled at straws. I still couldn't see where this line of thinking was going. I began to wonder if it was all a waste of time.

"Perhaps, but I doubt it. I looked at the deeds of the properties owned by Nosotros in the state of Georgia. All of them are large properties leased to corporate giants like Lerox, Qmart, and AT&Z. Those deeds were signed by someone other than Carlos Mendoza. The seven deeds signed by Mr. Mendoza, with the exception of their home, were for adult day care centers."

"Ah, that's how you knew about that place I mentioned earlier."

"Yeah, but I took it one step farther. Six of those properties are in residential neighborhoods, including the laundry. The only location that is zoned commercially is WeKare."

"Damn, I think you are in the wrong business. You have got a nose for this type of stuff. After this is over, I want to talk to you about it."

Tilo grinned. For the first time I noticed how attractive she was. Looking at her, it was hard to believe that she preferred women to men, but I wasn't going to judge her decisions. She was proving herself to be a potential good friend and that was the most important thing to me.

"You feeling me now?" She chuckled.

"Yeah, I'm feeling you." I picked up her notes and quickly scanned them. She had underlined those properties listed in the residential neighborhoods and the sums of money Mrs. Mendoza had been sent.

"There's something else," Tilo said.

I put aside the papers and made a mental note to review them more carefully. "What is it?"

"Gabriela said they hadn't seen their father since they were children. He stayed in Columbia to care for his aging parents. Their only contact with him was over the phone. She said when he came home, they didn't recognize him."

"What's so strange about that?" Once again, Tilo had lost me.

"She didn't go into any great detail, but she did mention that he had been to college, learned to speak English, and had corrective surgery on his eyes."

"And…I still don't see the point." I felt myself getting frustrated again. I didn't like the fact that Tilo had all the answers and I didn't even know the questions to ask. I could not help but to question my relationship with Ariana.

"All of those changes suggest there is money coming from somewhere."

I wasn't impressed with this last bit of information because there could've been a good explanation for it. Things change and so do people, but I filed that tidbit away in the back of my mind for further speculation. The ice in my glass had long since melted. I poured two fingers more of rum into my glass and belted it back. The warm liquor burned all the way to my stomach, but it served the purpose. "So where does that leave us?"

"Hell if I know, you are the detective." Tilo laughed but her face did not hold the smile.

I could tell that she was worried—hopefully about nothing—but worried nevertheless. "Okay, let me look into this and see what I can find out. Do you mind if I take your notes with me?"

"Sure, have at it. I've looked at them till I was blue in the face. I just need to make sure all is okay on the Mendoza front."

"I'm sure it is or they would have contacted one of us."

"You are probably right, but did you hear about that man in Jonesboro who killed his daughter last month because of an arranged marriage?"

Damn, why did she have to say that? I had forgotten about that case. The woman who was killed was twenty-five years old and her father admitted to killing her because she wanted a divorce from the man her father had selected for her. "All right, you have succeeded in getting me into panic mode. I'm going to start working on this first thing in the morning."

"What do you want me to do?"

I had to take my eyes off of Tilo before I got my horny ass in trouble. "Keep your eyes open and let me know if you hear from either one of the sisters." I grabbed a piece of paper off the pad and wrote down my telephone numbers. I could tell that Tilo had peeped my attraction to her.

"Are you okay?" she said, stepping uncomfortably close to me.

"Yeah, I'm fine."

"Okay then, since you have such a good relationship with Ramón, you might want to ask him what is going on at the house."

The obvious was right there in front of my face and I had missed it. Tilo was amazing me with her natural talents. "You really ought to consider changing your line of work."

She smiled at the compliment.

I gathered up the paperwork and got ready to leave. I was at the door before I remembered the last thing Ramón had said to me. I turned to face Tilo, who had followed me to the door. "I just remembered something that Ramón said—"

"What?" her voice rose as she asked the question.

"I asked him if he would get into trouble for coming home so late. He said that his father probably didn't even know that he was gone. He also said he could come and go as he pleased, but the girls were on lock."

"That doesn't sound good to me. We have to find out if their father really is keeping them there against their will," Tilo replied.

"Damn. When he said it, I thought he was just kidding. Now that I think about it, I'm not so sure. I'm going to question him further in the morning. Try to get some rest. If you think of anything else, call me no matter what time it is, okay?"

"I will and please call me after you have spoken to Ramón. I'm very worried about this."

"Wait, I need to get your phone number before I leave."

She turned around and trotted back to the table and grabbed the pad we were writing on. She handed me the paper that contained her home and cell numbers. She stepped to me, stroked the side of my face, then kissed me. "For the last couple of hours, I've wanted to do that and more, but I will settle with the kiss for now."

I swallowed the lump in my throat. Thoughts of Ariana hovered in the back of my mind.

"I have a proposition for you, Mr. Gadget."

I knew I was about to get in trouble. "I'm listening."

CHAPTER THIRTY

MOSES RAMSEY

Tilo's offer had been on my mind all night. It was tempting. Waiting for Ramón to arrive at work was probably one of the hardest things that I'd done in my life. I wanted to go to the school and sign him out. The only thing stopping me was how I would explain my relationship to him. The fact that I still had not heard from Ariana didn't help the situation. I flung the paper that I pretended to read across my desk in frustration. Noting the time, I decided to call Tilo to see if Gabriela had shown up at work.

"Hello?" Tilo answered her phone on the first ring.

"Hey Tilo, it's Moses. Have you heard anything from Gabriela?" I wasn't going to mention her offer unless she did. She didn't need to know that I had not gotten any sleep just thinking about it. Nor was I going to tell her that I was secretly working for Mr. Mendoza.

"No, she hasn't called me. And so far, she hasn't come to work. I'm afraid they are going to fire her if she doesn't have a very good explanation."

"Damn…something has to be wrong because everybody needs to hold on to a job. It's going to take some time before Obama can bring about some change in this country."

"Not someone with a million dollars in bearer bonds. Anyhow, my supervisor is pissed. She came over to my cubical and rolled her eyes at me as if I knew what the hell was going on."

She went there but I wasn't going to touch it. I said, "Too bad we don't have something to tell her. Just hang in there. Ramón will be here at three. I'm going over to WeKare this morning to see what type of operation it really is."

"Okay, keep me posted."

"I will and you do the same." After I hung up the phone, I pulled out my folder on the new case I started yesterday and jotted down some notes. I had to step away from this mess for a minute as thoughts of Tilo ran through my mind. Tammi Sykes wanted my attention the other day at the café and now she was about to get it. She was beautiful, intelligent, and feisty as hell. It was evident from my encounter with her that if she hadn't cheated on her husband already, it would only be a matter of time before she found a willing partner. A part of me pitied Mr. Sykes because he seemed to be such a nice guy, but I had learned in my business that there were two sides to every story. For all I knew, he could have been whipping that ass on the regular and she had gotten tired of it.

I grabbed my jacket and told my secretary that I would be out for a couple of hours. I told her to make sure to hit me up on my cell phone if anything happened that I needed to know about. My thoughts were still scrambled as I drove to WeKare. I wanted to get a look inside before I spent too much time staking them out.

The parking lot was deserted this time. I did a U-turn onto Glen Haven Road and pulled into the lot. I spent a few minutes creating a cover story before I went inside. There was a receptionist at the front desk. She was a young black woman who looked to be in her early twenties. I immediately put on the charm.

"Hi, welcome to WeKare. How may I help you?" She was reading a book, which she attempted to hide from me.

"What you reading?" I asked.

"*The Tribe,* by Gregory Townes" she replied with a smile.

"I don't believe that I've ever heard about this book. Is it any good?" In my spare time, I loved to read and was always looking for new African American authors to add to my collection.

"I'll say. The book came out a few years ago. If you like to read, I highly recommend it."

"Thanks, I just might have to check Mr. Townes out." She touched my hand. Mission accomplished. I could now get back to the purpose of my visit.

She nodded her head. "May I help you?" Now that the pleasantries were over, she was ready to get down to business.

"Yes, I would like to speak to someone about care for my father." The facility appeared to be deserted and wasn't at all like I had pictured it. I had expected the place to be bustling with elderly people engaged in social activities of some sort. If there was anybody else there, they must have been sedated. The place was too quiet, almost eerie.

"Have a seat. One of the counselors will be out to assist you shortly."

"Sure," I said as I took a seat on one of the chairs that lined the wall. The building's interior was nicely decorated and was quite a contrast from the outside appearance, which was rather run down and dull. I watched as she picked up the phone and called someone.

While I waited, I flipped through an old issue of *Essence Magazine* that had obviously been handled a lot. "How long has this place been open?" Maybe I was jumping to conclusions about folks being strapped in the back or possibly drugged out of their minds.

"I'm new here so I don't know much history, but we are new to this location."

"Ah, that explains why I never noticed you here before."

She nodded her head in agreement as her eyes went back to her book. She had dismissed me. The only sound in the room was that of a clock, which was directly over my head. I wanted to rip the battery right out of that sucker because it was a constant reminder of how long I had to wait to see Ramón. I observed that the phone never rang the entire time I sat there. I was getting ready to ask the receptionist another question when the front door opened and in walked Tammi Sykes. "Oh shit," I muttered when I realized that I had been caught.

She walked up to the receptionist desk and chatted with her a few seconds before she turned to me. Her dark face paled when she recognized me, but she kept it professional.

"Good morning. Sorry to keep you waiting." She extended her hand to me and I reluctantly took it.

"Thanks, did I come at a bad time?"

"Actually, we only work on appointments. I wasn't too far away, so you are fine. Come with me." She turned and started walking away.

I tried not to notice her bubble butt or the gentle sway of her hips. She was a striking woman, but her vicious tongue tarnished her beauty. I followed her past eight empty offices on the left and right sides of the hallway to what appeared to be the largest office in the building. The room apparently served as an examining room and office.

"Sorry, I didn't know. I was just driving by and decided to drop in."

Opening the desk, she placed her purse inside and pulled a brochure from another drawer that she slid across the desk to me. "You're fine."

Was she talking about me or the fact that I had dropped in unannounced? I took a seat opposite the desk. Seeing Tammi again put me off my game for a few minutes and I was struggling to regain my footing. I had banked on her being busy with her day job. Stalling, I looked around the office. As with the front area, I could tell that it had been recently remodeled. Absent from the walls were any degrees or certifications. "I'm looking for a place to bring my father while I work."

"How old is your father?" Tammi asked as she pulled a yellow pad out of the desk drawer. She was obviously comfortable in the office as she knew where everything was located and didn't appear to be fumbling around.

"He just turned seventy-two."

"I see. Can you tell me a little about your father's health?"

"He's as strong as an ox as and stubborn as a mule." I smiled at her hoping to break the icy wall she had erected around herself. I needed her to relax so I could find out the information I was seeking.

"Cute, but I was referring to his medical health." She was all about the business.

I quickly recited my story, but this was not how I had envisioned this interview going. I was merely interested in the connection to Nosotros Properties. "Physically, there is nothing wrong with my father. Mentally, he is slipping, and I'm afraid for him to stay by himself while I'm away at work. He refuses to live in a home, so I'm seeking alternatives."

She stopped writing on her pad and looked through me as if she were lost in deep thought. I started to wave my hands in front of her face, but I knew that would only antagonize her.

"Sorry, he reminds me of my mother."

I could see tears forming in her eyes. "I'm sorry. I didn't mean to bring up bad memories for you," I said—truly sorry for being the cause of her unhappiness.

"Oh no, those were fond memories. She used to fight me all the time. God rest her soul. That's where I got my fighter's instinct from," she said, laughing. Tammi really had a beautiful laugh.

"Good." I didn't know what else to say, so I allowed her to conduct her interview at her pace.

She pushed the brochure toward me again. I didn't want to read a bunch of fabricated lies. I wanted to know things that I was sure were not printed in that publication.

"Let me tell you about our organization. We were formed in the late eighties to offer an alternative to families wanting to care for the elderly. Many of our clients were afraid to allow their loved ones to move into a senior citizen home because of all the reported cases of neglect and abuse. At WeKare, we allow our patients to live in the comfort of their homes while giving the family the peace of mind that someone is watching over them."

"So you don't have patients here at this facility?" This was not what I had expected and it showed on my face.

"No, what made you think that?" She looked at me like I had just stepped off the short yellow bus.

"Forgive my ignorance. I allowed the name of the place to mislead me. Don't laugh, but I thought people just dropped off their parents to be watched like we do our children."

"That is completely understandable, and there are some programs like that in the city, but this facility isn't one of them. We have found that patients do much better in their own environment rather than taking them someplace else."

She made a valid point and if I were looking for care, I might have considered this as an option.

"Wow, I was way off base. I guess I'm not ready to take this step yet, but I will keep it in mind when things get worse."

"Things?" She cocked her head to the side as if she were trying to see inside my head.

The feeling unnerved me.

"I think my father is in the early stages of dementia. He won't admit it, and I'm keeping a close eye on him. I'm looking for a long-term solution if his condition gets any worse. Right now, I have a neighbor looking after him to make sure he doesn't wander off."

"That's exactly what we do. However, we are trained to assist in the event of a medical emergency."

"How large is the staff here?"

"We don't have anyone on staff per sec, except the secretary. All of our practitioners are certified doctors and nurses who come in as needed. We have a network of twenty-five people who are available twenty-four seven."

"Thank you. You have answered my questions, and again, I apologize for just dropping in." I stood up to leave and she followed suit.

"Should you ever need us, Mr....?" She hedged.

"I'm sorry. It's Ramsey. Forgive my manners."

She grabbed her card off the desk and handed it to me. I placed it in my breast pocket without even looking at it.

She also handed me the brochure that I had left on the desk.

"Our services are covered under most insurances and Medicaid so if you need us, call."

"Thanks, I'll keep that in mind." I needed to get out of that office so I could sort out my thoughts. Something about the place just didn't seem right to me, and I couldn't shake the uneasiness I felt just being in her office.

The sound of her heels clicking against the hardwood floor told me that she was following me out. I wanted to get out of there before she asked me out or something. She had made me feel like a piece of meat, and I felt sorry for her husband, who appeared to be trying to do the right thing.

When I got to the front desk, I turned to shake her hand. She was so close to me, I could smell her perfume. I extended my hand. She grabbed it with both of hers and pumped it firmly. Her grip was strong and decisive.

I glanced at her hands and noted that she wasn't wearing a ring. This chick had mad game. "Thanks again," I said, pulling my hand free. I wanted to wipe it clean against my pants, but I refrained from doing so until I was out in the parking lot.

Looking back on the building, I wondered what other secrets it held. I wanted to ask her questions about the founders, but I knew I would find out everything I needed to know—and then some—from tailing her.

As I drove back to the office, I called Tilo. "Can you talk?"

"Yeah, give me one second."

I waited for her come back to the phone as I sat at a stop light. I would have hung around WeKare but I knew I would have to use another vehicle if I planned on following

Tammi anymore because she would know my Jeep since it was parked in front of the center.

"I'm here," Tilo said clearly out of breath.

"What are you doing? You sound like you have been running."

"I had to go outside to have some privacy. My boss has been breathing down my neck all morning. The only time she's not watching me is when I go to the bathroom."

"Damn, that's deep. Are you available for lunch?" It was a quarter to twelve and my stomach was growling.

"Sure, where to you want to meet?"

"You pick the place because you have got dragon breathing down your neck, and I don't want you to be late."

She chuckled. "Good looking out. How about we meet at Ruby Tuesday's on Ponce at twelve-thirty?"

"Great. I just love those mini-burgers. Can I order for you? Their service sucks sometimes."

"Yeah, it does, especially at lunchtime. Order me the burgers too, and I'll see you in a few." She hung up the phone and I turned the car around and headed back to Decatur.

■■■

I thought I was going to have trouble finding a parking space, but God had smiled on me because there was one available across the street from the restaurant. I fed the meter then crossed the street. "Sure hope I don't get a ticket for jay walking," I mumbled as I dodged the cars that zoomed through the quaint city of Decatur.

Revitalization of the city was everywhere I looked. New condos were cropping up and the small shops appeared to be thriving.

Stepping inside the restaurant, I welcomed the cool blast of air-conditioning that hit me in the face. I removed my shades and placed them in my jacket pocket, surveying the busy restaurant. I waited for a few minutes for the hostess to seat me, then gave my order to the waitress. With any luck, the food would be served by the time Tilo made it to the restaurant. While I waited, I made some notes of my visit to WeKare on my legal pad that I carried inside with their brochure.

I stood up when Tilo come through the door and waved her over to the table. She was looking good, despite the late-night drinking we had shared.

"Hey," she said, sliding into our booth. She sat directly across from me.

I could not resist allowing my eyes to feast on her beauty while I remembered how her tongue had tasted. The flashback was sweet, but I didn't regret hooking up with Ariana. She was one in a million to me. "You look nice this afternoon," I said as I sat back down.

Tilo blushed, showing off her deep dimples. "So do you," she murmured. Changing subjects before our flirting went too far, I filled her in on my visit to the center.

"What does your gut tell you?" Tilo asked, cutting right to the heart of things.

The waitress had chosen that time to deliver our food, so I waited until she had left before I answered. "The place is a cover for something. It's too big inside for the operation that they described to me. Why would they have all that space if the only thing they did was schedule outpatient care?"

"Right. That's my feeling, too. From what you said to me, they only need a phone to operate. They could conduct their interviews in the patients' home for that matter."

"Exactly. Also, why would they hire a receptionist if most of their clients are by appointment? The phone didn't ring once while I was there."

"Sounds like a job I would like to have," Tilo joked.

She was too smart to hide behind a menial job like that.

"Yeah right, that shit would drive you out your mind and you know it. You are too nosy, remember?" I laughed with her.

For a few seconds the worry lines disappeared from her face, and I was struck again by how beautiful she was. Tilo threw her fork down on her plate so suddenly I thought she was reading my mind. Her pupils grew to the size of a nickel.

"What's wrong?" I tried to keep the alarm I felt out of my voice.

"We're missing the obvious." She threw her napkin onto her plate after wiping her mouth.

"What are you talking about?"

"Something you said it last night, but we didn't go into it. How is Ariana's husband reacting to all of this?"

Damn, she was right. If we were going crazy wondering what was going on at the Mendoza house, her husband had to be feeling it too.

"Wow, I guess I wanted to deny his existence so badly, I have not given him much thought." I threw my napkin to the side and signaled for the waitress. "Check please." I handed her my credit card so she could bring it back with the receipt.

"How are you going to confront him?"

I had not thought that far, but I knew that I needed to at least see the man who I wanted to be. "I'm not sure. For now, I just want to drive by their house. I have their address back at the office."

"I could go with you. You can tell him that I'm a friend of Gabriela's and that I came to you because I was worried about her."

Once again, Tilo surprised me with her ability to think on her feet.

"What about your job?" I wanted her to come with me, but I couldn't ask her. It had to be her decision.

"Fuck 'em. After this is over, I'm going to be working for you—if you don't take me up on my offer, right?"

I laughed as I slid out of the booth. I nodded my head in agreement. Either way it went, I felt like we should be working together. "Let's do this then," I said.

CHAPTER THIRTY-ONE
MOSES RAMSEY

We were parked across the street from Ariana's home in Lithonia. It was a modest ranch-styled home on a quiet cul-de-sac off Covington Highway. Judging by the swing sets and basketball hoops in the surrounding yards, we could tell the neighborhood housed mostly young people with school-age children. It would be an ideal place to raise children given its close proximity to two elementary schools and one middle school.

"Look at the mailbox," Tilo said.

I was lost in my musing about the life that Ariana led behind the door of her house and those thoughts hurt my heart. When she was with me, I was able to forget she was married to someone else. Seeing her house brought it all back to the forefront of my mind. I tore my eyes away from the door and looked at the box. The box was ajar and mail was practically spilling out of it. "That's a lot of mail," I stated. I surveyed the rest of the block, looking for nosy neighbors. I wanted to look at the postmark on the mail but was afraid to draw undue attention to ourselves by brazenly retrieving it. Outside the door sat a pile of phone books.

"I'm getting the mail," Tilo announced. Before I could stop her, she had darted across the street and stolen the mail from the box. She jumped back in the car with a triumphant grin on her face.

"You are a hot mess," I replied, holding back a chuckle.

She looked like a kid who had stolen her first piece of candy from the corner store.

"I got it, didn't I?" She was thumbing through the mail.

I looked through it as she laid each piece on the seat next to her.

"That stuff has been there a minute. Look at the way the envelopes are curled." I turned my attention back to the house. The lawn was overgrown and their house was the only one on the block that didn't have a trash can to the curb. Erratically, I pulled the Jeep in the driveway. If someone was going to call the police, I would at least have time to inspect the house before they did it.

"What are you doing?" Tilo hissed as she clutched the mail to her chest.

"Getting a closer look. Stay in the car and beep the horn if you see someone coming." I didn't give her a chance to complain before I jumped out of the Jeep and walked around the back of the house. I didn't want to be caught peering in the windows at the front of the house until I was sure it was empty. Luckily for me, they had a privacy fence and I only had to worry about someone noticing my car in front of the house.

The patio glass was shattered. Pulling my gun, I crouched down and gingerly approached the door. If my instincts were correct, whoever had broken the glass was long gone. Pushing aside the drapes covering the doorway, I stepped into the house. The smell almost pushed me back out. It was a scent that I had smelled before, but I needed to be sure. Stepping over as much glass as I could, I made my way to the front room.

The body of a white male was laying in the floor. His head was a bloody mess. There was no use in checking his vitals. I could tell he was dead—more than likely from blunt-force trauma. I looked around for the weapon and immediately spotted a bloody baseball bat. Whoever did this was very angry. Careful not to touch anything, I retraced my steps.

Once outside, I gulped in fresh air, trying to purge my lungs of the vile stench of death that prevailed inside the house. Finding a dead man I assumed to be Ariana's husband dead was not what I had expected. I wanted to get away from this house as quickly as possible.

"What's wrong?" Tilo demanded as I slammed the door shut and started the car.

I backed out of the driveway without answering her.

"What about the mail?" Her voice rose.

"He won't need it," I muttered. Fear had sprouted in my chest and I could not shake the feeling.

"What do you mean? You are scaring me."

"He's dead all right!" I instantly regretted shouting at Tilo, but we needed to get the hell away from that house.

■■■

Tilo let out a deep breath. "You know we are going to have to ask Ramón about what's going on at that house, right?"

We were seated around the small conference table in my office.

"Yeah, I'm just trying to figure out how to go about it. He's a real good kid, but he's shy. My first big breakthrough with him came yesterday when I took him out on a case with me."

"Shy or not, you have got to figure out a way to do it."

She was right but it was going to be a touchy situation. No one wanted to hear potentially bad things about their parents, especially a parent who they didn't know too much about.

I said, "I think I should talk to him alone. He might get scared if he sees you with me."

"I don't have a problem with that. Although Ramón and I are cool, we haven't formed a special bond that transcends my relationship with his sister." Tilo stood up to leave.

I hated to see her go. "I was serious about you coming to work for me."

"I was serious about my proposition. We can pull it off. But I'm glad you were serious about the job because I probably got fired when I pulled that no-show after lunch. When do you want me to start?"

"How about today? I need you to keep an eye on WeKare. My instincts tell me that the place is somehow connected with all this drama."

"I agree with you. I'll go over there right now." She turned back toward the door again, but came back in the room and shut the door. "I don't mean no harm, but this shit would not have happened to a black woman."

"Come on, Tilo, that's a racial statement."

"No, not really. It may be stereotypical, but it's not racist. Stereotypically, Latino people are hotheaded except when dealing with their parents. When's the last time you met a docile black woman?"

I could not help but to laugh at her logic.

"Exactly. History has proven we don't do that bondage shit very well."

"What about slavery?" I was playing the devil's advocate.

"Shit, we had no choice but to be docile then. They snatched us up and took us across water—you know we are afraid of that. They forced us to work and beat the shit out of us on a regular. They chopped off the feet of those who tried to run. But on the day Masta slipped, we got that ass."

"Now you know you are wrong for that one." I was enjoying Tilo's company. She was making a very unbearable situation tolerable.

"I believe in calling a duck a duck. All I'm saying is that a black woman would have found a way out. We are good at making a way out of no way."

"Point well taken. But until we know all the facts, we can't jump to any conclusions. There may be more to this than we can see."

"Okay, I won't rush to judgment."

"Be careful over there. I don't want you going in. I just want you to watch the place. I'll call you as soon as I have talked with Ramón."

"Okay, boss," she jokingly said.

I watched the door long after she had left.

"Whew," I mumbled. Even though it wasn't hot in the office, I was sweating. Acting like I wasn't troubled by the body I had found at Ariana's house took a lot out of me. I wanted to tell Tilo about the brutal scene, but I was not sure if she was ready for that.

The beating was personal, not a random act. I had seen enough bodies in my life to know the difference. Leaning back in my chair, I allowed my mind to go back to the house. I tried to decipher all that I had seen in the brief amount of time that I was there.

Taking a tape recorder from my desk, I closed my eyes and pictured the house. My hands were shaking as I held the record button. "Victim was laying face down in a pool of blood. I suspect blunt trauma to the back of the head will be listed as the cause of death. From the positioning of the body, I believe he was attacked when he came down the stairs. The victim suffered from blows to the lower torso, chest, and legs. Victim's head was severely battered, suggesting repeated blows to the head. Victim's feet were still on the bottom step. Multiple sets of bloody shoe prints further suggest that there was at least two killers." I cut off the recorder.

"And then the bastards peed on his head." The stench from the urine and the decomposing body continued to fill my nostrils. Rising from the chair, I stepped into my private bathroom to wash my hands and change my clothes. I really wanted a shower, but I didn't have time for that. Ramón would be here any minute, and I had to get my mind right for that. I took my dirty clothes and threw them in a plastic bag, then stuffed them in the trash. There was no way I would ever wear that suit again without remembering the gruesome scene I had discovered.

CHAPTER THIRTY-TWO
MOSES RAMSEY

Ramón was seated in my office when I came out of the bathroom.

"Hey Ramón, you are early." I decided to play it cool to see if he were going to confide in me.

"Yeah, a friend of mine was coming this way so I didn't have to wait for the bus."

"Good. You can continue on those files from yesterday for right now. I may have something else for you to do later."

He started to get up but sat back down. I could tell something was bothering him because he wore the same defeated expression on his face that he had worn the day before.

I picked up one of the files off my desk and pretended to be engrossed in its contents. When I looked up, Ramón had a stack of money wadded up in his hand. My eyes traveled from his hand to his face and back to his hand. "What's up?" I put the file back on my desk and gave him my undivided attention.

"I want to hire you." His voice was low, so low that I could barely hear what he had said.

"Say what?"

He cleared his throat and said it again, this time louder.

I looked at the measly pile of bills and chuckled.

His head jerked up and he snatched back his hand that held the money. "I'm not playing." He added a little more bass in his voice.

"I'm sorry, Ramón, I thought you were kidding or something. Hire me to do what?"

His lips curled in a frown and his bushy brows appeared to spike. His entire demeanor changed as he slammed the money down on my desk. "It's not much, but it's all I have. If that's not enough, I'll work off the rest." He stared directly at me.

It was hard for me to keep a straight face. It wasn't that I didn't take him seriously, it was the tough-guy persona that I was having a difficult time dealing with. "Okay, we can work out the details later. Tell me what is it that you want me to do."

"I want you to spy on my father."

Damn, I wasn't expecting that. I knew things weren't right in his house, but I wasn't ready to believe that it was that bad. "Ramón, I know what we did yesterday was a lot of fun, but it's not a game. People don't like to be spied upon, and your father wouldn't take it too kindly if I did it to him." Now I really felt like shit. This was the second Mendoza family member to hire me. What the hell are they into? Better yet, what have I gotten myself into?

"I don't give a fuck what my father thinks," Ramón spat.

So much for that meek mentality that Tilo was talking about.

"Wow, I don't know what to say?" I was honestly at a loss for words. All day long I tried to figure out a way to get Ramón to cooperate with me, then he walked in and gave me an open invitation.

"Are you going to do it or not?"

"I need to know why you want me to follow him." I felt myself begin to sweat again. This time it wasn't fear that was making my sweat, it was my cultural uncertainty in dealing with Ramón. Ariana, I could figure out—she was pretty cut-and-dry, but Ramón was an emotional stick of dynamite waiting for a match. Ariana didn't see color and neither did I. She was quick to say something about my high-yellow ass, and I would remind her she was just as yellow. I wanted to be able to have that same kind of banter with Ramón, but I wasn't sure of how to get there. I chuckled at the memory, but Ramón apparently thought I was laughing at him.

"Forget it. I knew you wouldn't help me." He grabbed his money off the desk and stuffed it in his pockets.

"Hey, where are you going? I didn't say I wouldn't do it. I just need to know why."

He turned and looked at me. I could see hope blossom in his eyes as he hesitated.

"Something isn't right with him. We don't even know who he is, and I don't trust him." He sank back down in his chair. Instead of lowering his head as I expected him to do, he stared at me in defiance.

I cleared my throat and tried to decide how I was going to handle him. I closed my eyes briefly and images of Mike's battered body flashed before my eyes. "Can I ask you a question?"

"Uh…I guess." He looked uncomfortable but I had to know.

"I haven't heard from Ariana in days and that's not like her. What's going on at your house?" I probably could have phrased it better—prepared him for my directness—but I felt like we were running out of time.

"Huh?" Ramón's gaze wandered around the office as if he looked for answers on the panel of the wall.

"Look, if you want my help, I have to know. I'm worried."

"Gabriela and I haven't seen or talked to Ariana in six days. Her husband Mike is not answering his phone, and we have called all the hospitals. The only thing my father will tell us is that she's alright, that she's relaxing." Ramón wouldn't look at me.

I knew I had to shock him to get him to open up more because what he had just said scared the hell out of me. "I'm going to say something that I know you are not going to believe, but I love your sister very much and she's in love with me. If anything has happened to her, I won't be able to live with myself. I need to find her." Any thought, no matter how tempting Tilo proposal was, went out the window. Ariana and our baby meant more to me than money.

Ramón looked at me as if I had just whistled "Dixie" backwards. He started to laugh but stopped mid-laugh. "Are you serious?"

"As a heart attack." I needed him to understand how far I was willing to go to protect what I felt belonged to me. We sat in silence for a few seconds. I assumed he was trying to figure out how he felt about my confession. "I need to know that she and my baby are safe."

Ramón bolted out of his chair. "Stop talking crazy. Ariana is married, and it's not to you!" He started walking back and forth, eyeing me out the corner of his eye. His lips were moving but no words were coming out.

I thought he was having a nervous breakdown, and I regretted telling him about the baby. "It's true, Ramón. Your sister and I are going to marry as soon as she files for divorce. I told you the truth. I love her and the baby." I stood up and walked over to the window where Ramón was standing with his back to me.

He still didn't say anything.

"She called me every day, Ramón—sometimes two or three times a day up until last week. I know something's not right, and I will find out what it is." I put my hand on his shoulder to show him I meant no harm.

His reaction surprised me. He turned around and hugged me. My arms wrapped around his heaving shoulders as he cried tears reserved for the young. I let him cry. When he was finished, I led him back to a chair. "I'm sorry. Things have been so crazy at the house. Ever since my father came, it's been hell living in that house. He doesn't bother me as much as he does my sisters. According to him, they can't do anything right." Ramón's voice was harsh, and I knew it would only be a matter of time before he decided to take matters into his own hands.

I needed to stop him before he made a bad situation worse. "Ramón, I ran into a friend of your sister's yesterday, and we talked. She said she hasn't heard from Gabriela either. She's afraid that if Gabriela doesn't come to work soon, they are going to fire her." If I lived to be nine hundred and ninety-nine, I never wanted to see the look of despair again that I saw in Ramón's eyes at that moment. My heart went out to him for all that he had been dealing with for the past couple of months. First the death of his mother, and now he had to deal with this latest drama. I was afraid to tell him about his brother-in-law.

"He said he wouldn't hurt them."

My heart skipped a beat. "Who is *he*, Ramón?"

"The man. I refuse to call him my father ever again."

I wasn't going to argue with him about that because as far as I was concerned, Mr. Mendoza hadn't earned the right to have that title. "I know this may be difficult for you, but you are going to have to start from the beginning." I needed a drink. But if I fixed myself one, I would feel compelled to offer Ramón one too. I wasn't about to go there.

"The man treats my sisters like slaves—uh—I didn't mean—"

"You can say slaves, Ramón. In fact, I would appreciate it if you would just say whatever is on your mind, and we'll sort it out later. I promise you won't hurt my feelings."

He looked relieved as he continued. One of the man's thugs told me that there was a big fight last week. The man found out about the baby. I heard he was mad—real mad. She ruined all of his plans or something. He…he hit her, I heard." More tears followed that admission. At that point, I was ready to do a drive-by and shoot the motherfucker myself.

My face grew warm as I willed myself to remain calm. "Why?" My head wanted to say more, but my tongue got in the way.

"He sold my sisters like cattle to a couple thugs."

Damn, he had just confirmed everything Tilo had read in the letters that Ramón's father had written. I flipped open my rolodex, looking for a colleague of mine who dealt with international matters. I wanted to know how I could get my woman without spending the rest of my life either dead or in jail.

"What are you looking for?" Ramón watched me closely.

"A phone number for a friend. I need some advice," I replied.

"I think you should wait."

My hand stopped along with the beating of my heart. I thought I was in control of my emotions, but I didn't know how much more I could take.

"The man said that if we ever wanted to see Ariana again, Gabriela would have to marry one of those goons that he has hanging around the house."

"What? He can't make her marry someone if she doesn't want to. We don't do that type of shit here in the states." I was yelling and didn't even realize it. My outburst scared Ramón, but it also scared me. I was seeing red and couldn't wait to get my hands on the manic that thought he was going to come into the picture and ruin all of our lives for his own personal agenda.

"I think he owes them money or something 'cause they watch him almost as much as hard as they watch Gabriela. I heard one of them talking about some bonds or something. Anyhow, she can't even go to the bathroom without leaving the door cracked." Ramón wiped the tears from his face and blew his nose with a tissue he had taken from my desk. His face was crimson and his eyes were bloodshot. He was much too young to have such a burden placed on his shoulders.

"I still don't understand why you are free to come and go as you wish and they are being held hostage." I was not sure hostage was the right word to use, but that's what it sounded to me. I was struggling to wrap my mind around that, and it just wasn't making sense to me.

Ramón jumped out of the chair with his arms flung wide. "I can give you two reasons. If I don't show up for school, the truant officer will come to my house. The second reason is that he don't give a fuck about me. All he cares about is saving face."

I understood enough Spanish culture to know that a man's word was all he had, but that twisted bastard forgot the most important rule—family first. I immediately regretted becoming involved with Mr. Mendoza. I got up from behind my desk and went to the wall cabinet, which was hidden from the naked eye. Pressing the hidden access button, I opened the cabinet. From the center drawer, I got two small microphones no bigger than a quarter. I also grabbed a small, white teddy bear, which concealed a camera. I brought the items back over to my desk. Placing them on the desk. "Ramón, each of these things are listening devices. I need you to plant them in the house."

"Does the teddy bear have a camera in it? I saw some shit like that on television once."

"Yeah, it became popular back in the nineties when there were so many cases of alleged abuse with children. Mothers put the bear in the baby's room to make sure their child wasn't mistreated."

"That is so cool."

"It does pretty good, but you have to remember not to draw attention to it. If someone were to pick it up, they would notice how heavy it is and start looking at it more closely and your cover would be blown."

"Where do you want me to put them?" Ramón picked up the bear.

"Give the bear to Gabriela. If you can, put one bug in the room that your family eats in and one in your father's room."

"I might not be able to get in the room he stays in because he keeps the door locked when he's not there."

"Where else does he go to talk about things that he doesn't want you to know?"

"The basement. I could slip down there while he's sleep and he wouldn't know."

"Perfect. I need for you to be sure of the place you want to put it and turn it on by flipping this switch. It's voice activated, so you don't have to worry about the battery running down."

"Okay, I got it."

"And make sure you act like it isn't there. Although these pieces are difficult to detect, if you keep staring at it, he will know something is up."

Ramón nodded his head in understanding.

I looked at my watched and realized that it was only four o'clock in the afternoon. Despite the early hour, I felt like I had been up for days. The tension from not knowing about my child was taking a toll on me. "Ramón, I've got to ask you a very serious question, and I need you to think about it before you answer, okay?"

"Yeah," he mumbled.

"If your sister has the baby and your father realizes that it's black, what do you think he will do?" Asking that question was one of the hardest things that I had done in my whole life, but I needed to know the answer because it would determine how I would go about rescuing Ramón's family from the madman who called himself a father. Not able to stand it any longer, I jumped up and poured myself a drink from the carafe on the credenza. I drank the first shot and poured another before I brought the bottle and another glass to the desk. Without hesitation, I poured Ramón a shot.

"He will kill her."

CHAPTER THIRTY-THREE
TILO ADAMS

I was back in Moses's office, savoring a drink after having spent the last four hours sitting in my hot-ass car observing the activity at WeKare. During the time I was gone, Moses appeared to have aged. His eyes had dark circles under them and a smile no longer lingered on his full lips. He was such a handsome man. I hated to see the stress etched on his face.

"Do you really believe a father would hurt his own child?" I prayed that the answer to that question would be *no* but when it didn't come I had to accept that it was a good possibility.

"Ramón was very clear about what he thought would happen if his father learned that his child was carrying a black man's baby."

I completely understood Moses's pain. I was also worried about Gabriela because I was no closer to the money. I was scared of what they would do to her if she showed her ass. "What do you hope to gain from putting the bugs in the house?" I asked.

"To be honest, I don't know. Initially, I wanted to use them to learn something about Mr. Mendoza to make him leave the country. But now, all bets are off. Knowing what

I know, my perspective has changed. I intend to monitor the house to see if I can learn where Ariana is. If I even think he's planning on hurting either one of them, I'm going in there with my guns blazing."

I smiled at Moses over the lip of my glass. "What if they are involved in organized crime, then what?"

"Actually, that would be the best scenario."

"Huh?" He had lost me. I would've thought that would have been the worst scenario because those people tended to be ruthless in getting what they wanted.

"If it's organized, there is a trail. If there is a trail, I'll find it. Then, we just place a call to the feds and the rest will be on the news."

The trail ain't the only thing I'm counting on you to find, I thought. He was wavering back and forth and I was beginning to doubt his sincerity. "You got that kind of clout with the feds?" Just the thought of having anything to do with the feds made me nervous.

"You don't need clout to deal with the feds. All you have to do suggest that there is a potential to seize some money and they are there like flies on shit."

The visual didn't make me smile, but I understood where he was coming from. "Can I ask you a question?" This man intrigued me and I wanted to know more about him.

"Sure."

"What made you decide to become a private investigator?"

"Do you want the real truth, or the one I would give the media if I ever got as famous of James Bond?"

I started laughing as I imagined Moses behind the wheel of a snazzy sports car with all sorts of gadgets. "Give me the real truth. I can make up my own fiction." I snickered.

"I'm nosy as hell! When I found out I could dip in folks' business and get paid for it, I said sign me up."

"That makes perfect sense to me. I wonder why my nosy ass didn't think of that."

"Well, it's in your blood now. It's a good thing our paths crossed. I think we are going to make a good team."

"Thanks."

We fell into a comfortable silence in an uncomfortable situation. We were waiting for Ramón to place the microphones so we could hear what was going on inside the house.

"Did you see anything noteworthy while you were staking out the center?"

"Uh…I'm not sure if it means anything, but there was something that bothered me."

"Don't keep a brother hanging, what happened?"

"It wasn't so much as what I saw; it's more of an observation."

"Tilo, stop pussyfooting around and tell me."

"Only two people actually went into the center. Both were women. One was black and the other was Asian. They didn't stay long, but they went in with briefcases and left without them."

"That is nothing to throw up a red flag about. They could work at the center just like Tammi and only come there to get their assignments. Remember I told you there were at least eight offices in the building."

"As high as gas prices are, they could have done that over the phone," I insisted.

"Hey, good point. What else you got?"

"Four ambulances, all from the same company, within thirty minutes of each other." I could see disappointment written all over his face, and I was sure he was having second thoughts about having given me a job.

"There's no crime in that, Tilo, especially given the nature of the business," he said, shaking his head. He was not as smart as I had originally thought.

"That's it, don't you get it?" Realizing that Moses wasn't on my level, was a bitter pill to swallow. I danced around from foot to foot eager to spring my hunch on him.

"Okay, damn, I give up. What am I missing?" Moses's mood turned sour, and I could tell he wasn't one to play with.

"Why do they need so many ambulances when the center doesn't house any seniors?"

"Well I'll be damned. I knew you were smart. Hell, the average emergency room doesn't have four ambulances in four hours."

"That's what I thought. The ambulances didn't come in with emergency lights, either. They just came in and drove around to the side entrance. I didn't even know it was a side entrance until I pulled up some to see what was going on."

"That's pretty slick. I wonder what they are doing?"

"What if it had something to do with the briefcases the woman brought to the center? I think one of us needs to pay them a visit and leave one of your fancy listening devices." I was feeling pretty damn good about myself.

He nodded his head in agreement. "By any chance did you get the name of the transport company?" Moses asked.

"Yeah, it's called Kareport, ain't it cute?"

Moses used his computer to do a Google search but nothing came up. He then typed WeKare to see if that was a service they offered to their patients. If it was, it wasn't listed online.

Moses said, "We are going to have to get some license plate numbers if we are going to find out who owns those vehicles. I have a hunch they are connected to all this other drama."

CHAPTER THIRTY-FOUR
GABRIELA MENDOZA

I was sick and tired of being trapped in the house. If I wasn't so concerned about Ariana's whereabouts, I would have fought like hell to get as far away from here as I could. Even though my father made his expectations perfectly clear to me, I still couldn't believe that he would force me to marry someone I didn't know, let alone love. The only good thing that came out of this forced imprisonment was that I was beginning to get a better understand of my father's relationship with those two goons. They were looking for some bonds that they were sure my father knew where they were hidden. Only problem was there was no one I could share that information with. And I guess my involuntary marriage to Chico Velasquez would be sort of like an insurance policy.

I was interrupted from my thinking when I heard a door close. I was sitting in the living room for a change so I could keep an eye on things. As long as our father stayed out of sight, I was free to room the upper rooms of our house.

"I need to get into his room to see if I can find out what this key fits." I couldn't shake the feeling that the answers to my questions were hidden in my mother's room. I ran upstairs to search and I caught my father moving out some of Madre's things. "What are you doing?" I demanded. I had walked up behind him and scared the shit out of him. Madre used to say that when you were doing something that you weren't supposed to do, the devil had a way of riding on your shoulders and telling on you. I didn't understand it at the time, but the look on my father's face proved that she was right.

"Stop sneaking around here and shit." His menacing look should have scared me, but I was sick and tired of being afraid.

The house was quiet today. Ramón had left for school, and—for a change—my father's buddies were nowhere around. I decided to be nice to him to see if I could get better results. "Sorry, I didn't mean to scare you."

He stopped pulling the bags that he was removing and looked at me strangely. "What do you want?" he practically growled at me.

"I don't want anything." My feelings were hurt. It took everything in me to be nice to that motherfucker and he threw it back in my face. I turned to go back to the living room before I told the short fucker exactly what I thought about him.

"Wait," my father said.

I stopped because, for a split second, he actually sounded like the man I once knew. "Yes." My voice was chilly to my own ears, so I was sure he had detected the animosity I felt toward him.

"I packed up your mother's clothes. Do you want anything?"

A whole bunch of thoughts rolled around in my head. I knew he didn't want to hear them because number one on that list was to see his yellow ass out our house. Instead I said, "There may be a few things. Can I look at them? We have not had a chance to go through anything since she died." I threw the *we* in there just in case he had forgotten he actually had another daughter that was being held only God knew where.

"Here." He pushed the bag toward me and I dragged it down into the living room.

I was pretty sure that I didn't want any of my mother's clothing, but I wanted to keep this brief window of communication open with my father. If there was a way that I could get him to let us go, I was willing to take the first step.

To my surprise, he followed me into the living room and watched as I pulled out each item and held it up in front of me. He stared at me intently. After a few minutes, I got self-conscious. "Why are you staring at me?"

"Because…you remind me of her."

That was the first kind thing that he had said to me since he arrived and I didn't know how to take it. Was this his way of letting me know that he really did love our mother after all? While it was on my mind, I decided to ask him. "Did you love her?" In my head, the words sounded loud but it was only a whisper.

"What did you say?"

I searched his face before I answered. I didn't detect any anger, so I asked again. "Did you love my mother?"

"Of course I did. How can you ask me that?" His face started turning red. He balled his hands up into fists.

I lowered my head and pretended to be more interested in the bag than what he would say.

"Gabriela, there are a lot of things that you don't understand."

Surely he didn't think that that was an acceptable answer to me.

"Would you please explain it to me because I really need to know?" At first I thought he wasn't going to answer so I put the last of the items back in the bag, preparing to take them to my room. Even though I didn't see anything I wanted, Ariana deserved the opportunity to look through them as well.

"I never thought this would happen," he said as I started walking away.

I could have taken that statement several ways, so, in order to be fair to my father, I gave him a chance to explain it further. "What?"

We had come to a fragile place in our conversation, I didn't want to ruin it. If I could get him to admit that what he was doing was wrong, there was a good possibility we could come out of this hell with some semblance of a relationship.

"I never expected to be here…like this." His shoulders slumped in defeat.

I didn't know how I felt about his admission. He really wasn't saying what I wanted to hear. I wanted him to tell me why he had allowed those goons to snatch my sister out of her home and why he felt entitled to sell us off to the highest bidder. I felt myself getting angry all over again. "You know what, I really don't give a rat's ass about what you expected! Did you once stop and think about what we were expecting?" I was so mad, I could have punched him in his right eye and not thought twice about it.

"Gabriela, you have every right to be angry, but—"

"But hell! We haven't seen your ass in years. When we do, you give us your ass to kiss. We didn't deserve that! I wish, I wish we had never called you."

"No, you don't understand," he wailed. Tears gathered in his eyes as he looked at me. His eyes begged for understanding, an understanding that I didn't have for him.

"Then make me," I demanded. I felt my neck roll as I placed my hands on my. I almost laughed out loud. I felt myself turn into Tilo with an attitude. I struggled to keep the grin off my face as I stared my father down. His look of desperation turned to one of fear. Despite his new worldly ways, he was still a victim of his past. A past where the only right a woman had was to shut the fuck up.

"I'm still your father!" He stood up and walked toward, but I was way past caring about what he was going to do.

"Then act like it." The words had slipped out of my mouth before I could catch them. Even though I had no regret for saying the things that I did, it was all in the delivery. I wanted to kick myself for pushing the envelope. I wouldn't have been at all surprised if he reached over and smacked the shit out of me.

We stood staring at each other for a few seconds, each of us shaking with anger, neither of us willing to concede to the other.

"I'm in trouble, Gabriela. I need to ask you something." He sounded as if he were begging.

"What? What the fuck could you possibly want to ask me?" No regret. It's all in the delivery.

"I sent your mother some bearer bonds worth a lot of money. They belong to some dangerous people. I've looked everywhere. Do you have any idea where she would have hidden them?"

Padre finally showed his hand. He wasn't sticking around Atlanta out of any heartfelt sentiment toward us, he was after some money, plain and simple.

I thought about the key that was in my pocket and burst out laughing. "You're crazy. Look around you. If Madre had something worth money, we would have used it." He stared at me for a few minutes and I could tell that I had struck a nerve. I stood there waiting for the other shoe to drop.

He marched up the stairs and slammed the door to my mother's bedroom. I might not have won the battle, but I didn't lose either.

CHAPTER THIRTY-FIVE
GABRIELA MENDOZA

After spending a few hours in my room, I decided to cook dinner. I knew it would only be a matter of time before Ramón came home and he would be hungry as a horse. I hoped he got back before the goons came back. Actually, I was surprised that the entire day had passed and I hadn't seen them once. My father believed that I would grow to care for Chico if I spent enough time around him. As far as I was concerned, it would be a cold day in hell before that happened. Part of me wanted to scream at my father and tell him that I liked pussy, too. The other part of me wanted to live for another day.

Ramón came in as I was fixing my plate. Normally, I would have waited until my father came out of the room to start serving, but I assumed he was still licking his wounds from our earlier confrontation. "Hey," I said.

Ramón put his finger up to his mouth to hush me. Confused, I did as he had asked. He looked around the room. I assumed he was looking for our guest, but I shook my head to let him know they weren't here. He looked toward our mother's room. I nodded my head to let him know that our father was home. He grabbed my hand and practically dragged me deeper into the kitchen.

"I've got so much to tell you," he whispered.

"What's happened?" Fear pricked my heart.

"I spoke to Moses, Ariana's boss, and he's agreed to help us."

"What?" Ramón clamped his hand over my mouth.

We both turned toward the stairs that led to our father's room, waiting to see if my loud ass was going to bring him out of his room. After a few seconds Ramón continued.

"He knows Tilo and she is working with him to get Ariana back."

I was so surprised, I almost fell down. Ramón grabbed my shoulders and held me steady.

"How did you know to speak with them?" My mind was racing furiously. I wondered how much of our lives he had inadvertently revealed. After thinking about it for a few moments, it was perfect. Having the outside help was the ideal solution, especially since both of them had a vested interest in the outcome.

"I've been working with Moses for about a month. He was concerned because he has not heard from Ariana and started asking questions so I told him." Ramón's eyes searched mine.

I could have kissed him for his ingenuity. "How did he find out about Tilo?"

"I'm not sure, but we can talk about that later." He pulled from his book bag a teddy bear and something that looked like a quarter. He gave me the teddy bear.

"What do you want me to do with this?" I turned it over in my hands. It was unusually heavy for a stuffed animal.

"It's a camera and a listening device. I need you to put it in the dining room. I'm going to put this one in the basement." He left me standing there with my mouth open as he disappeared down the steps.

My feet felt like they were rooted to the floor. Even though I knew that time was of the essence, I couldn't move. I could not help but marvel at Ramón's resourcefulness. He came back up the stairs and saw me standing in the same spot.

He snatched the bear from my hand and took it to the dining room. Once it was positioned, he smiled at me. "Act like you don't know it's there. If you draw attention to it, our cover will be blown."

I nodded my head in understanding as my heart swelled with pride. My little brother was growing up right before my very eyes. Numb, I got my plate and continued to fix it. Ramón stood beside me and fixed his own plate.

We sat down at the table together and said grace.

"Aren't you going to call him to dinner?" Ramón said.

"No, we had words earlier. If he wants to eat, he knows where the kitchen is." Just thinking about our earlier conversation was making me mad all over again.

"Why? What happened?" Ramón put down his fork with a solemn look on his face.

"He was getting rid of some of Madre's things and I guess I got mad. I tried so hard to be nice to him. For a minute, I thought he was going to open up to me. He told me that he didn't mean for this to happen."

"Did he say anything about Ariana?"

"No, I kinda blew up at him before I could get that far."

"Damn, Gabriela, you might have blown the only chance we had of getting him to talk."

I didn't need him to make me feel bad about our failed conversation since I was feeling bad enough on my own. "I know, but I couldn't help myself. I feel like I'm going crazy sitting in this house every damn day."

"That would get to me too. I'm glad that they haven't started fucking with me."

I wanted to ask him how much he knew about the relationship between Moses and Ariana.

"Moses asked me what I thought our father would do when he finds out Ariana's child is black."

I felt like Ramón had reached into my mind and snatched away my thoughts. I was thinking the same thing, especially since she was due to deliver at any time. I said a silent prayer for her and the baby. "What did you tell him?" I whispered. I wanted to know if Ramón felt the same way that I did.

"I said he would probably kill her."

Ramón and I were on the same page. Finding Ariana before she delivered was paramount to her safety. I had suddenly lost my appetite and from the way that Ramón was pushing his food around on his plate, it was clear that he had lost his as well.

"If I could just understand why this is happening, I could deal with it better," I said.

"I have my own theories," Ramón admitted.

I felt like I was seeing Ramón for the first time. I never thought about discussing any of this with him before, and I could have kicked myself for the wasted time and opportunity. "I wish you would tell me because I'm going around in circles with it."

"Moses mentioned something about some letters to Madre. He even suggested organized crime."

I chuckled as I dismissed the idea. "He must have been speaking to Tilo. She sees conspiracy behind every closed door." Just thinking about Tilo brought a smile to my face.

"Well, she might not be that far off, base if you really think about it. Have you ever stopped to think about how much our father has changed?"

He wasn't even lying about that, but I wasn't ready to concede that point.

"We all have changed." It was a weak defense but it was all I could come up with.

"Come on, Gabriela, he's reinvented himself," Ramón spat. He was right and I knew it.

"Yeah, but that doesn't explain a connection to organized crime."

"Gabriela, where did he get the money? It sure wasn't from this pitiful laundry business. And while we are on the subject of the business, why am I still making deliveries? Are you washing clothes now?"

"I didn't know that you were still doing it. Why didn't you tell me?"

"You didn't ask. I am making the same drops that I've been making for the last seven years, expect now the packages are heavier. The only difference is that I don't have to do the bank run."

"What bank run?" To my knowledge, my mother had never been inside of a bank, let alone made a deposit.

"She has a safe deposit box at Wachovia. We would go at least twice a month and make deposits. She said she was saving for a rainy day." He started laughing.

Once again, my mind was spinning with the possibilities. Although this information was surprising to me, I still couldn't believe that there would be a significant amount of money in the bank because the laundry couldn't have been making a lot of money. My thoughts returned to the key I had taken from our madre's desk room. I reached in my pocket and pulled out the key.

"Is this the key to the box?" He reached over and took the key from me, examining it.

"It looks like it," he said, shaking his head in agreement.

"Are you sure? I asked you about it before and you said it was to the lock box."

He looked at it again. "I'm sorry. I was upset and not paying any attention. I'm sure this is the safety deposit box. See this yellow mark? That matches the row the key fits in at the bank." He gave it to me, but I pushed it back to him.

I was disappointed. I felt like he wasted a lot of time by not paying attention to me but I wasn't going to argue the matter now. "Keep it. I think you should go down there and see what's in the box." His look was thoughtful as he palmed the key and placed it in his pocket.

I was so lost in my own thoughts, I didn't hear my father came into the room. He stopped any further conversation between me and my brother.

He looked at the both of us with a scowl on his face. "I obviously missed the call to dinner," he remarked as he sat down at the table.

I waited for a few seconds before I got up to prepare his plate as was expected of me. It took everything in me not to spit in his food, but it didn't stop me from dousing salt in his refried beans. If I were lucky, he would keel over right at the table. However, to my chagrin, he acted as if he enjoyed the extra seasoning.

If I hadn't lost my appetite before, I'd certainly lost it now. I grabbed Ramón's plate and my own and headed to the sink to wash the dishes. Ramón got up to help, but I quickly halted him with a look. That would only make my father mad, seeing Ramón do common work that women were supposed to do.

"Gabriela, I need for you to pack some things for your sister," my father said.

"What type of things?" On one hand it made me feel good that, at least, he was speaking of Ariana as if she still existed. On the other hand, I was nervous. Was he indirectly saying that she was no longer welcomed in our home? He was really going to have a fight on his hands if he thought I was going to give up the opportunity of ever seeing my sister again.

"She will need some clothes and her personal items."

"Will I be able to see her?"

"That won't be necessary." He cut off further questions with the wave of his hand.

"Won't be necessary for whom?" I looked at this man like he was crazy. "Where the hell is she anyway?" I got up in his face and dared him to touch me. I was sick of his ass, and I wasn't afraid to let him know it.

My father's demeanor was calm on the outside, but I was willing to bet he was pissed on the inside.

"I have had enough of your smart mouth, young lady, for one day," my father warned.

"And I've had enough of your evasive bullshit!"

My father shoved his plate to the floor in a rage and jumped up from the chair, knocking it to the floor.

Instinctively, I backed up but wasn't quick enough to avoid his hand connecting with my face. The world seemed to stand still in time as my hand lifted to my aching jaw. He had slapped me so hard, I was sure to have his fingerprints fossilized in my face. Ramón attempted to rush my father, he pushed Ramón back as if he were nothing more than a worrisome little bug.

"Sit down," he commended.

I wanted to defy him again but my head told my ass not to write a check *we* couldn't cash. Until I was in the position to make sure he never put his hands on me again, I would have to do as he said.

His look dared us to provoke him again.

"Listen carefully…as I will not be explaining myself again. Your sister is away because I will not have a bastard child born in my house. After we have disposed of the baby, she will be given the choice to return home provided she agrees to marry Jesus. As for you..." he directed his attention to me.

My heart skipped a beat when I allowed his words to replay in my head. He distinctly said *dispose of the baby* as if he would be putting out the trash. Although he had continued his tirade, I had stopped listening. As far as I was concerned, it was time for us to start making some moves of our own. Without saying a word, I got up from the table and went to my room. There was more than one way to skin a cat, and I was about to find out how many there were.

CHAPTER THIRTY-SIX
ARIANA MENDOZA

An overwhelming sense of panic dragged me out of a sound sleep. I had a terrible dream and it left me shaking. Instinctively, I reached out to Mike—but the tiny bed was empty. As the last vestiges of sleep crawled over me, I realized that I wasn't at home. I struggled to remember the dream, but the details escaped me. Yawning, I swung my feet over the side of the bed with the intentions of going to fix myself a cup of tea.

I searched for my slippers in the dark. The floor was curiously bare and cold. I was trying to be quiet so I didn't awaken Gabriela but my hands were not touching any familiar objects. "Shit," I mumbled as I reached for the lamp that normally sat on the small night table next to my bed. It was missing. I turned in the direction of the window but even that was dark.

A shiver traveled up my spine. I wiped my eyes, thinking that things would become clearer once I cleaned all the gook from them. As I touched my face, I winced in pain. The whole left side of my face began to throb, and I remembered the series of events that had brought me to this place. Fear returned as I struggled to see in the darkened room.

"Where the hell am I?" If there was anyone else in the room, they were silent. Feeling braver, I stood up and made my way to the wall in search of a light. I had no idea how long I had been there. After a few swipes at the wall, my fingers finally touched the light switch. Then it hit me. I had been drugged. I closed my eyes to protect them from the bright light I anticipated, but nothing happened when I flicked the switch. I tried it several times, then I noticed a similar switch right next to the one that I had been trying. As the dim light penetrated the room, a mounting sense of panic came with it.

The room I was in was very nondescript. It reminded me of either a hospital room or some sort of dorm room. When I saw the bathroom, I let out a small squeal. As I stumbled to it, I realized I had never been so happy to see a crapper in my entire life. With the exception of some tissues in a box on the sink, the bathroom was absent of anything that would let me know where I was.

If this were a hospital, their logo would be on everything, I thought as I dropped my pants and relieved myself. For the next several minutes, I could do nothing but sit there. It wasn't until after I finished that I realized I had sat on an unprotected toilet in a strange place. While that should have worried me, in the scheme of things it was minor. I needed to find out where I was, and how to get out of there.

A series of flashbacks rushed over me. Although I was still disoriented, I knew that the brief swatches of memories were not figments of my imagination. Once I regained more of my senses, everything came back to me.

"Mike!" His name slipped out my lips at the same time the first tear fell from my eyes. I jumped up so fast I got dizzy. Nothing was making any sense. I struggled to pull my pants up. My baby was uncharacteristically still. This added to my already growing feeling of dread. If they had done something to hurt my husband, I would never forgive myself. Even though my feelings for him had changed, I didn't want anything bad to happen to him.

The room was as barren as the bathroom. There wasn't anything on the small dresser, not even a clock. Ever since I had gotten pregnant, I hadn't been able to wear my watch because my arms was so swollen. It irritated me to wear any jewelry, including my wedding ring. I approached the only other door in the room cautiously. Before I attempted to turn the knob, I put my ear against the door. I couldn't hear a thing. That shit didn't work in the movies, so I don't know why I had tried it. Not wanting to waste any more time, I tried to knob but it refused to open.

"Shit."

I started banging on the door as if my life depended on it. I knocked for several minutes, but no one bothered to come. I could not stop the tears from flowing down my face. Just when I thought things couldn't get any worse, the baby kicked me. I should have been excited but it wasn't the normal type of movement that I had been experiencing. It was almost as if the baby was knocking on the door of my stomach. I clutched my belly and backed away from the door.

"Whoa now, little one, it's not time yet," I advised my bundle of joy. Even as I said it, I knew it wasn't true. My stomach had dropped lower and I knew my time was near. "Lord, don't let me deliver my baby here," I pleaded. I was so afraid I didn't know what to do. I had not even finished taking my Lamaze classes, so I damn sure wasn't ready to have this baby now. I could only hope and pray Gabriela would be able to talk some sense into my father. Another swift kick followed the first one. It was so hard I could have sworn my baby was wearing shoes. I had to sit down. I started praying like I had never done before.

"Oh, please, God. I know I have been disobedient, but please don't take this out on my child." Once again, I thought about Mike. Perhaps God was punishing me for cheating on him. My thoughts went to Moses. I knew he would come to my rescue if only I had a way of contacting him. Thinking of Moses only made me more agitated, and the baby seemed to respond to my every thought.

The baby kicked my ass today, and I was starting to get worried. Since I had missed my last few appointments, I was scared that something was wrong. I just couldn't get comfortable no matter what I did. If I stood, my lower back bothered me. If I sat, the weight of the baby pressed down against my bladder, causing me to spend most of my time in the bathroom.

"This is not how I envisioned pregnancy to be," I wailed to the walls of my tiny prison. I wanted to make enough noise to bring my captures running, but they had placed me on ignore status. I could not remember the last time that I had something to eat, let alone something to drink. My thoughts started to go down the dark corridors of despair. I had to struggle to bring myself back from the brink of depression.

Suddenly, a pain ripped through my lower abdomen like a sharp knife. It left me shaking. "What the fuck was that?" The baby had kicked things up into overdrive. The minor pains that I had felt this morning were nothing compared to what I was experiencing now. I tried to keep the fear from rushing through my veins, but that was kind of hard to do, being all alone and uncertain as to what your fate would be. I had tried to remember exactly how many more weeks I had to go, but my brain hung out a *do not disturb* sign at the first sign of real pain.

"Oh, Lord, not now," I prayed. I tried to lay still. For some reason, I thought that things wouldn't progress if I lay absolutely still. That theory went straight out the window as the next pain ripped across my body. I stuffed my hand in my mouth so I wouldn't give voice to the scream that was building in my throat.

"This shouldn't be happening, God!" All the preparation and planning went straight out the window as my thoughts ran rampant.

"Lord, if you could just stop this right now, I swear I'll go to church more often. I'll go once a month—I'll go every Sunday! Hell, I'll go every day." I wailed as another pain ripped through me. I was thirty-two weeks pregnant. I needed to carry the baby for another two weeks at the very least.

Since God had me on what I felt was the *do not call list*, I started calling out to all the angels I knew, hoping just one of them was watching over me. I was comforted but I had lost any semblance of peace of mind with the last pain. I assumed my contractions were coming about fifteen minutes apart. If I was going to get through this, I was going to need some help. I inched onto my side. I needed to get my feet on the floor, so I could bang on the door some more. Surely my padre didn't leave me here, wherever I was, alone.

I waited until my contraction was over before I attempted to stand. My breathing was coming faster. I knew I should start using my breathing exercises or I would completely lose whatever control I thought I had over the situation.

I made it to the door just as the next contraction was building. That was the only way that I could describe the pain. It started in my lower back and snuck around to my stomach. I felt like I had to take a shit but I was too afraid to use the bathroom. I was sure that I wouldn't have the strength to get up from the toilet.

I screamed as the next pain hit me.

"It's coming!" I was in straight panic mode, and I wanted that baby out of me by any means necessary. No longer did I consider my baby a gift from God. It was a devil spawn and it had to go!

"Will somebody help me?" I screamed at the top of my lungs. My throat felt like it was on fire. I was sure that my words rocked the entire building. If they didn't rock the building, they had certainly wreaked havoc in the tiny little room that I occupied. I sank to the floor as the tide ebbed. If this was what labor was like, I was ill prepared. "Madre didn't tell me this shit would hurt like this." When I thought about how excited I had been to find out that I was pregnant, I felt like killing myself. To know that I signed up for this shit made me feel stupid. Nothing was worth this sort of agony. The pressure started building again. I had to sit up to relieve some of the pressure on my back.

"Oh, God, won't somebody please help me?" I shouted. I was crying helplessly. A sudden urge to push hit me and almost made me stand straight up from my crouched position.

"God, no!" I followed this cry with another plea for mercy. I started babbling. The words were coming so fast, I couldn't even understand myself. As the pain peaked, I could do nothing more than scream.

Then my water broke.

If I had any doubt of what was happening before, it was clear now—my baby was coming.

"What the hell is all this screaming about?" a young black woman entered the room. She immediately dropped to the floor and grabbed my hands to keep me from beating myself about the face and arms.

I was trying to focus the pain someplace other than my pelvic, which kept rising off the floor. "It's coming," I screamed again. I wanted to rip my clothes off and show this ignorant woman what all the fuss was about. I didn't care that I didn't know her from Adam. My baby was coming, and it didn't care who was around to see it.

"Oh, Lord, you're about to have a baby," she exclaimed.

I fought the urge to say "No shit, Sherlock." She grabbed a two-way radio that she had attached to her sleeve and started speaking in a language that was foreign to me. I didn't give a shit what she was saying as long as she was calling for help.

She kneeled behind my head and attempted to get me off the floor, but I wasn't having that. Every time I moved, the baby kept pressing down on my back. I wanted her to leave me the fuck alone so I could deal with that. I punched the woman, who easily outweighed me two to one, square in the mouth, and she just flipped over like a fallen domino piece. Without forethought or planning, I snatched the keys that were around her neck. I prayed that one of them would unlock any door that stood in my way.

This is my chance, I thought. I had a few moments of clarity between contractions, which I believed were coming every ten minutes. I struggled to my feet and scrambled to the door, which was left open by my capturer.

"Finally," I muttered. In my demented state I thought I was getting the assistance I needed from God. I instinctively knew the woman was the only person that I had to worry about at the moment. I knew that if I could get out of this place, I would have a fighting chance of making it to safety.

I hit the corridor at a slow trot, but I was moving as fast as I could for a woman in my condition. As I trotted, I prayed that whoever prevailed in setting me free was still on the job and watching over me. I knew that the next contraction would fold me against the wall.

And then it happened.

"Oh, Lord, please help me!" I waited until I was in control of the pain before I moved forward. The door to freedom was in my sights. I was going to make it. I hit the push-bar with my shoulder as I clutched my belly. Once again, I had to fight the urge to push.

My eyes squinted against the bright sunshine as I broke through the door. I really hadn't expected the door to open without using the keys that I had managed to steal. I still didn't know where I was, but there was enough traffic on the road for me to get some assistance. I bent over during the pain and when it ebbed, I headed for the busy street ahead of me. If I had to walk through traffic, I was determined to get away from the place that had detained me. I knew I had hit the lady hard, but I didn't believe I had delivered a punch that would have her disabled for too much longer. I threw a final look over my shoulder.

My mind began to play tricks on me as I attempted to maneuver to the road. The last thing I needed was to collapse in the driveway without reaching the help I needed. What looked to be three hundred yards was actually less the ten feet. I stopped for support when I reached a telephone pole. Leaning up against it, I used one of my hands to flag down a passing motorist. The other hand was clinched around my belly to keep my child from sliding out onto the concrete.

"Please!" I didn't recognize the guttural sound that escaped my lips, but it seemed as if my voice had wings. Every car within the sound of my voice suddenly put on brakes. I fell into the first car that had stopped in my path. Fortunately for me, the stranger immediately reacted to the situation. Jumping from the car, she opened the passenger door and pulled me inside.

My vision blurred as the pain radiated through my body. The fact of my savior was obscured and I could only pray that I would be safe. My body melted into the seat as my head lulled to the left.

"Go," I hissed as another shooting pain wracked my body. I wanted to get as far away from that place as possible. My eyes slowly closed as she pulled away from the curb.

CHAPTER THIRTY-SEVEN
MOSES RAMSEY

I was tired, bone tired, and I couldn't wait to go home and soak in my hot tub. I had been listening to the house that I had officially labeled The House of Mendoza for the past twelve hours. I didn't learn a thing that would help me find the love missing from my life. Part of me wanted to get depressed, but the professional side of me knew this came with the territory. My problem was that I was having a hard time keeping this investigation from being personal. My biggest fear was that my woman and child were in danger and that there was nothing I could do to save them.

Tilo was on stakeout at WeKare and Ramón was doing a run for his father. We were still trying to figure out exactly what he was delivering, but until we knew what we were dealing with, things had to appear as normal as possible. Ramón wanted to open one of the packages, but that would have ruined everything. I was just about to call it a night when my cell phone rang.

"Hello?" I didn't recognize the number on the caller ID.

"Moses, I found her. We are headed to Emory, meet us there?" Tilo was shouting into the phone.

"Found who?" As much as I wanted to believe she was talking about Ariana, I didn't want to get my hopes up.

"Ariana, I got her. She's in labor, Moses. I'll explain everything when you get there." She hung up on me.

I snatched my keys and raced out of the office. "I'm having a baby!" I yelled out loud but no one was around to pay attention to me. Something that I had dreamed of was about to become a reality. I was so happy, I didn't have time to get nervous.

"Please, God, let everything be okay." I could feel the tears building behind my eyes, and I did nothing to stop them. I was breaking all the rules as I drove, but I didn't care. If one of DeKalb's Finest tried to stop me, they would be in for the ride of their life 'cause I had no intension of stopping until I'd reached the hospital. Fortunately, no cop did, and I took that to be a sign of luck.

I pulled into the emergency-room parking lot and parked in the No-Parking space, but, once again, I didn't care. I would pay whatever fine I had to because time was of the essence. I wanted to be there when my child entered this world. My eyes scanned the faces of the many people sitting in the emergency room.

I was looking for Tilo, but I didn't see her. I pulled out my cell to call her, which went straight to voice mail. More than likely, she was in the delivery room with Ariana if she was truly in labor. I ran up to the desk demanding information. "I'm told my fiancé was brought here."

"Good evening, sir."

I didn't have time for pleasantries. I knew I was being rude, but I really didn't give a damn. "Her name is Ariana Mendoza." I gave her the information, even though she didn't ask for it. I noticed the change in her attitude, when she realized that I was inquiring about a Latina. She looked me up and down and turned her nose up at me as if she smelled something foul.

I was about two seconds away from jumping over the desk and wringing her stupid neck.

"Do you see her listed?" The bitch didn't even pretend to put Ariana name into the computer. I could tell this woman wasn't going to be helpful, so I moved on down the line and asked the next person because waiting on that woman would only lead me to a night in jail. "Sir, can you please help me?" I tried another approach since the first one didn't work. I was sure they were used to dealing with folks just like me on a regular basis and could understand that we weren't in the best frame of mind.

"Sure, what's the patient's name?"

"V-e-r-ó-n-i-c-a Mendoza." I impatiently patted my hand on the desk. I noticed the look of disapproval on the brother's face, but he quickly corrected himself. It was a good thing because I was out of patience.

"She's being examined now. Are you the father?"

Proudly I replied, "Yes I am."

"Great then. I'm sure you would want to be with her," he responded.

I thanked him for his kindness and professionalism.

"I sure would." My heart was racing as I realized this was really happening.

"Stand over there. I will have someone come for you." He pointed to an area near some double doors. I hoped that they wouldn't take too long, because I was ready to jump right out of my own skin.

Tilo came running out the double doors directly into my arms.

I was so happy with her. I could have kissed her right on the mouth. "How is she?" I pushed Tilo away from me so that I could see her face.

"They are still examining her. She was badly dehydrated and they are trying to get some fluids into her right now."

"Has she asked about me?" I really didn't want to stand there in the hallway asking a whole bunch of questions, but I was nervous about seeing her.

"She hasn't said much. She's in a lot of pain and she doesn't know who I am. We have met a few times, but I really don't know her that well?"

"How did you recognize her?"

"Actually, when she came running out of the center, I didn't know who she was. She just looked like she needed help."

"Thank God you were there. I need to see her."

"They put me out but I'm sure they will be coming to get you in a few minutes. Moses, I just want to warn you, she was beaten. Her face is healing, but she's definitely been through it."

"I'm going to kill the bastards." A raging storm flooded through my veins. It took everything in me not to leave the hospital and put my hands on Ariana's father and the bastards he had helping him.

"Yeah, I could climb up in their asses myself. But with Ariana safe, things will be easier. All we have to do is get Gabriela out of the house and we'll be safe."

"Do you think it's going to be that easy because I'm not feeling confident that it will be." I wasn't ready to go into any detail, but I felt sure they were going to come looking for Ariana—nine times out of ten, this hospital would be the first place they look. Just as I was about to fill Tilo in on my decision to get the feds involved, I was summoned into the delivery room.

"Who's here with patient Mendoza?" a short, stout black lady asked. She looked to be in her early forties.

I knew I was going to suffer from some more nasty looks. People killed me, especially my people, with their silly prejudices. Most of the women I met were just mad because I was dating outside of my race, but choosing Ariana was not meant to be a slap in black women's face and they needed to understand that. "I am," I said perhaps a little too loudly. The lady surprised me because she didn't so much as bat an eye.

"Come with me."

I followed her to a station. She handed me some scrubs to put on. "Wash your hands over there—wash them good, okay?"

"I will." As I washed my hands, I began to get nervous again. I was afraid of what I would see and how I would handle it. My biggest fear would be that I would pass out like some sort of wimp. If I did, I knew Ariana would never let me live it down. The nurse must have sensed my fear.

"Pick a spot in the room and stare at it and you will be fine." She gave me a big ole smile and it bolstered my confidence.

"Thanks."

She turned me around and put a surgical mask on my face. "Good luck. She's going quickly, so it won't be long."

"Is that a good thing?" I knew that some labors could last for hours, so I wanted to make sure that *quick* didn't mean trouble.

"Hurry up before you miss it." She pushed me toward the door.

Sucking up my last bit of courage, I backed into the room. She never answered my question, but that didn't matter now.

"Oh, God," Ariana screamed and my heart went out to her. I was having a difficult time believe that anything as large as a baby could come from inside of her, because she was such a tiny woman. The doctor was coaching her to breathe as I slipped up beside her and grabbed her hand. She didn't even acknowledge me, but her eyes were closed. The grip she had on my fingers was fierce. I didn't know she had that much strength in her entire body.

As the pressure on my hand decreased, I leaned in and whispered in her ear, "It's going to be okay, baby."

Her eyes flew open and she uttered a short whimper. "Moses, how…did you…know…where to find me?"

"Shush, don't worry about that now. I'm here and that's all that matters."

She started crying, but I couldn't tell if it was from seeing me or if she was about to have another pain. I kissed her on the forehead, which appeared to be the only part of her face that wasn't bruised.

The doctor was down between her legs. I was determined not to go down on that end of the table.

"Here comes another one," the doctor warned.

I braced myself for the pressure, but this time it wasn't that bad, perhaps because she knew that I was there.

"They are…coming…faster," she growled and panted at the same time.

"Of course, that's the way we like it. I can see the baby's head," the doctor announced.

"Dammit…can I push?" she yelled as the pain seemed to have reached its peak.

"Yes, give me a good one."

Beads of sweat were popping out on Ariana's forehead.

I wiped them away with a towel she had laying next to her head. "I love you, Ariana,"

She smiled back at me, even though she was in a lot of pain. "I love—I don't like—you very much—right now."

I knew it was the pain talking. I had heard horror stories of women cussing out their husbands, so I was really waiting on that to happen. "Don't worry, you'll get over it."

She let go of my hand and rose up off the table.

"Where are you going?" I was baffled.

"Home. This shit…hurts." She had all these wires hooked up to her and she was talking about leaving.

"Leaving ain't going to make it stop. It will just go home with you," I patiently said.

She ignored me and kept trying to get off the table. "Drugs. Is it too late? Please…give me some drugs?" Ariana begged as the pain ebbed and she lay back down.

"Sorry, but you're too far gone. Anything that I gave you now would go directly to the baby, and we don't want that," the doctor said.

"But…I can't take this—" Her statement was cut off as she let loose another scream that rivaled the first one.

"Push, Ariana, push," the doctor urged.

"Dammit, I am pushing," she grunted.

I could tell she was about to get combative, and I felt sorry for the doctor. I was just glad that she was directing her anger at someone other than me.

"You must not want to see this baby," the doctor chided.

Ariana rose up on her elbows and bore down.

I could tell she was straining because two veins stood out on the side of her neck as she worked.

"You are doing good, sweetheart."

She looked up at me as if she wanted to hit me, so I decided to keep quiet. I knew that the pain had passed when she fell back on the pillow.

"I've got the head. Don't push now. I need to clear the shoulders."

I fought the urge to run around to see who my child looked like. That was when I saw the mirror over the bed. It was pointed right at us. I don't know how I had missed it in the first place. I could feel my eyes get bigger as I saw how stretched Ariana's pussy was. "There is no way that I'm going to be able to fit in there ever again," I mumbled. As soon as the words left my mouth, I felt bad for saying them.

"I heard that," Ariana said as she braced herself for another pain.

"Don't push, Ariana. Let me do the work for you," the doctor said.

"Hurry up—it's coming!"

"That's good, Ariana. Breathe for me." I glanced at the mirror again as a white baby slid out into the world.

I hit the floor.

CHAPTER THIRTY-EIGHT
MOSES RAMSEY

Tilo handed me a cigar as I was wheeled out of the delivery room. I had never been so embarrassed in my life. I had been played like a first-class pussy.

Tilo said, "Congratulations!"

I could tell she wanted to ride me about passing out but she kept it in.

"Have you seen it yet?"

She looked at me funny. "No, they are checking him out. They just told me it was a boy and that you would be joining me soon."

I stood up from the chair and pushed it into the corner. I wanted to get as far away from this hospital as possible.

"You sure you don't want me to hang on to this chair just in case you get woozy again?" A smile played at the corners of Tilo's mouth.

"I know you think this shit is funny, but if you saw the same shit I did, your ass would have passed out too."

"Didn't you know you are not supposed to look? They put that mirror there for nosy bastards just like you. It's a setup."

She gave up trying not to laugh at me.

"Shut up Tilo. That bitch lied to me. That child isn't mine."

Her laughing abruptly stopped. "What?"

"The baby…has light hair and blue eyes like his father." I remembered how Mike's lifeless blue eyes stared at the ceiling and how his blond hair was matted with blood. I felt betrayed in the worst way and I wanted her to pay for deceiving me. She had destroyed everything good within me. I paced for about fifteen seconds then turned to Tilo. "Is your offer still on the table?"

"Are you serious?" Her whole facial expression changed.

"After the way she played me, I deserve to get something out of all this."

"We both deserve this come up." She offered me her hand. "Seventy-thirty, my way."

"Oh, no you don't. We split this down the middle or count me out."

"You can't blame a sister for trying."

I shook her hand. "This is some bullshit right here. What the hell am I supposed to do?" I couldn't get the baby's face out of my head.

Now, Tilo was pacing.

"If—"

"Let me think, Moses. I just need a minute." She paced again, then said, "I got it." Her smile looked almost demonic to me.

"The first thing we have to do is get Ariana and the baby moved before someone comes looking for her. I need you to make some calls. We need a private hospital and an ambulance."

"Moses, they are not going to let you just take that baby out of the hospital. Not today anyway. They are going to want you to wait at least two days."

"Tilo, we don't have two days. This is the closest hospital so they are bound to come here first. We have come too far to fuck up now. "

She had this patronizing look on her face. "This can be solved rather easily."

"How's that?" Tilo was scaring me. I was almost afraid to hear what she would suggest.

"Marry Ariana. If you give them your name, she won't be registered as a Mendoza in the hospital—case closed."

I looked at Tilo like she had lost her happy mind. It would have been different if I were still feeling Ariana like that, but right about now, I hated her. As much as the idea sickened me, it would, however, solve the immediate problem. I wasn't sure how Ariana would react to my proposal, but I was willing to take one for the team. "Are you sure about this?" I asked.

"It's really the only solution to our problem right now."

"Do you think Ariana will go for it?"

"There is only one way to find out. If she says yes, I'll have a priest waiting." Tilo pushed me toward to door. If she felt any apprehension about this at all, she didn't show it. The only thing left for me to do was convince Ariana.

Ariana was nursing the baby when I came into her room. She looked at me with tear-filled eyes and said, "I'm sorry. I thought he was—"

"Let's not talk about that right now. I have some bad news to tell you."

She wiped her eyes and kissed Mike's son on the top of his head. "I'll understand if you hate—"

"Your husband was murdered." I didn't know how she would react, but I wasn't prepared for her total silence.

She sat looking at me as if she had not heard a word that I said.

"Did you hear me?"

She only nodded her head as more tears flowed. "My father did this. I heard him tell Jesus and Chico to take care of him right before I passed out. I was hoping that he was bluffing, but I guess he wasn't."

"I'm so sorry." I didn't know what else to say so I just let her cry. I was glad that she was in pain.

"He didn't deserve to die," she said.

"I know, and trust me, I'm going to get whoever was responsible for it, but we have to take care of first things first. Your father and his friends are going to come looking for you. It would be foolish to think that they won't."

She shuttered as if she were remembering something vile and wicked. "What should I do?"

It took everything I had not to spit in her face. "You are not alone, I love you and the baby. It doesn't matter that I'm not the father. He's my son, Ariana. We are in this together."

Her eyes were on the baby, but I knew she saw me as well. When she didn't say anything I continued.

"Ariana, I know this is sudden, especially in light of all that has happened, but I want you to marry me."

She looked up at me in shock. I didn't know if she was reacting to the timing of my proposal or if she found the thought of marrying me as repulsive as I did.

"Are you serious?" She breathlessly asked.

I held my breath. I had no idea what her answer would be. "Yes, I am quite serious. I've told you from the very beginning how I felt about you and I would like nothing more than to officially claim you in my life."

She appeared to choose her words carefully. "But…what about Mike?" Fresh tears gathered in her eyes.

I knew this was going to be difficult, but we really didn't have much any time to discuss any other options. "Sweetheart, Mike is gone. I know that sounds harsh, but it's the truth. If you take my name, your father will have no way of finding you when he comes looking." Although I didn't want her to think of marrying me as a last resort, I needed for her to understand why it would be acceptable if she were to go ahead and do it now.

"What will people say?" Her eyes held a glimmer of hope and I planned to take advantage of it even though it sickened me.

"Do you really care? Because I sure as hell don't."

Ariana appeared to be deep in thought and I found myself getting nervous all over again. In the back of mind, I recognized that she could possibly turn me down, but I tried not to think like that. "Do you love me?" I had to know if she were telling the truth all this time or she was feeding me a bunch of shit to get what she wanted.

"Of course I do."

I resisted the urge to take her in my arms while I waited for her answer. Time stood still. My eyes searched her face, but she was so good at hiding her emotions, she would have made an excellent poker player.

"When do you want to do this?" Without bothering to respond to her question, I whipped out my cell phone and made the call. "Tilo, we are all set." I hung up the phone wearing a forced smile. "Is now too soon?"

"Moses, we can't get married now!"

"Why can't we?"

"Uh..."

"Tilo has a priest ready and you won't have to leave the bed."

She giggled like a teenager.

"Who is Tilo?" She wore a confused look on her face.

"She's the lady that found you and brought you to the hospital. She is also your sister's roommate." I almost told her that they were lovers but I knew that wasn't for me to tell.

"Wow. I thought that she looked familiar, but I assumed I was delirious." She started laughing and I joined her.

"So much has happened in such a short time," I replied.

"I still want to know how you found me."

"I know, and I want to know all that has happened to you, but let's get this wedding out the way. We also have to think up a name for our son."

"I don't have to think about it because I already know what it's going to be," she said, smiling.

"Oh, I don't have a say in this? We have not even gotten married yet and already you are calling the shots."

"I would like to name the baby after you." Her voice was so low I almost didn't hear her. "Any objections?" Her smile was almost as wide as her face.

"That would make me very happy, almost as much as having you for a wife."

"You don't have to sweet talk me. I already said yes," she joked.

I think the expression on my face told her how much her decision meant to me. I got up from the edge of the bed to kiss her but was interrupted by a knock on the door. It was a nurse coming to get the baby. Although she wasn't ready to give him up, it was perfect timing.

I struggled to keep a smile on my face as I pulled my hand from her grasp. I kissed her on the forehead and quietly let myself out of the room. She was happy as hell now but I was going to have the last laugh.

CHAPTER THIRTY-NINE
GABRIELA MENDOZA

Ramón was skipping school and going to the bank. If my mother felt so strongly about putting something in the bank, it must have been important. I would have been lying to myself if I said that I wasn't curious about what he would find.

I still could not believe how much Ramón had matured. He had managed to find a job and keep it from all of us. I realized that I had seriously underestimated him. I tried to keep him as a child, but he had shown me he was ready to be a man.

I said a prayer that Moses would be able to find a way to get us out of this situation without anyone getting hurt. I went into the living room to do some cleaning since there was nothing else to do. Once again, the house was strangely quiet. I was beginning to think my father had a change of heart because his friends weren't coming around like they used to. However, my tranquility was destroyed by an urgent beating on the door. I rushed to answer it, but my father beat me to it.

"Go on back to your room," he instructed.

I wanted to tell him to kiss my ass, but I held my tongue. Instead of doing as he had said, I went back into the living room.

He yanked open the door. "Why are knocking on my door like that?" he demanded.

"We have a situation," Chico said. He pushed pass my father and came into the house. His broad shoulders bumped against my father.

I could feel the tension mounting in the room. I don't know when it had happened, but they no longer appeared to be buddy-buddy. They stared each other down as if both of them were waiting for the other one to say something first.

"Well, what is it?" my father finally asked.

"She's gone?"

I couldn't see Chico's face, but my gut told me he was talking about Ariana.

"Who's gone?" I heard my father ask.

"Your daughter, she's escaped."

"You idiot! How did that happen?"

"I suggest that you watch who you are calling an idiot. I wasn't the one who messed things all up for us."

I froze, too scared to breathe. I could not afford to miss one second of their heated exchange.

I could tell Chico was pissed.

"What of the child?"

Chico didn't answer, and I didn't know what that meant. I wanted to run into the room and bash that bastard upside his head, but I knew that would only make things worse.

"Why are you shaking your head? What does that mean?" my father demanded.

"It means that she got away before we could get the baby," Chico said.

"For crying out loud, I asked you to do one thing and you fools couldn't do it right. She was pregnant. How the hell did she get away?"

I wanted to know the answer to that as well. All of a sudden things were looking much better, and I couldn't wait for Ramón to get home so that I could tell him the good news.

"You wanted me to kill the baby. I don't do children. If you wanted it dead, you should have done it yourself. Besides, I had a buyer all lined up for the baby so fuck you," Chico spat.

I could not believe my ears. My father had planned to kill my sister's baby. What kind of man was he? I was glad for the hidden microphones. Now I would have proof of what my father was doing when we managed to get away. I eased into the room.

"Well, that's your problem," Chico said. "You fucked this up but this had better not affect the rest of our plans. You better find the money by Friday. They will be here."

"Shut up talking to me. This is your fault."

I saw the same look on my father's face as I did the night he had slapped me. I knew there was going to be some fighting going on in a few short minutes.

"I came over here to warn you that it's about to be some shit. What you do with this information is strictly on you. But if this deal doesn't go down on Friday, I would not want to be you."

"Get out of my house," my father shouted.

I eased closer. Both of them stood staring at each other as if one was waiting on the other. I wanted them to keep talking so I could find out the details of this deal that was supposed to be going down. I slid back into my hiding place before they saw me. The next thing I heard was the front door slamming. From my vantage point, I couldn't see and I was afraid to come out of hiding because my father would realize that I had been listening. I snuck through the dining room and into the kitchen. With any luck he would go back in his room or to the basement.

"You can come out now," my father shouted.

Terrified, I could not move. I couldn't believe that I had been caught. Although his voice was loud, it wasn't angry and that surprised me. I walked into the living room and sat down on the sofa.

"You are just like your nosy mother." He chuckled when he said it and reminded me of the man that I used to know.

I didn't know what to say to him, because he was acting so strangely. If he were truly upset about Ariana's escaping, there was no evidence of it now. "I just came downstairs."

"And you are a lousy liar too."

He had no idea of how devious I could be. But if he kept fucking with me, he was going to find out. I said nothing because we would have been exchanging barbs all night long. "Are you ready to tell me what this is all about?"

"I'd hoped that it would never be necessary, but I can see now that I don't have a choice." He sat down on the love seat facing me. For a few minutes, he just stared into the air. "Years ago, before you were born, I worked for the CIA."

"The what?" He could not be talking about the Central Intelligence Agency. What kind of fool did he take me to be?

"You heard me the first time. As I said, it was a long time ago. I wasn't really working for them, but I worked through them. They hired my firm to provide trained pilots and to get them small aircrafts they could use, which couldn't be traced back to their organization. It was very top secret."

"You are going to have to come better than that. What do you know about flying a plane?"

"There is a lot that you don't know about me—and your mother for that matter."

I could only look at him like he was crazy. It was true that I didn't know him, but I knew my mother almost as well as I knew myself. I stood up to leave. As much as I wanted answers from him, I wasn't in the mood to hear a bunch of lies, especially about my mother.

"You don't have to believe me but it is true. I worked there until you were born and your mother convinced me to get out. She said it was too dangerous and that we had kids to think of."

"Please stop. You don't have to do this." This was the most pathetic lie that I'd ever heard.

"Will you just shut up and listen? I don't know how much time we have."

He got my attention with that line. Although I didn't believe any of that crap about the CIA, I still didn't know how Ariana's escape played out in the scheme of things. "Go head," I said.

"Things got tough when I quit. I had five mouths to feed and very little money coming in. I began to accept money from the Cali cartel. Small change in the beginning—harmless amounts when you think about the amount of money they had running through Columbia. All I had to do in exchange for the money was fly a plane every now and then. I never knew what I was transporting, never wanted to know." He stopped talking for a minute and I thought he was going to leave me hanging just when the story was getting interesting.

I wasn't sure how much of his story I believed, but I knew there had to be some element of truth in it so I continued to wait. So far, nothing I had heard excused the fact that my father ordered the death of my nephew.

"Your mother was livid. She also worked for the CIA. Did you know your mother spoke several languages fluently?"

"Yeah right. She couldn't even speak English well," I shot back. If he was around, he would have known how much our mother struggled just to understand what we were saying.

"That's where you are wrong. If you pretend to be ignorant, you can find out so much information. Your mother was the master in that game. She used to be the translator for the flights that we scheduled. When we were called to work, we never knew who we would be transporting. She had to be prepared to deal with all of them."

I could not believe what I was hearing. There was no way I was going to believe that my mother was some sort of undercover anything. "I'm sorry, I'm not buying this act," I adamantly stated.

"Whether or not you believe me is irrelevant. Your mother is gone so I will never be able to prove it. But if you are very honest with yourself, I'm sure you will recall some times when you thought you were pulling the wool over your mother's eyes and she knew exactly what it was that you girls were planning."

Damn, he did have a point there. We always thought it was some sort of fluke or something whenever she caught onto our games. What if she were really listening to us plot and understood the games all along.

I thought about it for a few minutes and realized that he was right. What she knew or didn't know at this point was irrelevant. My only choice now was to believe or disbelieve what my father was telling me. "Okay, I am not going to argue with you about whether or not what you are saying is true because as you said, it's irrelevant. I want to know what is going on now."

He cleared his throat before he continued. "I've been trying to get out of the game for years. Each time I got one foot out the door, something happened to pull me back in. Part of it was greed, I'll admit that. But the other parts were to ensure your safety. Every time I said I had had enough, they would threaten to do something to one of you. I had to pretend that I didn't care for you just to make sure they couldn't use that against me to make sure I did as they asked."

"This sounds all good and shit, but I'm not believing it. What about how you treated Ariana? What about how you treated all of us? When you came here, we didn't even know who you were."

"Weren't you listening, I had to do it. Your mother was adamant that I stayed out of your lives. I've been here all the time. She wouldn't allow me to contact you because she said it would be too dangerous."

"Are you kidding me? Didn't you know that we needed you?" I felt like crying for all the lost years.

My father just hung his head in apparent shame. When I thought about all the wasted time that we couldn't get back, I got mad. I didn't know who to be angrier with, my father or my mother.

"I am so sorry," he said as tears slid down his face, and I could tell they were genuine. However, it still didn't excuse his actions and for those things, I would never forgive him.

I wanted him to feel our pain. "Ramón needed you the most. He cried for you and you were nowhere around. He needed you to teach him how to be a man!" I probably should have stopped fussing when I saw him crying, but he didn't need any mercy as far as I was concerned.

"I didn't want it to be this way—you have to believe me."

I just shook my head at him. If he really wanted to be a part of our lives, he would have made a way. "I don't have to believe anything. To me, seeing is believing and you haven't shown me a damn thing. And another thing, you said you stayed away to protect us. Well, if that was true, you have been here for months and nothing has happened so now what?"

My father just stared at me.

"Just what I thought, your story doesn't hold water. You stayed away because you wanted to." I was so angry, I just wanted to hit him.

We sat in an uncomfortable silence. I didn't know what he thought he would accomplish by coming clean with me. If he thought that all would be well and we would walk away in the sunshine, he had another thing coming. "When I think about how we had to struggle to make ends meet, I could just kill you," I admitted.

"But I sent plenty of money. None of you should have wanted for anything." He was adamant about that.

I looked at him skeptically.

"Does it look like we had everything?" I followed his eyes around the room, and I was certain that he saw the same things that I saw. We weren't dirt-poor, but we could hardly call ourselves comfortable.

He continued to cry as I paced the floor. Although I felt a little sorry for him, I still couldn't get over the fact that he had written us off.

CHAPTER FORTY

GABRIELA MENDOZA

I thought long and hard about what he had said while I looked at the teddy bear sitting on top of the television. "So, if Madre hadn't died, we would have never seen you again?"

His eyes sought mine. I could tell he wanted to lie to me again but couldn't. I had seen behind his façade.

"You could have called me," he mumbled but there wasn't much conviction in his voice. He had to know that we couldn't afford the long-distance charges.

"Don't be ridiculous, we were children. We thought you were back at home taking care of your parents or was that a lie as well?"

His shoulders started to shake uncontrollably. It took everything in me not to reach out to him and offer him comfort.

"They are dead; they were killed to teach me yet another lesson."

I sat back down. He had knocked the wind from my sails with that admission. "You talk in riddles." I was trying to make sense out of everything that he had shared with me, but I was still missing some vital pieces to the puzzle.

"I cannot share everything with you. Do you see how dangerous it would be for you?"

"*Liar.*"

He scowled. I really wanted to say *bullshit*, but out of respect, I didn't.

"It is true. I have already said too much. I need to find a way to get you out here."

"What are you talking about? You are the one that is keeping me here." I was losing my patience with him.

"Keeping you here kept you alive. You will not be safe on the streets until my job is finished. I hired someone to watch over you."

I looked at him as if he had lost his happy little mind. "Enough of this shit! Tell me everything right now or I'm walking out that door." I bluffed. I wasn't ready to go yet because I still wanted to know about all the money he claimed he had sent for us. If he were telling the truth, I could understand the need for Madre opening an account.

"Where do I begin?"

Once again, he looked at me as if I would be giving him an immunity pass or something. Regardless of the circumstances, he still made a choice to leave us behind. I wasn't going to lose sight of that regardless of how he explained away his actions.

"How about starting with why we are being held captive?" I firmly stated.

He wiped away his tears and stared at me. He looked as if he were trying to decide on how best to explain it to me. Even though I didn't believe his entire story, parts of it was ringing true to me.

"It's very political so some of it won't make sense to you. I will only tell you enough to make you trust me."

"You've got to be fucking kidding me. I don't even know you." The words slipped out of my mouth before I could clean them up, but I meant each and every word. As far as I was concerned, he had done nothing to garner trust.

He didn't react to my outburst. I had expected him to reach across the room and slap the taste out of my mouth, but he didn't. He shook his head from side to side. I breathed a sigh of relief 'cause if he had hit me this time, I would have commenced to kicking his ass. I was through playing games.

"There is great unrest in Columbia. The government has tired of the Cali cartel and is making things very difficult for them. They can no longer operate the sweatshops. The government is closing down their drug manufacturing plants as quick as the cartel can open them. Many of the cartel leaders are trying to leave the country. I am being used to make this happen." That's why I was entrusted with the bonds I sent to your mother.

"What kind of bullshit are you trying to feed me? If they truly wanted to leave Columbia, what is stopping them from hopping aboard a plane just like you did?"

He looked at me as if I was stupid or something.

"These people can never leave. They would never make it past customs."

He had said this as if I knew how difficult customs could be. To my knowledge, I had only been on one flight—the one that had landed me in Atlanta. I guess he could tell by the look of confusion on my face that I didn't comprehend the difficulties they faced.

"These are known criminals. The United States does not want to open its borders to them. The only way they can enter the country is illegally. I provide the means for them to do so."

Once again, I felt like he was selling me a fantasy ticket on a ship to nowhere. "You keep saying that shit. There is no way I'm going to believe that you have that kind of power. You were a dork the last time I saw you."

"Dork? I don't understand."

"A nerd—not someone I would go to if I needed something." I wasn't trying to hurt his feelings. I was just stating the facts as I knew them.

"I don't understand," he said.

"And that's another thing. When the fuck did you learn English?" I was getting mad all over again.

"I've known English for a very long time, but you didn't need to know that. It would have made things too dangerous."

"You keep saying that. What does that mean?"

"If you must know, I played stupid and so did your mother. We speak several languages very well and that is why we were chosen by the CIA. We didn't look the part, so they could send us just about anywhere and we would blend in. Everything was fine until your brothers were taken. After that, your mother lost her taste for the spy business. She wanted out so she could raise the rest of our family in peace. I stayed to guarantee all of your safety."

"If our safety was guaranteed by your staying, why did the cartel kill your parents?"

His shoulders shook as if he were remembering something. "Because I wanted to be with you."

Without him saying it, I knew the *you* he was referring to meant our entire family. But I wasn't ready to clear him of all the wrongdoings that he had done since he had been reunited with his family. "You know…all of that sounds good, but the facts still remain the same: you allowed those people to take your eldest daughter, and you instructed them to kill her child."

"Finding out Ariana was pregnant almost messed everything up, but she was never in any danger. That was all part of the plan. I knew exactly where she was being held and her escape was prearranged."

Either this man was a phenomenal liar, or he was telling the truth. I allowed him to continue.

"Having you and Ariana marry the elders was a last-ditch effort to secure my alliance to them. At the time, it made perfect sense to me. I would be able to dictate how you were to be treated. They would have provided for you well."

"But wouldn't that have caught us up in the same shit that you have been trying to avoid all our lives?" I felt like I had hit the nail over the head and he couldn't fight my logic at arriving at the conclusion that I did.

"Yes, I admit my plan was flawed. I wanted to see you all so badly, I allowed that to color my decisions. It was me who phoned your mother. I thought that if I scared her enough, she would allow me to come back in your lives."

"Oh my God, you killed her!"

"I know, I didn't mean for it to be this way." He started crying again.

Whatever happened from that point on, I knew I would never have a relationship with the man who was supposed to protect us. He had single-handedly ruined all of our lives.

"Okay, with all that said, where does that leave us?" I was getting tired of the chase. I had a lot of things to think about, but getting out of this mess was a priority. Now that Ariana was safe, there was nothing holding me in this house. I only had to discover what Ramón's role was in this farce and if we would be finished with my father. "If I have a place to go, what about Ramón? What happens to him?" I could tell this was a loaded question as soon as it escaped my mouth. Obviously, they had plans for Ramón that I wasn't aware of and I got a sick feeling in my stomach just thinking about it. As far as I was concerned, Ramón was still a kid and deserved protection even if it had to come from me.

"Ramón will be okay as long as he delivers the passports that he has. After that, his debt is paid."

"Debt paid? You say this as if we willingly signed up for service." I had never felt so much hatred in my life.

"Don't look at me like that. It came with the territory. Trust me, we were well awarded for our compliance. I sent your mother money, their bonds—everything."

"Who is *we*? I'm telling you that we, your family, received nothing."

The back door opened with a bang.

"Gabriela, where are you?" Ramón yelled.

"I'm in here," I answered. I could have told him I wasn't alone but he would see that as soon as he rounded the corner.

His whole body language changed when he saw my father in the same room with me. His eyes searched mine. I gave him a small smile to let him know that things were okay.

"Did you make the delivery?" my father said. His hands were clinched into fists.

I could tell that Ramón was surprised that my father and I were in the same place by the look on his face.

Ramón looked at both of us before he answered. "Yeah, I made them." He grunted and turned away as if he smelled something in the room that he didn't like.

"And you had no trouble?" Padre's hands unclenched several times.

"No, why would there be trouble?" Ramón raised his brow at me, but I said nothing.

I wanted to ask him if he went to the bank as well, but I would get to that when we were alone.

My father said, "Sit down for a minute."

It wasn't quite a demand, but it left no room for consideration. Ramón chose a seat right next to me, and I reached over and grabbed his hand. Again, he didn't say anything.

"Your sister has escaped, and I need to get you two out of here before they come back here looking for her."

Ramón looked at me for confirmation, and I nodded my head.

"If she's escaped, why would she come back here?" Ramón snorted with contempt.

"Where else would she go?" Padre responded.

I could think of a million places I would have gone if it were me, but I didn't bother telling him that.

"You better hope that she doesn't bring the police with her to lock your ass up," Ramón snorted again.

I didn't know where he picked up that little trait, but it made him appear older and more cynical. I could only shake my head because he would never have a relationship with his father. I sensed that my father realized it as well.

Ramón said, "Why do you care? You treated her like an animal."

I could see the hatred burning in Ramón's eyes. Ramón released my hand and clenched his fists. I could tell he wanted to leave the room, but I for him to stay.

"I'm not going into this with you. I did what I felt was best for everybody." Padre stood up from the chair in defeat.

"I hate you," Ramón declared.

He had said what I was thinking but was afraid to say. The words resounded in the room. Once again, I felt no sympathy for the man. Maybe in time I would learn to forgive him, but I seriously doubted it.

"I am sorry for that. Now go pack—we have to leave!" They'll hunt us until they find the bonds. If either of you know where they are, now is the time to tell me."

"We're not going anywhere with you," Ramón said as he got to his feet.

I rose to stand by his side. "Why should we have to leave? You said that once Ramón made his delivery it was over." My chest heaved in frustration.

"This is only a precaution. I don't know how Jesus will react to Ariana's disappearance. He is the wild one in the bunch."

"Fuck Jesus and fuck you too for that matter. Come on, Gabriela, let's go find Ariana."

Suddenly, I was afraid. Ramón was itching for a fight and from the look on my father's face, he was about to get it.

Padre's anger was written all over his face. "You can't be here when the shit hits the fan."

I had no idea what he was talking about. As far as I was concerned, the shit had already hit the fan.

"What are you talking about?" Ramón asked.

"The delivery…it's a trap. When the plane arrives Friday, everyone will be arrested. The whole dynasty will come tumbling down."

Ramón looked at me, but I didn't have any answers for him. I was just as confused as he was.

"What have you gotten us involved in now?" I wanted to leave so badly and let him stew in his own shit, but I felt compelled to stay. I needed to know and I refused to leave until he told me everything that I wanted to know.

"I explained some of this to your sister, but I will repeat it for you as well. The leaders of the Cali cartel are coming to Atlanta. Things in Columbia have changed and not for the better. They cannot come into the country legally because of their criminal records. You delivered fake passports and the location of the plane. They will be able to board the place. Once they land, they will be taken to a hotel and I'm going to call the police and tell them where they are."

I looked at him like he had bumped his head. "Do you think these people are stupid enough to trust you like that? There won't be a place on this earth that you can go if you trick them like that and keep their so-called bonds." As much as I hated him for what he'd done to our family, I still didn't want anything bad to happen to him.

"I am not concerned about me. I just need for you two to be safe."

Ramón sat back down on the sofa, his brow creased in a frown. "Why now?" He asked a very good question.

If my father had been doing their bidding all these years, why did he choose now to suddenly grow a set of balls. "Yeah, why now?"

"They will never leave us alone until we do something to make them stop," he admitted. He lowered his head and stared at his feet.

We all sat in silence for a few minutes.

Ramón got up and grabbed the phone. He held it up to my father. "Where is the cord?"

My father had pulled all the cords several days ago to keep us disconnected from the outside world.

"Who are you calling?" my father asked.

"Someone who has a clue 'cause you obviously don't."

Ramón hung up the phone and announced, "He is coming."

CHAPTER FORTY-ONE
MOSES RAMSEY

Ariana was finally getting some much-needed sleep after her grueling escape, a painful labor, and a quickie marriage ceremony. I had been to the nursery several times to see Mike's son. He was resting while all the other babies screamed at the top of their tiny lungs. *Why couldn't he have been mine?*

I couldn't decide who he favored more. He had his mother's wide round eyes but his father's eye color. Why did she do me like this? The vibration from my pocket jolted me from my thoughts. I stepped outside the room to keep from disturbing Ariana.

"Hello," I said. I listened intently before closing the phone. I was not expecting this turn of events, but it was better than I had expected. I went back inside the hospital room. "Sweetheart, I need to leave you for a while but I'll be back in a few hours." I kissed her on the lips for the very last time. I took the syringe that Tilo gave me and pierced the IV line of the woman I swore to love for life. Her lids barely fluttered as the effects of the poison surged through her body. I thought I would feel something as I did it, but I didn't. I left my feelings for her on the delivery room floor.

***

Surprisingly, my car was still where I left it. I had expected it to have been towed or, at the very least, have a ticket or two stuck on the window. I pulled out my phone to call Tilo. I wanted to let her know where I was going, but she had beaten me to the punch by calling me.

"I was just about to call you," I said.

"Are you headed to Ramón's house?"

"Yeah, how did you know?"

"I'm at the office listening. When I heard Ramón using the phone, I assumed he was calling you."

"I thought you went home to get some rest."

"I was going to but I was scared that something might happen at the house that we needed to be aware of."

"That was a good idea. How were things going in the house?"

"There were a few rough moments, but still no mention of the money's whereabouts. Things have settled down right now. Your boy Ramón has a lot of anger stored up inside of him."

"I think you should come with me to the house since you are a part of this, too." I didn't know how Tilo would feel about going, but I really wanted her there.

"I was hoping that you were going to ask me. I'm leaving the office now. I'll meet you there. What about the other thing? Did you do it?"

"Yeah, I did it."

"Are you all right?"

"Fifty-fifty, Tilo." I remembered how Ariana's eyes fluttered close. "Fifty-fifty."

Tilo and I approached the door together. Since I didn't know what to expect inside, I grabbed my gun from my glove compartment and slid it into the back of my pants.

"Are you ready for this?"

Tilo nodded her head but didn't say anything. I could tell that she was nervous. I rang the doorbell and Ramón answered the door. If he was surprised to see Tilo, he didn't let it show.

"Come on in."

I patted Ramón on his shoulder as I walked past him. He seemed like he was glad to see me. I walked in first so Gabriela didn't see Tilo until after I had cleared the doorway to the living room. Carlos smiled when I walked into the room. He rose from his seat and came to greet me.

Over Ramón's head, I gave Carlos a warning look to not blow my cover. Fortunately, no one noticed the exchange.

"Ramón, who are these people?" Carlos said.

Gabriela stood like a deer caught in headlights when she saw Tilo.

"Tilo, what are you doing here?" Gabriela said.

She already knew me, but I assumed Ramón hadn't told her that Tilo worked for me.

"Meet my new boss," Tilo answered with a smile.

"Say what?" she returned the smile.

I could feel the sexual chemistry between them. If they wanted to keep their relationship a secret, they were going to have to tone it down.

"This guy is Ariana's boss and the lady is a friend of Gabriela's," Ramón replied.

Carlos looked uncomfortable, but he managed to sit back down without any further comment. Since Ramón was the one who called me, I was going to let him do all the talking.

Ramón started filling me in on his father's plan, and Gabriela filled in some of the missing pieces. When they were finished, I could do nothing but shake my head. During the whole time, Mr. Mendoza didn't say a word.

"So, that's your plan?" I looked at Mr. Mendoza skeptically. When he had first hired me, I thought he was brilliant. I realized now that I had been dealing with a fool. I searched his face for any resemblance to Ariana's child but there was none. In fact, none of his children looked like him.

"Yeah," Mr. Mendoza replied.

I let his words settle in the room before I started speaking. "No disrespect intended, but all you are going to do is piss the cartel off with that move and sign a death certificate for you and your family." My mind wrestled with the new complications Carlos Mendoza's plan added to finding the bonds. Stealing from the cartel was serious business.

"How do you figure that?" Mr. Mendoza jumped up from his seat on the sofa, clearly agitated that I had called him out.

I debated whether or not to stand up and face him, but I didn't feel like staring down at the little man so I remained in my seat. "If you are successful in getting the police to come to the designated place—and I strongly emphasize the word *if*—the only thing they will be able to do is deport those people back to Columbia. If these people are as connected as you say they are, they will be back on the street by the time you close your eyes."

"But the Spanish government has been looking for them for some time. Things have gotten out of hand and people are tired of living in fear. The government will know what to do with them when they get them.

"Have you ever asked yourself why they haven't been detained before?" The answer was sitting right there in front of his face, but I assumed he chose to ignore it.

"Uh…"

"That's my point. Obviously, they have someone on the inside looking out for them. The cartel's pockets are deep, and, unless you know who you are working with, you could be just setting yourself up." Once again, I allowed the implications of my words to sink in before I continued. "You also have to think about the influence the Cali cartel have in the Atlanta area. Do you really think that they are going to allow some body to come up in their house without a major gunfight ensuing? Who do you think they will come looking for at the first sign of trouble?" I could tell that my words had finally broken through the tough veneer Mr. Mendoza was trying to hide behind.

"You have spoken very wisely. What do you suggest that I do?" His shoulders slumped as he sat back down. Apparently, he wasn't used to asking for anything. He would not even look me in the face.

I was still trying to decide how much to tell him. "Let me give you a little background on me. I am a licensed private detective. I have my own practice and have been in business for several years. I have worked with the FBI and with various other fractions of law enforcement that I cannot discuss with you. If you would trust me, I believe I can help you, but you will have to listen and follow my instructions to the letter. Do you think you can do that?" I gave my credentials for Gabriela's benefit because Carlos already knew everything I had said. If things were going to work out as I had planned, I needed her cooperation.

"Do I have a choice?"

I laughed because he was still trying to be Billy Bad-ass when he was clearly out of his league. "Oh yeah, you have a choice. But if you decide to do this by yourself, I will be taking Gabriela and Ramón with me. I will not allow you to do any more damage to their lives."

"What are you talking about? They are my family?" Mr. Mendoza shouted as he jumped up again. He had the nerve to try to play that card as if he had been acting like a father all the time.

Without my saying a word, Gabriela and Ramón got out of their chairs and came around to stand behind me. Their actions spoke volumes. He acted like he was about the bust a blood vessel and for a split second, I felt sorry for him. It had to be tough to see his own children pick another man over him, but he brought it all on himself.

"Fine, if that's the way it going to be. I just want this over with." He sat back down in defeat.

I nodded my head as Gabriela and Ramón took their seats. "Good, let's go somewhere to talk," I said. It wasn't necessary to go over everything in front of everyone. Carlos still had some information about the bonds I needed to get. I could tell that Gabriela wasn't thrilled about my decision to leave her out, but I left Tilo to deal with her.

"We can talk downstairs," Mr. Mendoza said as he rose and started toward the basement.

I winked at Ramón and he immediately caught my drift. With the hidden microphone in the basement, the entire conversation would be recorded. He smiled back at me.

"Tilo, will fill y'all in on what's been going on," I said as I stood up to follow Mr. Mendoza down the stairs.

CHAPTER FORTY-TWO
GABRIELA MENDOZA

I couldn't wait for the basement door to finally close. Having Tilo this close to me after our forced separation was driving me nuts. My pussy was practically dripping. I still hadn't figured out how she had managed to hook up with Ariana's boss, but it was obvious that she felt comfortable with him. I wondered if there were more to their relationship than met the eye, but I quickly dismissed that idea.

"Go 'head and kiss her already," Ramón said, smiling.

My heart slammed into my chest as my eyes grew big.

"What?" Tilo and I said in unison.

"I maybe young, but I ain't dumb," Ramón replied.

I was so shocked, I didn't know whether to shit or go blind. "How did you know?" I asked.

"Shit, Stevie Wonder could've seen that shit. Madre knew too. I think the only person that doesn't know is Ariana. But she would have figured it out if she had spent some time with you two. Y'all ain't that good at hiding it."

I felt stupid. "Why didn't you say something?" I asked.

"Why didn't you?"

Duh, he had me there. "So what do you think?" I wasn't sure what scared me more, his acceptance or my admission.

Up until this time, I hadn't told a single person about my feelings for Tilo. We were careful not to put a label on what we were doing—as if that would have changed anything.

"Why should I care as long as you are happy?"

I had never loved my brother more than in those few seconds. He just continued to amaze me with his logical approach to situations. Without waiting a second longer, I hurled myself into Tilo's arms and we shared a deep kiss. She wrapped her arms around me and I felt like I was melting into her skin. I felt my knees tremble as our bodies melded together.

"Damn, I said a kiss, dammit. Y'all might need to go get a room," Ramón said, laughing.

He had turned his back to give us some privacy, but he must have peeked. How else would he have known what we were doing? Reluctantly, I stepped back from Tilo's arms. She whimpered as I pulled away. It had been a long time—our longest time apart since we had become intimate. I took her hand and led her to the couch to sit down beside me. Ramón sat across from us on the love seat. He pulled a long envelope from his back pack and handed it to me. It was sealed with my name on it. I recognized my Madre's handwriting.

"What's this?" I asked but I already knew. It would be my mother's final words.

"It was in the safe deposit box. Ariana and I both have one, but you have two. Open it." He urged me to do it even though I would have preferred to read it alone.

I wasn't sure what it was going to contain, and I didn't want to start crying in front of Tilo. "Don't you think I should wait to read it alone?"

"For what?" Tilo and Ramón asked at the same time.

I did a double take. Why did it feel like they were ganging up on me? I exhaled deeply to gather my nerves as I slid the letter out of the envelope. I took a minute and scanned the first three lines before I began reading aloud. "It's written in English." I was shocked, but it only added validity to what my father had said earlier about me not really knowing my mother. Now I knew how it was that my mother knew about my relationship with Tilo. I had never bothered to censor what I said to Tilo over the phone because I thought my mother couldn't understand what I was saying. Boy, did she have me fooled. I went back to the top and started from the beginning:

> *"My dearest child, if my suspicions are correct, you found the key and were able to find the contents of my box. This can only mean that I am either dead or dying. Of all my children, I knew you would be the one to make the connection. You were always nosy.'"*

I laughed through the tears that were running down my face.

> *"I can also assume that you are finding out a lot of things about me and, perhaps, your father that you didn't know. Please know that we did what we did out of love, and I pray that you don't think too badly of us. If you have managed to reconnect with your father, please don't judge him too harshly. He respected my wishes and stayed out of your lives for a reason that I hope you will never find out about.'"*

Humph, well it was too late for that. I put the letter down on my lap. I needed a minute to reflect on what she had said.

"Is that all?" Ramón inquired.

"No, there is more. I just need a few minutes to think." I understood why she had written the letter, but I couldn't understand why she couldn't have told me all of this herself. She had to know that we would have protected her secrets and loved her in spite of them. I could not help but to think off all the wasted years we had spent, and I vowed to never do that to my children if I ever had any. If Ramón was fazed at all by the contents of the letter, he didn't show it. I picked the letter back up and continued to read:

> *"Gabriela, I trust you to keep our family intact. Of all my children, you are the most logical, and, even though you didn't always agree with me, I could reasonably talk to you. I am worried about Ramón. He carries a lot of anger inside of him. I ask that you make him understand the dangers of giving into anger. Try to make him understand that things aren't always as they seem. Teach him to think with his heart sometimes and not with his head.'"*

Ramón said, "If she thinks I'm going to forgive that bastard downstairs, she had better keep on praying." I chose to ignore his outburst because he had just confirmed what my madre had said in the letter. I continued reading.

'

> *"Ariana must follow her heart. I too know what it's like to marry a man that you don't love—"*

"Whoa, back the fuck up. What is she trying to say?" I asked.

"She must have known about Ariana and Moses," Tilo whispered.

"Fuck that, she's saying she didn't love our father," Ramón replied.

Damn, I felt like I had been living in a house built of cards and the wind was blowing them down.

"Ariana is with us. She had the baby, and she's married to Moses," Tilo said.

The letter dropped to the floor.

Too much had transpired in so little time that I was having a difficult time processing all the information. "Holy shit, when did this happen?" My mouth was gapped open, but I could see that Ramón was just as shaken up as I was.

"I found her late last night. She came running out of a building on—"

"Covington Highway," Ramón finished the sentence for her.

I looked at both of them in bewilderment.

"How did you know?" Tilo said.

"I knew that building was connected somehow, but I never knew that is where they were keeping my sister," Ramón said. He had the biggest grin on his face, but I was still confused.

"Ariana's already married!" Why was everybody so happy all of a sudden? Didn't they know that Ariana could get into a lot of trouble behind that stunt?

"Mike is dead." Tilo lowered her head when she said it.

The smile slipped from Ramón's face.

"And that bastard downstairs is the one who ordered it. He told Jesus to take care of him and now he's dead." Outdone, I fell back in my chair. My head started pounding as the words rushed around in my head. "Oh my God." I couldn't have said any more if my life had depended on it. How was I ever going to look my father in the face again knowing what I knew now? One thing was clear. I would never trust him, despite the final words that were written at the bottom of my Madre's letter. I could see them staring back at me from the floor.

'We did what we did out of love. Please believe that.'

I laughed because if this was their idea of love, something wasn't right with their thinking. She had signed the letter *with love*, but I felt like she didn't even know the meaning of the words.

Ramón handed me the second manila envelope. It was filled with thousand-dollar bills and a stack of those bonds my father was looking for. I looked at him in shock. "Is this money real? I never heard of a thousand dollar bill."

"It's real and very rare. I checked at the bank and we can sell them for twice the amount they are worth. It's over one hundred thousand dollars in there. I counted it. There was an envelope in there for me and Ariana. We got the same thing in ours, we are rich." Ramón was smiling again as he waved the other manila envelopes in my face. I shook my head in disbelief.

"Well I'll be damned." My eyes widen in shock as I watched Tilo put a gun up to my brother's head and pull the trigger. The loudest sound came from the empty shell casing hitting the floor. His tiny body crumbled. My feet were stuck to the floor. Instinct told me to run, but I couldn't get my body to cooperate. I keep thinking this was some sort of cruel joke, especially when she pointed the gun at me.

"Sorry, baby," Tilo said, shaking her head.

"Why?"

"Things aren't always the way they appear. Haven't you learned that? If it makes you feel any better, that guy downstairs—he's not your father, he is the Cali cartel."

"Sorry" was the last word I heard.

CHAPTER FORTY-THREE
MOSES RAMSEY

Tilo had her instructions. After she got the money, she was to go to my office and wait. Things were working out better than I had hoped for. After grilling Mr. Mendoza for over an hour, I had a better idea of who we were dealing with. In order for my plan to work, I would have to call in a lot of favors from people who I had worked with throughout my career.

He sat patiently in the corner while I made those phone calls and agreed to accompany me downtown for a meeting. Once I assured him that his family would be safe, he agreed to participate. We left through the basement so he had no idea that they were more than likely already dead.

From what he had told me, the Cali cartel was involved in just about every illegal activity known to man, and they were trying to bring their entire operation to the States. He had confirmed Tilo's suspicions that they were using the adult day care facilities as a front for their illegal operations.

"This is all useful information, but I still don't see how we can tie it to the guys you said are coming over on that plane."

"Don't you see, nothing is done without their permission? Jesus and Chico take their orders from the council. If you shut down the council, you shut down the cartel," Mr. Mendoza said.

We were sitting around a large conference room table at the Peachtree Towers Hotel where I had secured a room for Mr. Mendoza. Agents Stewart and Meadows from the FBI were also seated at the table. After hours of discussion, a plan was set into motion. If all went as planned, everything would be over by the following evening.

I escorted Carlos to his hotel room. He wanted to phone his children, but I warned against it.

Carlos, none of this is making sense to me. I'm going to need for you to at least tell me the truth. Carlos stared at me for five minutes before his façade gave way. He stumbled over to the sofa and sat down with his head between his fingers.

"You saw right through me. Didn't you?"

"Yeah. Who are you?" Silence filled the room as we locked eyes again.

"My brother is a good man." I wasn't expecting him to say that.

"Your brother?"

"Carlos is my brother. He doesn't know that I'm here."

I sat down across from him with my hand on my gun. If he made one false move, he was a dead man. He had told so many lies in the last twenty-four hours I didn't know what to believe anymore.

"Go on."

"He's the person they remembered, it was me that got caught up in the money. Carlos told me everything." His shoulders started to shake as he cried.

"I didn't mean to kill her, I just wanted to scare her—"

"It was you that called?"

"I thought if I told her they were coming she would give back the bonds. I didn't mean to kill her."

"When that didn't happen, why didn't you leave the children alone?" His head snapped up.

"I couldn't. I was in too deep and I had to have that money." His eyes pleaded with me to understand.

"Fuck that, man, you messed up so many lives with that one phone call." I was angry as well because my life had gotten entangled in the same mess. I stood up. I had heard enough. There was nothing else that he could say that would change anything.

I said, "There will be an agent posted outside your door. Do not attempt to leave your hotel room."

"I won't. Thank you for agreeing to help me."

I wanted to tell him to fuck himself. He had trusted the wrong person but he would find that out sooner rather than later. My intentions were to call the cartel and tell them where to find him. I needed him out of the picture so I could collect the reward money being offered for the capture of the members of the council. "Don't answer your phone either unless it's from me. I will call you here at the hotel when it's over."

He nodded his head in understanding. I wouldn't have wanted to be him for all the beans in Columbia, because, as a result of his greed, he had lost everything, including face.

"Good night," I said as I turned to leave.

"Tell my family I love them," he muttered as I pulled the door closed behind me.

I hadn't even made it to the elevator before I heard the gunshot. I pulled my weapon and raced back to Mendoza's room. Since I still had the key card in my pocket, I used it to open the door. I couldn't believe that I had been so careless as to not have checked the room before I had allowed him to enter. I crouched down low as I pushed open the door. Agents Steward and Meadows filed in behind me. Mendoza was lying on the floor with a bullet in his head. The gun was still clutched in his hands. I holstered my weapon as doors along the hallway started to open.

"Damn, I didn't think the little fucker had it in him." I sunk down on a chair and waited for the authorities.

"So much for my reward." I mumbled to myself.

Several days later, I updated my files:

The raids started one hour after Mendoza's body was taken away. Seven buildings, four hundred forty arrests, and twenty causalities later, over twenty million dollars was seized in drugs and money. Among the causalities were Jesus and Chico. They had died during the final raid at the airport when the council arrived in the states. For my assistance, I received two million tax-free dollars from the federal government.

CHAPTER FORTY-FOUR
MOSES RAMSEY

It hadn't rained in Atlanta in fifty-nine days but it started raining the moment I left Mr. Mendoza's body at the hotel. Judging by the way it was coming down, it appeared as if God intended to give us every inch that we'd missed in a single dousing. Taking my time, I eased my car onto the expressway. Tilo was meeting me back at the office. I was anxious to find out how much money we had taken.

The drive was tedious. Every bad driver in the world was on the road, traveling too fast for the conditions. Every other car I passed had on their flashers, an indication of the poor visibility but that didn't stop all the drivers from driving recklessly. After barely avoiding a sliding car, I exited the expressway.

"Shit, these fools are going to kill themselves. It would be just my luck to get killed before I could cash in on all that money." I picked up my cell phone from the passenger's seat and dialed Tilo. I wanted to make sure that she had made it back to the office but she didn't answer her phone. Irritated, I dialed my office but hung up when the answering machine came on.

"She's probably stuck out here just like me." I tossed the phone back on the seat and slowly made my way to the office with thoughts of Ariana running through my mind. I didn't regret killing her, but I did feel sorry her baby would grow up without ever knowing its mother or father.

The television was talking when I went to sleep and it woke me up this morning. All evening long special announcements flashed across the screen outlining the biggest drug bust Atlanta had ever seen.

"Federal drug enforcement agents in Atlanta seized the largest stash of Mexican crystal methamphetamine ever recorded in the eastern U.S...." At first, the newscasts served as a distraction that I needed to keep my mind off the fact that Tilo never showed. Now, it was just a reminder of how badly I had handled the entire situation.

For the umpteenth time, I dialed Tilo's cell but once again, she didn't answer. I could not believe that she had been able to move so quickly, without a trace.

"Some private fucking detective I turned out to be." If it were possible to kick myself in my own ass, I would have. My attention was drawn back to the television as I heard the reporter announce late-breaking news. I turned up the volume:

"This just in: The body previously reported to be that of Carlos Mendoza, which was discovered late yesterday evening at the Peachtree Towers Hotel, has now been positively identified as Monte Fernando. Monte Fernando purportedly was the leader of the now defunct Cali cartel—" I dropped my glass as the enormity of that statement hit me.

"Oh my God. Ain't this a bitch!" I stumbled over to my desk.

The reporter droned on: "Special Investigator Tilo Adams, who was instrumental in breaking this case, is reportedly missing. Sources close to the scene suspect—"

"Damn, how stupid am I? How the hell could all of this shit be happening right in front of my face and I didn't even know it. Tilo was an agent? On whose team?" At first, I was depressed that I allowed such a great opportunity to come past me but now I was pissed beyond pisstivity. Tilo had played me for a fucking fool and I was going to pay the bitch back in full.

I searched my desk to find the first correspondence from Mr. Mendoza. It saddened me to believe that I was so hungry for work that I didn't even bother to pay attention to the post mark. My heart sank when I saw that the letter was indeed from the Atlanta area. I was so ready to believe the outlandish request that I didn't bother to check my sources. If I were honest with myself, I deserved everything that was happening to me. I reminded myself that the situation could have been worse. As it was, I had only lost out on the opportunity to make some money.

A sharp knock on the door interrupted my thoughts. For a brief second, I believed that it was Tilo coming to make things right between us.

"Who is it?" I yelled. I could not imagine who would be knocking on my door on a Saturday morning. Without waiting for response from the other side of the door, I snatched open the door. I was prepared to unleash all the fury that I held inside on this unsuspecting stranger. "What!"

The man before me stumbled back. He was a short Latino man with graying hair, thick horn-rimmed glasses with high water pants. His hair was cut in a bowl shape—all the description that Ariana had used to describe her father.

"Are you Mr. Ramsey?"

"Son of a bitch—" This just kept getting better and better.

"I beg your pardon?"

"Uh…I'm sorry. Are you Mr. Mendoza?"

"How did you know?"

I was beyond caring what he thought. He had been used as a pawn and to my knowledge, he wasn't aware of it.

"I received a letter from this woman named Tilo. She said my children were in danger. I stopped at the hospital to see Ariana before I came."

"Ariana?" I stared at the man in horror. Something was terribly wrong. I delivered the fatal injection myself…or did I? Or had Tilo screwed me again?

■■■

Several days later, I updated my files:

The raids started one hour after Fernando's body was taken away. Seven buildings, four hundred forty arrests, and twenty causalities later, over twenty million dollars was seized in drugs and money. Among the causalities were Jesus and Chico. They had died during the final raid at the airport when the council arrived in the States. For my assistance, I receive two million tax-free dollars from the federal government. No other mention has been made of the whereabouts of Tilo Adams. The bearer bonds, which were reportedly valued at over one hundred million dollars, are still missing.

THE END

ABOUT THE AUTHOR

Tina Brooks McKinney began her writing career as a dare. As an avid reader, writing was the next step for her. Armed with a very active imagination and a story to tell, Tina penned her first novel All That Drama. Readers fell in love with Tina's no-nonsense characters and her comedic style of weaving a story. Since then, Tina has written ten novels and two novellas. Her titles include, All That Drama, Lawd, Mo' Drama, Fool, Stop Trippin', Dubious, Deep Deception, Snapped, Got Me Twisted, Deep Deception 2, Snapped 2: The Redemption, Betta Not Tell and Catch Fire and Catch Fire 2, which will be released in the next few months. You can reach me at www.tinamckinney.com or by email at tybrooks2@yahoo.com.

www.ingramcontent.com/pod-product-compliance
Lightning Source LLC
Chambersburg PA
CBHW020846090426
42736CB00008B/261

* 9 7 8 0 9 8 2 1 0 8 9 1 8 *